W9-COF-459

SAVAGE SHADOWS

SAVAGE SHADOWS

EILEEN ROSS'S TRUE STORY OF BLINDNESS, RAPE AND COURAGE

Eileen Ross

NEW HORIZON PRESS
Far Hills, New Jersey

Library of Congress Catalog Card Number: 91-66895

Eileen Ross
Savage Shadows

ISBN 0-88282-105-9
New Horizon Press
1997 1996 1995 1994 1992 / 5 4 3 2 1

Author's Note

This is the actual experience of a real person, Eileen Ross. The personalities, events, actions and conversations portrayed within the story have been reconstructed from extensive interviews and research, utilizing court documents, letters, personal papers, press accounts and the memories of participants. In an effort to safeguard the privacy of certain individuals, the author has changed their names and the names of certain places and, in some cases, altered otherwise identifying characteristics. Events involving the characters happened as described; only minor details have been altered.

Dedication

To my Dad, Rosario Musumeci

To the Memory of David Wilson

To Ricardo Rivera

To all of the women, men and children
victims/survivors of sexual abuse

"Between cowardice and despair, valour is gendred"

John Donne

Acknowledgements

I would like to express my gratitude and deepest appreciation to these very special friends and acquaintances, who, either in the past or present, have offered me support, patience, wisdom and kindness. You have made my world a better place.

I acknowledge Thorn and Ursula Bacon's contributions as writers to this book.

Al Geissler
Barry Weinstein
Bill Clemons
Bob Kappel
Peter Kross
Carol Shafer
Diane & Alice Hayes
Gail Turner
Gary Trachten
Gregory J. Cannata
Helene Thornton
James Hughes
Janet Lapinski
Janis Lasky
Joanne Shelly
John C. Tortora
Judge Torres

Kristy Miles
Leah Walmer
Linda & Michael Cook
Linda Fairstein
Louise Broadley
Lynn Gottleib
Mary Johnson
Minerva Morales
Moe Tanke
Nancy Patterson
Natasha Kern
New Horizon Press
Norman Pearlman
Pam Freeman
Pat Sulsona
Paul George
Phillip Turner
Ray & Joan Lucero
Dari Smith
Mt. Sinai Rape Crisis Intervention Program
Richard L. Grant
Richard Fox
Richard N. Hirsh
Richard Fowlks
Schneider, Kleinic & Weitz
Sr. Jean Marie
Stuart Kudman
Tessi Clavicilla
The Rivera Family
Thomas Devincentis
W. Chad Mitchell
Werner Weingartner
All My Fantastic Friends and Co-workers at Willamette Falls Hospital

Very Special Thanks to:

Arnold Bunting
Bob and Joyce Ulbrich
David Wilson
David Arocho
Denise Decker
Iona Segal
Joan Wright
Kay Ketchum
Luis Gonzalez
Pat Logan
Marjorie Musumeci
Mary Baumann
Phil Goodbody
Ricardo Rivera
Rosario Musumeci
Sammy Alvino
Patty Kehoe
Sal Catalfumo
James R. McGeown
Bruce Milau
Bob Merz
Richard Harker
Jack Baker
Frank Paganucci
All of my Wonderful Animals
Ginger Trench
Anthony Nozzi

Contents

Prologue

The luminous dial of the alarm clock radio on the shelf above Eileen's head spread a faint glow on her neck and shoulders and softened the darkness. Her hair was a wide dusky fan on the pillows as she lay on her back soothing her dogs. Bonnie and Bethie had finally settled down, no longer snipping and growling at one another from opposite sides of the bed. They were nestled against her thighs as she listened to the late Sunday news report. The meagre content of the events belied the swollen importance of the announcer's voice:

The temperature was certain to climb into the nineties in New York City on Monday; Jane Geddes was the winner of the United States Women's Open with a purse of $50,000; illegal aliens in the Empire State who met minimum income eligibility rules would now be able to receive Medicaid benefits; a woman was suing David Letterman for $1 million for a remark that ruined her poodle's show business career; President Reagan had sent a letter to Secretary-General Gorbachev setting the stage for the resumption of arms control talks; and two men were raping and terrorizing women in Brooklyn and on Manhattan's East Side.

Eileen Ross barely heard the final news item; she drifted asleep with her hands resting affectionately on her beagles, who were cuddled against her form. A few minutes later, the timer on the radio shut off the volume control and the apartment fell silent. The only sounds were the metallic whir of the air conditioner, the tiny hum of the clock and the soft breathing of the beagles.

Chapter 1

He waited, as he always did, until about 2:00 A.M.

It was the beginning of the dead part of the night when people descended into the deepest part of sleep. They were less prone then to hear little strange noises. Also, the whole city was slower, fewer cops were on the street, crowds thinned out, the bars were beginning to close down. It was a perfect time to start a score. He always timed it so he would make the actual entry between 2:00 A.M. and 3:00 A.M. This gave him a couple of hours, if he needed that much time.

He strode purposefully up the street with long athletic strides. He had first seen the woman on her patio, glancing up at her on his way to his sister's house a block or so away. Even from fifty or sixty feet there was something about her that excited him. The way her long dark hair swayed about the soft fullness of her hips as she bent down to pick up one of her dogs and cuddled it in her arms while the other barked for attention at her feet. Stupid looking dogs. Long and white with brown spots and droopy ears.

He grimaced. He hated dogs. They were a nuisance. There were too damned many of them in the world. He paused. A thin smile played about his mouth. One less now. He thought about the other woman, the one whose apartment he had broken into just the week before.

Her apartment was on the sixth floor of a building separated from an adjacent one by a distance of only seven feet. Quite a feat for some, but child's play for his climbing agility. He climbed out on the roof of the second building, found a piece of weathered lumber next to the door of the stairwell. It was about ten feet long, an inch thick, and eight inches wide. It was an interesting thing about the security habits of apartment dwellers. They felt absolutely safe high up in the air and didn't bother to lock their windows. He walked to the end of the roof and looked down. The window he chose was open; he saw the curtain stirring in the light breeze.

It was located about six feet lower than the top of the roof where he was standing. He hoisted the flat board over the low roof wall and angled it down to the window sill. The incline was severe, at least seventy degrees. When it was in place, he pushed it slightly until it was resting firmly on the sill.

Barely glancing at the narrow canyon of space that plunged seventy feet deep and separated the two buildings, he stepped on the flat board, tested his balance with his toes, and walked carefully, without fear, down the incline. The board swayed in the middle from his weight, but he didn't let the sinking sensation bother him. He was crouched on the window sill balancing on the tips of his tennis shoes and raising the window less than fifteen seconds after he started. He was rummaging in the freezing compartment of the refrigerator looking for valuables packed in aluminum foil when he saw the woman in a short blue nightgown framed for an instant in the kitchen door.

Her mouth was open and her eyes widened in terror. She clutched the fabric of her gown at her throat and turned and ran toward the front door of the apartment.

As he started after her, saying, "Hey, lady I won't hurt you," he heard the dog growl and turned with his Rambo knife and slashed quickly as the animal, a shepherd-labrador cross, jumped at him.

The dog yelped and the woman screamed, "Get him, Blackie, get him." She threw the door open and ran into the hall.

The dog was bleeding from the long cut in its side. It was growling and whining and biting at the wound. He ran to the door and saw the woman disappear down a stairwell, screaming at the top of her voice, "Help, help. He's trying to kill me!"

Furious, he slammed the door, locked it behind him and headed for the kitchen. The dog blocked his way. It was lying in the doorway, moaning, licking its fur, growling.

The knife flashed in his hand, cutting, stabbing, slicing. First he slit its belly open from breastbone to pudendum. Blood scattered all over the kitchen in strings and puddles. The animal lay on its back, its front legs folded back against its chest, the wet paws hanging limply, like hands in supplication. He emptied the cavity. Some of the organs—liver, stomach, spleen—were strewn on the floor. Then he threaded a long string of intestines through handles on cabinet doors. He hung them in grotesque loops, dripping blood on counter tops. Even in the low light, the spilled blood was everywhere, on table legs, counters, the door to the refrigerator, in splotches on the stove, on the face of the dishwasher, in spots on the sink.

Breathing heavily, still angry from having been thwarted by the woman, he thrust the knife in the ankle sheath and climbed through the kitchen window, leaving a bloody footprint on the window sill. He crawled up the flat board and dropped on the adjacent roof. He pulled the board back and let it fall next to the wall.

He thought about his frenzy now, and his face tightened.

You had to show women who was the boss. Give

'em an inch and they'd take a mile. Every time. Power was the only thing they understood. It was amazing how quick a bitch would fall apart once you threatened her, and she knew you meant business. Well, that bitch would remember what he left behind for a long time.

He stood still for a moment and looked around. Tonight he was not about to be stopped. Either by a dog or a woman. He bent down and checked under his trouser leg. Raising it slightly, the knife strapped to his ankle glinted as he ran his finger across the blade. He had sharpened it especially for this occasion. Quickly, he rolled his trouser leg down again.

The place he'd been seeking was just ahead.

His sister had said celebrities lived there. She'd sworn she'd once seen Mary Tyler Moore walk out of the front of the building, escorted by a doorman floating around her like a corpulent butterfly.

He smacked his lips—a rich area, a damned rich area and it was time he branched out, he decided. Now was as good a time as any. Maybe better. After all, he was getting hot in Brooklyn. Every time he pulled a burglary over there he raised the threshold of police impatience and determination to get him. He knew about odds. They were at least ten thousand to one that any of the women he raped, or their husbands, would ever recognize him. But just when you've started figuring the percentages were in your favor you could walk into a grocery store or restaurant and run right into one of your victims. You could take a bet on who would be the most surprised and scared.

According to the cops, professional criminals seldom changed the geographical area of their operations. He knew about the theory, and the statistics on repeat offenders which were supposed to make it true. It was the best reason in the world for changing locales.

He stood in front of the building now. In the dark, with human activity almost shut down, the apartment house lay in night shadows of its own making. It was an enormous place taking up a whole city block, with a wide, columned entrance facing the street. From where he was standing, concealed in the shadows of bushes planted in front of an apartment house across the street, he could almost hear the splashing of the illuminated fountains that cascaded through a stream of light in front of the building.

Interior light from the lobby cast soft beams outside on shrubs and on young maples. Above it and to the left, the building's looming size was defined by a few scattered lights from windows in apartments whose dwellers were up late. Her apartment was to the extreme right of the lobby on the first floor, but the terrace was elevated from the sidewalks below by a retaining wall structure that surrounded the four sides of the building. A first floor occupant like her actually looked down on pedestrians who used the sidewalks.

Slowly, carefully, he would make his entry. Tall burgeoning maple trees at the corner sheltered that portion of the building and there were few lights. It was a natural blind spot, perfect for a burglar. There was a window partially concealed by shrubs which would hide him as he tinkered with the latch to get in.

Depending on the building, he mused, you could slip a knife between the window frames and turn the latch. The more expensive latches were not that easy to open. Well, if the window was too hard, he would try the others around the corner. But something told him the first window was going to be vulnerable. He had hunches like that sometimes and he was always pleased when they came true.

He glanced to his left and right and walked across

the street, his muscles rippling as he covered the ground confidently. Nobody was stirring as he crossed diagonally, the shooting fountains and deserted lobby to his left. Agilely, he hoisted himself into the lower branches of the corner maple tree and swung over to the terrace. He slipped behind the shrubs concealing his target window and looked carefully at the frame. He was in luck. Steel windows, but the latch was the old-fashioned kind. Before he reached for his knife, he shrugged and decided to see if the window was unlocked.

People were inconsistent about locks. He had entered dozens of buildings without forcing the windows because tenants would secure the locks on the window overlooking the fire escape, but leave the ones adjacent to it unlocked.

He pushed. The window gave and rose slightly. He slipped through it, removing his Rambo knife from the sheath on his ankle. He stood absolutely still, breathing quietly until his eyes adjusted to the darkness. He had entered an office bedroom. There was a desk, a word processing machine, books, papers, a dictating machine. Blue and beige throw pillows were strewn on the bed. A window looked out on the patio where he had seen her earlier. She and her dogs. Where did they sleep?

Briefly, he reconnoitered the living room and discovered the door that led to the patio, which he opened in case he needed a quick escape.

He kept walking and began to search for some kind of hammer he could use on the dogs. He found what he was looking for in a wooden planter box, sitting on a counter with a bundle of twine next to it. It was a wooden mallet with an aluminum face. When he hefted it in his hand it had a good striking weight to it.

Just as he was about to leave the kitchen, he was

startled by a small yelp. He turned and was surprised to see one of the dogs standing in a doorway looking up at him. She started to bark. He made a soothing sound, bent down and grabbed the animal quickly, before it could retreat. Then he whacked it once, quickly on the head. The animal quivered and fell over. He paused and listened, trying to discover if the dog's yelp had awakened anybody. Nope. No sound of stirring.

Suddenly, he remembered the twine on the counter next to the planter. He retrieved it and walked quietly into the living room, rechecked the door to the patio and slipped out. He made a tight loop at one end of the twine and tied it around the dog's neck. The other end he secured to a railing in the street fence.

The living room was an easy reconnaissance. Tables, chairs, a sofa, a baby grand piano, some wall paintings. There were two doors. One, obviously, led to the hall, the other probably to the bedroom. He began to get excited by the idea of her sleeping alone, quietly, without a hint of what she would be doing in a little while. Maybe she was dreaming of getting fucked. Maybe she would be grateful to wake up to find a man ready to give it to her.

He took a deep breath. That wouldn't happen right away. You had to get to know them first. He had to get familiar with little things about her that would be fun to think about later on. The way her mouth was formed, the color of her eyes. How they got bigger or squeezed smaller when she was scared. These and other things were signs to her personality, clues as to how she would act when he ordered her to take off her clothes.

He could hardly wait for the fun to begin, but there were other things he had to take care of first. He searched the darkness. Where the hell was the other dog?

He weighed the mallet in his hand. It had worked like a charm on the first little dog. It made a popping sound when it connected with its head. A lot of times, single women had their animals sleep with them. Maybe the other dog was in with her. He walked stealthily to the door and peered into the bedroom. He could dimly see her form on the bed, and a curled lump beside her, the other dog.

There was a lamp on a dresser across the room from her bed. Grasping the mallet securely, he reached beneath the lamp shade and found the switch. He turned it on suddenly and stepped back. His pulse was racing as she stirred . . .

Chapter 2

Eileen was puzzled as she became aware of brightness through her eyelids. Light was shining in her face. Her eyes fluttered awake and she realized the lamp on the dresser across the room from her bed was on. *That was wrong.* Then, Bethie barked. Startled, Eileen saw a shaggy blur, heard the dog's teeth snap in the air, heard the grunt, heard the knock on the skull, heard the yelp of anguish, heard the high screech of pain; heard the thud of the fall.

"Bethie! Oh, my God!" Eileen cried out. She was screaming, her arms flailing, her voice shrieking in her ears; scared, terrified, shaking; the hair standing stiff on the back of her neck.

"Shut up! Shut up!"

She heard the man's voice—her heart thudding, her mouth dry—felt the sharp blow to her scalp and the sudden intense pain. Her hands flew to cover her head and she thought, *Oh, my God! somebody's going to kill me.* She screamed again, louder, praying now, *Why doesn't somebody hear me?*

She tried to lift a leg out of bed, then realized, strangely, she was falling on her side; she must be dying; her brain was woozy, lights were swimming behind her eyes. She heard a pattering noise, could not imagine what it was . . . pat, pat, pat, pat, pat . . . and she tried to wipe away the heavy crimson wetness that poured and puddled in her eyes. It was like rain . . . Hot crimson rain. She tried to wipe it away with her fingers, then brought her hands close to her face and screamed, "I'm bleeding."

Blood splashed all over. Over her arms, down the front of her nightgown, on her legs, on her thighs, on her knees. Blood dripped from her hair onto the hard cotton bedspread. It streamed down from the top of her head; it fell in a spray when she changed the position of her head. She rubbed her hands on her nightgown and then made out the form of Bethie. The dog climbed on her lap and lay on her chest, breathing in muffled gasps. Eileen moved her face close to the dog. Her right eye was smashed and swollen. Blood ran down her nose.

"Oh, Bethie" she cried.

"Shut up! Where's your money? Where's your jewelry? If you scream again I'm going to kill you. I mean it."

Now, Eileen saw his blurry form, an indistinct shadow with a knife, a terror she couldn't describe. Blind since birth, except for partial tunnel vision in her right eye, to Eileen this stranger was a violent phantom in her night.

"Bethie, Bethie," she pleaded. "You hurt Bethie."

"Never mind that. Where's your cash? Rings and bracelets? Get out of bed."

"I'm trying. I'm bleeding. Can't you see I'm bleeding? There's blood all over. I must be badly hurt."

"You're all right. And stop looking at me. Don't look at me!"

"I'm not looking at you. I'm blind. I'm blind. I can only see a little bit."

Surprised, the man stepped back and stared at Eileen, uncertain of her truth, weighing what she had said.

"Get up," he barked. "Get up."

"Let me get my slippers." She groped toward the wooden drawer in the bottom of her bed and searched until she clutched her blue cloth slippers. She pulled them on her feet, still woozy, her head smarting from the blow she had received. She was amazed at the amount of blood. It was discoloring her slippers, making spots on the hardwood floor.

With so much blood, why didn't her head hurt more? She licked her lips and swallowed. Her throat was dry, aching. As she straightened up on her bed, she felt the man grab her wrist and pull her roughly to her feet.

Harshly, he demanded, "Where's your money? Quit stalling. Where's your jewelry?" Pulling her toward him, he dragged her through the bedroom door.

"I asked you, where's your money and stuff?"

Up close she could make out some of his clothes now. He was wearing a khaki T-shirt, brown pants and sneakers. He had bulky shoulders and he was taller than she was.

"What I have, most of it's in my pocket, my jeans. In the bedroom."

Suddenly, there was a barking from the direction of the terrace.

Bonnie! She must have jumped off the bed and hid when the man struck Bethie. Hid and ran out to the terrace when she discovered the door had been opened.

"Stop the dog from barking."

Eileen started forward and ran into the man's hard forearm.

"No, never mind," he said. "You're not going outside. You're staying right here. If you move, I'll kill you."

Eileen heard him step quickly across the room, his feet light on the parquet floor. She heard Bonnie's barking stop. There wasn't time for her to run to the hall door, unlatch it, swing it open and escape into the corridor. He had promised to kill her if she moved. Besides, he could see her, she was sure, through the open door.

He hadn't hesitated to hit Bethie and smash her eye, and hadn't he cracked her own head just because he thought she was looking at him and screaming? What would he do if she ran? He still had the knife and whatever it was he had struck her with. She shivered and ran her hand across her forehead. Her scalp was still bleeding, but the blood was darker now, running slower, thickening in her hair and on her skin.

She heard his step, heard the door to the terrace close, felt the bulk of him come close to her.

She felt his eyes on her. He was staring at her. She could tell. He was taking her in. He was feeling her with his eyes. She wondered what he thought about the harm he had done to her. The blood seeping from her wound, sticking her hair together, making gluey tracks on her face. Then, oddly, she thought of the celebrity picture of her and Anne Bancroft, the one in her scrapbook. The stage picture taken on the New York set of the *Miracle Worker.*

She'd been in the play. Years ago. She'd been ten and eager. Told by Miss Bancroft that she was pretty—dark hair, large dark, romantic eyes, full red Italian mouth, glowing fair skin. Lovely child, lovely woman, now standing with fear quivering in her spine, blood smeared on her hands and face, hostage to a man who could take her life as easily as snapping his fingers. *Oh, God, help me!*

"I killed your dog," he suddenly said. "I'll kill the other one."

No! She screamed inside her head. It wasn't so. She hadn't heard Bonnie whimper or cry out from the terrace. There had been no scuffle or sounds of resistance. Surely, the little dog would have made some small noise. Maybe he was just telling her Bonnie was dead to keep her under control. Maybe he had tied her up, little rabbit dog. Said she was dead to deepen Eileen's fear. Scared people don't think. They give in, do what they're told. Afraid if they don't they'll get hurt. *Get killed.* Was that what was going to happen to her? She thought of Bethie, lying injured and still on the bed, and cried, "Please don't kill the dog. I'll do anything you say if you'll leave her alone. My dogs are my life. Please."

Quit kidding yourself, she said, forcing her mind away from the dog. If you want to survive you've got to forget Bonnie. She's dead. You've got to forget her or you'll lose your mind and then everything will be lost.

Suddenly, she realized that this man, whoever he was, knew what he was doing. He was manipulating her with threats and fear. He had proved twice that he was violent and swift. He'd struck her quickly and crushed Bethie with a blow. And he said he'd killed Bonnie. Breaking in seemed something he was good at. He must have done it dozens of times.

Then, Eileen remembered the newscast she had heard before she had turned out the light and her legs almost lost the strength to stand. *The Silver Gun Bandit and Spiderman!* Two men who'd been stealing from women, raping and terrorizing them in Brooklyn and Manhattan's East Seventies! *This must be one of them. Oh, God!*

Eileen swallowed hard. Her throat was dry and her stomach was tight. Her arms were stiff, almost rigid with fearful anticipation. She had to face the inevitable. Unless she did, she would never survive. She would do something stupid or foolish and get herself killed. She breathed a little sigh, thankful that she had not run. He would have caught her—she was certain of that—and smashed her head again and again.

She was going to be raped. She knew it was going to happen. There was something direct and certain about this man, almost complacent, as if he knew in advance what was going to happen, as if he had a plan.

She couldn't say why she knew she would not escape from this intruder. She just knew it. It was the same sick certainty that had come over her when a wild and crazy-acting psycho grabbed her at night seven years ago when she had decided to walk home after the boyfriend with whom she'd had dinner had gotten so stupid drunk that he couldn't walk with her.

She'd been dumb, creeping home in the freezing cold, clutching her coat in the dark. The man had jumped her near a remodeling site. Then he had punched her face against a piece of metal on a scaffolding and had slashed her coat with a knife. Then, still calling her obscene names, he had pulled out his penis, masturbated in a frenzy, and ejaculated on her leg. She'd been too scared to run.

He had left her weak and trembling and run to a parked car and sped away.

When Eileen called the police, after she had stumbled into her apartment, she was advised by the patrolman, to whom she'd poured out the story that since she couldn't describe her assailant, she couldn't expect them to catch him.

Now, all these years later, this had happened. Tonight she'd been confronted by another man who had attacked and threatened to kill her, if she resisted him. Was there any way she could stop him from raping her? No! That was a forlorn hope. He had the knife and the weapon he had struck her with. Even without these, he was stronger than she was. Some men, she knew, were excited by resistance when a woman fought back. Well, she wouldn't do that. She'd give in, she decided. Be placid, be limp, unresponsive. *Oh, God! She didn't deserve this.*

She licked her lips and rubbed the side of her mouth with her fingers. She tasted blood on her tongue. She jumped when he asked, "Didn't you hear me? Where are your jeans?"

"On the floor in the bedroom."

"Okay, stand still."

He was gone for only a moment, returning with the jeans in his hands. He placed something that glistened and a thick object on top of a white leather chair. Now, she was close enough to identify a knife and the mallet. *It was from her kitchen.* A meat tenderizer, with a metal face of sharp aluminum spikes attached to a wooden head with a handle. She drew a quick breath. This had smashed Bethie's eye and lacerated her own scalp.

If he had a knife and enough time to rummage in the kitchen drawers and find the mallet, what other discoveries had he made? How long had he been in the apartment before he turned on the dresser lamp?

How had he entered? Probably through the window in the room next to the kitchen, the one with the broken latch she'd been complaining about for months.

Now, holding her jeans with the pockets turned inside out, he thrust them at her, and said disgustedly, "Heh, this isn't much money." He had found four ones and a ten dollar bill.

"I don't have much money. I'm a poor person."

"Come on, you're not a poor person. You live in this building, don't you?"

"Yeah. That's why I'm poor."

"You know, you're very funny. Now, tell me where you've got some more money."

"I've got sixteen hundred dollars in checks in the desk drawer over there."

"I'm not interested in that."

He turned suddenly and brought his face close to Eileen's.

"What's this about your being blind? You can see. I know you can see."

"I only have a tiny bit of vision."

"Don't lie to me. That's why I hit you. You were looking right at me and screaming."

"I'm not lying. If I was looking at you, it was coincidental. I can't make eye contact."

"Well, it's too bad. If I'd known you were blind, I would have covered your mouth with my hand. Something like that. You shouldn't have looked at me. So, how much can you see?"

"I can't see enough to identify you if that's what's worrying you."

"Nothing is worrying me. But you can see me. I know you can."

She shook her head no. "I can just see images in a vague sort of way. And my left eye isn't even real."

"It looks real to me."

"It's supposed to look real. They're good with eye cosmetics. Do you want me to take it out and show you?"

He gave a sigh of disgust. "No! Now where's your jewelry?"

"I don't have much jewelry." She fingered the watch on her hand. "I have this Gucci watch. I don't like jewelry. I'm a plain Jane."

"Give me the watch."

Eileen obeyed, removing the watch from her wrist. She touched her ears with her fingertips. "I have these earrings. I don't know if they're any good."

"Let me have them."

She removed the two small fake diamonds and reached out with them in his direction. He grabbed them from her hand, then grasped her wrist and yanked her into the adjoining room that served as an office where there was a large ceiling light.

He turned the light on and said, "How come you wear earrings to bed? They'll hurt your ears when you turn on your side."

"No reason, I guess. I just did."

"Well, I'll tell you, whoever gave these to you didn't like you very much."

"That's okay. I didn't like him very much either." He pressed the earrings into her hand and said, "You're very funny."

"I hope so," Eileen whispered to herself. "I hope I'm funny enough to stay alive."

She was getting a feeling about the man now. He was dangerous. Never to be underestimated.

He was intelligent. He acted quickly. She was absolutely certain that if he thought for a moment that she was hiding money or valuables from him that he would punish her. But was he a killer or a rapist? Maybe not, maybe he was just a burglar. He flinched from contact with her, almost as if she were contagious. When he had grabbed her to pull her from the bed, to lead her, each time he had grasped her by the wrist, as if hands were too intimate for him. A man who was repulsed by flesh, was afraid that touch would leave her imprint on him, would not rape, would he?

She tried hard to get a sense of him. Altogether, the man was a contradiction. He was a practiced thief, a break-in expert, but he did not speak crudely and he did not use abusive language or profanity to intimidate her. His speech was not emotionally charged with hate or frustration as she might have expected from a street punk who robbed, raped and ran. His behavior and manner were matter-of-fact, almost without personal emphasis, and this made his commands and actions more chilling. He was scary, brutal and unpredictable. And this made him the most dangerous kind of intruder.

Still her ability to analyze him made Eileen feel a little easier in her mind, easier but more wary. She decided to give him something. Maybe it would prove to him that she was genuine. Maybe he would believe she had nothing more worth looking for and leave.

"I have some pennies in a butter cookie box in a closet in the kitchen. I don't know if you want them?"

"Every little bit helps." He pushed her toward the kitchen. He opened the closet door, hefted the round, tin cookie box and said, "All full of pennies, huh?"

"Oh, there're some dimes and nickels in there."

"How much money do you figure there is in here?" He had removed the lid and dug his fingers into the coins.

"Oh, I don't know. Nineteen or twenty dollars."

He put the box down. "Well, make me something to eat."

Eileen was astonished. She hid her disappointment. He wasn't going to go easily. She felt outwitted. Why was he delaying; taking his time? Didn't he feel a sense of emergency, a sense of minutes rushing by? Wasn't he afraid of somebody coming?

Of course, he wasn't. Stupid of her. Who was going to come knocking on her door in the middle of the night?

What was there to threaten him? They were alone in an apartment with thick walls, surrounded by hundreds of other people living in the same building who couldn't hear her and probably didn't care. Her screams had attracted absolutely no one.

Why should he worry? The dogs were silenced, one probably dead. She squeezed her eyelids against the sudden smarting tears. Bonnie, poor Bonnie. Yes, he had time. What was wrong with a little snack at three o'clock in the morning before he decided where to search for valuables in her apartment?

"What do you want to eat?" she asked.

He was standing with the refrigerator door open identifying the food on the shelves.

"Pepsi, Slice, bologna, milk, hamburger, lettuce, celery, tartar sauce, oranges, peppers, chicken, shrimp. Heh, shrimp! That's my favorite food. Here, fix me some eggs." He extended his palm with the white objects in it.

Eileen grasped the eggs and moved to the stove. On a cold front burner was the frying pan containing the residue of her veal supper. She hadn't cleaned the pan. Her few dishes were stacked in the sink.

"Scrambled okay, and toast?"

"Sure, just pop'em in the pan. That grease'll be okay when it's melted."

He had glanced in the cupboard where she kept her condiments; now he was leaning on the open door of the refrigerator holding up a two-liter bottle of Slice.

"Don't you listen to the news?" he suddenly demanded. "This stuff might be poisonous. Didn't you hear that somebody's been juicing Slice with cyanide? They recalled thousands of bottles. Sure, you can give this to somebody by mistake and kill'em if it's the right bottle. Or may be you thought of that, huh? Was going to slip me some while I wasn't looking. Or maybe thought I hadn't heard about it being contaminated?"

"Oh, no," Eileen said. "I wouldn't want you to get killed here. What would I say to the cops with a dead body in the kitchen?"

"You're a very funny person."

Maybe it was the bottle of Slice that gave her the idea, actually two ideas. One was to lift the pan of grease when it got hot enough and throw it in his face. Then run for the corridor while he screamed and bumped around the kitchen with blistered eyes. The other was to get his hands on something that would transfer his fingerprints clearly so the cops would have a record to catch him with.

She didn't know why her anger had been so slow to come, and with it determination. But it had arrived. She quickly discarded the idea of the hot grease. He was too fast. He could dodge if she didn't aim right. His movements, from what she could see of his form, at times seemed lazy, slouch-like, but she was sure that this was just an act. He was on guard all of the time. If she picked up the pan and threw it where his voice told her he was sitting, at the kitchen counter, she could miss. Or merely sting him. *Then, she'd be in for it.* She could almost imagine his wrath and retribution:

"And just when I was getting to trust you, you pull a stunt like this. Well, you got to learn a lesson . . ."

No, she had to think of something else, some other way to trap him. Eileen's hand trembled slightly as she broke the eggs into a mixing bowl. She took a shallow, shaky breath, glad that she had abandoned her first idea. Now, he had opened a bottle of 7-Up. Careful to sound as natural as she could, she said, "Here, I'll get you a glass to drink from." Eileen said slowly.

The other thought crossing her mind crystallized; his fingerprints. She had to get his fingerprints.

As if anticipating her plan he interrupted, "I don't want a glass."

Undaunted Eileen persevered, "Well as long as you're sitting here, you might as well have a glass and plate. You need a plate for the eggs." *That sounded reasonable.*

"Oh, okay."

She covered her small triumph and nervousness by making unnecessary rattling noises as she reached into the dishwasher for a fresh glass and plate. She grasped the round bottom of the blue water glass carefully, hoping he would not notice how contrived it all was as she handed it to him. She felt his fingers touch hers as they wrapped around the glass and removed it from her hold.

She sighed as she heard him pour the 7-Up from the bottle into the glass. Felt less vulnerable, less afraid. She didn't need eyes. She was smart enough to trap him with the faculties she had mastered. With caution, intelligence and daring she could outwit this man, this brutal intruder, who sat on a stool at her kitchen counter fondling a snack pack of breakfast cereals while he waited for his eggs to cook.

Legally blind since birth, vision to Eileen was a combination of audio and tactile signals. She could count the fingers of her hand at three feet. Beyond that distance objects faded. She had no peripheral vision. What sight she possessed was straight ahead, viewing as through a tube. She could read newspaper print by holding the paper a few inches from her right eye. She depended upon temperature, texture, density, distance, brightness, color, voice intonation, and timbre to provide her with an estimate of the quality of the person. She was better at measuring human character than physical dimensions.

She did not feel deprived by her lack of sight, or that God and an imperfect world had been unfair to her. She was Eileen Ross, a mature thirty-seven-year-old self-employed woman, who had once been in love, who enjoyed music, made good friends, was proud of her vocation as a medical transcriptionist and asked no more of people than she was willing to give.

Now she was determined to outwit this man. If she could do that, devise a way to physically touch him in order to gain an impression of his size, hair type and features, she could report this information later to the police. It was a tall order in view of the fact that her intruder had shrunk from contact with her, had almost jumped to prevent her from touching him.

For a moment, she wondered at a fate that seemed to attract violence to her. Two rapists in seven years. Did her blindness create a mistaken aura of defenseless innocence? Did that make her seem more vulnerable? She knew there was no answer to those questions. She had, however, learned it was crucial to get physical details for the cops. They would not respond to vagueness. Would give her the equivalent of a shoulder pat and pity at being "a poor blind woman." Then it would be all too easy for them to place the case in some soon-to-be-forgotten file. She bit her lip, purposefully. She'd be damned if she'd allow that. Now she quickly studied her options. Meager though they were.

If she was going to be able to identify and lead them to the man in her kitchen, she had to be able to show them identifiable proof of who he was. As she debated in her mind how to do it, stirring the eggs on the low flame, he interrupted her thoughts.

"I really do feel fucked up that I hit you on the head 'cause you're blind."

"Well, now listen," Eileen said, "you shouldn't hit anybody on the head."

He paused. "I do this to make a living, but I still feel fucked up for hitting you on the head because you're blind.

Eileen gasped, then covering up her fear she decided to risk asking a question, "Are you the guy I've been hearing about on the radio?"

Eileen knew she was taking a chance, might rile him or worse, but the more she could pin down who he was the better were her chances of getting the police to find him. She had deliberately refrained from repeating the word "rapist" used by the news announcer to describe the men who'd been stealing from women and sexually assaulting them. The last thing she wanted was to give him any ideas about her. But if he acknowledged that he was the thief, she would have a better idea of what to expect from him. The tone of her question was calculated to display interest in the notoriety of the man, as if the actions of criminals fascinated her.

"I might be that guy," he said impetuously. "I just might be."

"Well, aren't you afraid you'll run into somebody's boyfriend or husband?"

"That doesn't bother me. It happened to me once. This guy pulled a gun and threatened to shoot me. Hell, I just punched his face out and took the gun away from him. Then I tied him up and let him watch while I went on about my business."

"Look," he said, "I've decided to have some cereal. Bring me the milk and a spoon."

Eileen picked up a spoon from the drawer in front of her and removed a carton of milk from the refrigerator. She decided this was the moment she had been waiting for. As she placed the spoon and milk on the counter near him, she pretended to lose her footing.

"Oh," she said, and lurched toward the intruder. Her hand flew out to catch herself and brushed his left shoulder and the short hair on the back of his neck.

He stiffened on his stool. "Get your hands off me," he shouted. "Don't touch me. Don't look at me. Get away."

He leaned backwards, tensed, muscles taut, face tight and angry.

"I'm sorry," Eileen cried, "I must have slipped. I was just putting the spoon down."

She picked up the empty blue water glass he had drunk from by the rim and took it to the sink where she pretended to run water over it. Carefully, purposefully she set it aside in the sink. His fingerprints were undisturbed, as far as she knew.

He was still disturbed and glowering. "Just stay where you are," he said. He remained on the stool, scowling, tense, a few moments longer then gradually relaxed and poured milk into a bowl of corn flakes. Eileen stood silently listening to the sound of him munching on the cereal. She was thankful his reaction to her had not been violent. Strange man. *Afraid of being touched, almost phobic about it.*

The eggs were almost ready when he dropped his spoon in the empty bowl and rose to his feet. He reached out suddenly, without warning, and grabbed Eileen's wrist in a hard grip.

"Come here," he said, glancing at the eggs on the stove. He pushed through the open doorway connecting the kitchen with the small second bedroom Eileen used as an office to transcribe medical dictation tapes. His hand still clamped about her wrist, he opened the closet where she stored office supplies. A strange, sinking feeling filled her chest. Inside the door were screwdrivers hanging from a metal bracket.

The largest one had a nine-inch blade, the smallest six inches. Each had a bright handle of striped yellow and black plastic. She could make out his hand reaching for them. Hear the snap as they were detached from their places.

Eileen swallowed hard. Her mind was racing. Why

would he want screwdrivers? How did he know where they were to be found? He must have been in the apartment much longer than she had imagined. Her sense of helplessness increased. She didn't know what to do. Should she say something? Her voice seemed to be stuck in her throat.

She was shaking as he gathered the screw drivers in one hand and walked to the queen-size bed that was pushed against the west wall of the room. He pulled her along with him.

Several decorative pillows were tossed attractively on the bedspread. He flung them on the floor.

She heard him drop the screwdrivers on the spread, heard them clack and roll together. He dropped her wrist and she saw his hands move in and out of her short tunnel of vision. Her stomach churned and she felt weak. She thought he was placing the screwdrivers in some kind of a ritual pattern on the bed. She couldn't clearly see his motions, except for his hands forming a sort of circle with the screwdrivers. *Oh, my God!* At the top of the circle where one's head would be, she thought she saw the blurry form of the smallest one. Then, it seemed on both sides at approximately three o'clock and ten o'clock, he placed two more. She moved her head closer, it seemed to her at five o'clock and seven o'clock, he laid out two more, and the longest one, he placed at six o'clock with the shining blade pointing upwards.

What was the significance of the screwdrivers? Desperately she thought of reading how the Boston Strangler had thrust broomsticks into the vaginas of his victims.

She shivered and wiped her moist palms on her thighs against her nightgown.

"What are you doing?" she asked. She didn't recognize her voice. It sounded husky and dry.

He didn't answer. He pushed her against the bed and she stood braced, staring at his chest with her arms at her sides.

"All right, take off your clothes."

"Oh, no, please! You don't want to do this. It's not worth it."

She could feel his eyes on her, looking her over. His voice was tough and cold. "Don't give me a hard time or I'll kill you. I mean it. I'll kill you without thinking about it. Just like I did your dog."

Eileen nodded her head. She could not miss his flat determination. He meant every word he said. She pulled her nightgown over her head and dropped in on the floor. Then she stepped out of her panties and straightened her shoulders.

She stood shivering.

Her throat ached.

She wanted to cry, to scream, to beg, but knew it wouldn't do any good.

Then, strangely, she thought again about her plan to get his fingerprints. She had succeeded. They were on the screwdrivers. On each one.

I hate you, you son-of-a-bitch. If I live through this, I'll get you and she screamed high inside herself.

Chapter 3

Eileen waited for the man to grab her. She was wet with perspiration. Trembling with fear. She had backed up against the end of the bed. He loomed in front of her, his head blocking the light coming from the dimmed starlight lamps in the metal track that ran across the kitchen ceiling. Then, he did something that surprised her. Almost hesitantly, he reached for her left breast and brushed the nipple with the tips of his fingers. He drew back momentarily and then repeated the gesture, touching her right breast awkwardly with the fingers of his left hand.

Eileen was astonished. A little boy would do something like that, she thought, touching a girl quickly in a forbidden place. Was he afraid of her? In the kitchen when she had stumbled against him he had jumped. Maybe he *was* afraid of women. Afraid of them and drawn to them to prove he was a man. Maybe if she resisted he wouldn't go through with it.

His steel-edged voice broke into her optimistic thoughts, "Lie down on the bed."

"You don't want to do this. *Please,*" she pleaded with a mounting panic.

"Shut up. Lay down."

Roughly he pushed her right shoulder, upsetting her balance and she fell on the bed. He fumbled opening his belt and dropped his pants, climbing on the bed, his knees straddling her. Eileen's left leg angled over the corner of the bed; only part of her buttocks rested on the mattress. His weight was heavy and uneven. The smell of corn flakes and garlic filled the air. He was breathing heavily, rapidly. She turned her head, thinking she was going to be sick. She swallowed the lump of nausea in her throat.

"Now put it in," he ordered.

Eileen found the man's penis with her left hand and guided it to her vulva. She tried not to tighten when he pushed inside her. She thought about the screwdriver that lay near her right hand. "You're hurting me," she cried.

He grunted and kept pushing.

Her fingers tightened on the screwdriver. *Jab him with it, now!* It was sharp. She could stick it into his left side with one quick blow. It might penetrate deep enough to strike his heart. And if it didn't? What if it struck a rib? Glanced off? He'd yell, roll off her and probably kill her. He still had the knife poised in his right hand. She knew he was strong; his bare arms supporting his body were smooth and hard.

Suddenly he pushed himself away from her and rolled off the bed.

"Don't move," he said and walked into the kitchen, returned, looked at her and went into the living room. She could hear him doing something, then he returned and grabbed her wrist. "Get up," he ordered. She stumbled as she followed, pulled by his rough grip on her arm.

In front of her seemed to be the overstuffed chair cushion on the floor. "Get on your stomach," he growled. Eileen almost cried out. She groped her way to the floor feeling even more helpless and vulnerable than before.

Suddenly, he threw himself heavily on top of her, squashing her into the pillow, flattening her breasts, pressing his weight into her body until she gasped for breath. "Oh, my God," she thought terrorized, "he's going to sodomize me." She wanted to scream, to block all the openings in her body.

Don't tighten up, she cautioned herself, *it will hurt more if you tighten up.* The image of a little female terrier she had seen in the park when she was walking Bonnie and Bethie flashed in her mind. The dog had been pinned against a tire in the wheel-well of a parked auto by a big yellow dog who jabbed her excitedly. She had squealed with fright and pain as he forced himself into her and hammered her swollen pudendum.

The man's hard thighs pressed against her buttocks as he suddenly thrust his penis into her vagina. She felt a sharp streak of pain, then he was sawing at her, his hands clamped on her hips, pumping and thrusting.

Trying not to scream Eileen buried her face in her arms. She squeezed her eyes shut as his thumping, jarring strokes pushed her into the pillow. As she endured his grunting and mechanical pumping, tears ran down her cheeks. She felt stained and humiliated. She was being raped, plundered, in the most secret part of her body. And she hated herself for being afraid, for crying, for being helpless, for lying still when she wanted to kill him.

Time passed. How much or how little she was uncertain. Now she sensed the man was slowing. As he began to withdraw he grunted. Her despair reached its lowest point. She had been used by an animal. She wanted to collapse, melt away, become nothing. How many other women had he made feel so degraded? She wondered, as she felt his penis pull out of her.

She lay still for several moments, while he stepped over her like a piece of garbage, walked into the office bedroom and grabbed up his pants. She heard him pulling them on, buckling his belt, giving little grunts of satisfaction as he dressed himself. Then another horror came into her mind. What if he had AIDS? She shivered and felt hollow again . . . and suddenly, furious. The quick, cunning anger that had come to her in the kitchen when she plotted to trap his fingerprints on a drinking glass had fled. In its place was a swelling rage that gave her new control and direction. Had the other women he raped felt as used as she did? Had they felt the same rage but been afraid to think about it because it would show?

Eileen stifled her sobs. If he heard her it might excite him, give him a feeling of power. She wouldn't give him the satisfaction. She pushed herself up on her knees. She was sore inside. Her vagina felt raw, swollen, traumatized. She tried not to think about it. She was alive. And she was determined to find a way to make him pay for every tear she had swallowed. At the same time she felt lost, angry, fearful of the man who had just raped her. She concentrated on the anger.

There were several things she could do to make him pay. All of them involved learning more about him to tell to the police . . . if she lived. He could be identified by his fingerprints . . . and maybe by DNA typing his semen. She had read that this modern form of scientific identification was foolproof. His blood or semen . . . if he'd put some in her . . . could be tested. But she was not certain he had ejaculated. Certainly he had not come to a discernable climax.

Eileen decided she would not urinate. If she could delay voiding her bladder until the police arrived, then maybe a vaginal smear could prove his semen was inside her. She would be making a major installment on her scheme of retribution. Even as she swore to hold back, to contain her urine, she felt the first small warm warning of bladder pressure.

Just because she had survived rape twice did not

He paused, seemed to be thinking about something, then said, "Look I'm sorry I hit you on the head. If your dog hadn't barked and you hadn't screamed, I wouldn't have done it. I couldn't have you yelling your head off, and waking up everybody."

His voice softened again. "Tell you what," he said. "I'd better wash the blood off your forehead. I don't think the cut's bad. Come on, get up."

"Oh, you don't have to do this. It's stopped bleeding."

Strange man, Eileen thought red-faced, a surge of anger surfacing. Apologizes for hitting me on the head, but no remorse for raping me.

She pushed herself off of the couch. He placed his hand on her shoulder and prodded her along gently in the direction of the bathroom.

The telephone receiver was lying on a rolled towel beside the tub. As he entered the bathroom behind Eileen, he saw it was attached to the plastic telephone cord that hung from the empty cradle on the wall. Suddenly his anger exploding, the intruder's fingers dug deeply into Eileen's shoulder and he whirled her around to face him. She stumbled, frightened, bewildered and grabbed the sink so that she wouldn't fall. "You bitch," he hissed, the telephone receiver up to his ear.

"You called the cops!" he yelled. "When did you do it? I ought to kill you right this minute."

The hand that had guided her to the bathroom was suddenly waving the knife in her face. He pointed the sharp end into her throat. The metal point punctured her flesh as he pressed it into her skin.

"No," she cried. "I didn't call anybody. I forgot to hang it up after I took my bath earlier. I didn't call anybody." She gasped, "I forgot to put it back. I always take it off the hook when I bathe. I just forgot to put it back."

Her whole body shook. "I wouldn't try to trick you. I don't want to get hurt anymore."

He slackened the pressure on the knife. She felt the point drop away leaving a stinging reminder. Her eyes smarted from the pain; she struggled to hold back the tears.

"If you fooled me, I'll kill you, bitch. I want you to understand that. I don't want any surprises from the police." He pronounced the word "po-lease", the first example of street vernacular Eileen had heard him use.

"Look I just forgot to put the receiver back." She took a deep breath. "I haven't lied to you about anything have I? I'm not a fool. I wouldn't take chances with my life."

"Well, you'd better not," he said coldly, warningly. "Now, sit down there on the toilet seat and I'll take a look at your head."

She flinched not wanting him to touch her again.

"You really don't have to . . ."

"That's okay. I don't want anybody thinking I go around hurting people without a reason. Here, hand me that wash cloth from the shower."

Trembling, Eileen gave him the still-damp cloth from the soap-dish handle where she always hung it. He held the nubby cloth under the water spout in the porcelain basin, wrung out the excess water, then carefully sponged Eileen's head until the water ran clear of red. When he had cleaned her hair of the crusted blood and could see the cut in her scalp clearly, he said, "Oh, that's not bad at all. Two or three stitches will fix it up good as new. Now come with me."

Eileen dried her face with a towel and started after him into her bedroom. There she heard Bethie snoring on the rumpled bed. Moving close she could see Bethie's right eye was swollen shut from the blow she had received from the intruder. It protruded like a walnut from the side of her nose. The sheets and covers of her bed were spotted with drops of her own dried blood. Bethie groaned when the man picked her up and put her in Eileen's arms.

"She'll be all right," he said gruffly. "Put her down after you've petted her and we'll go back to the living room."

Strange, twisted man, Eileen thought. His kindness in washing her wound may have helped him to expiate his guilt for striking her, but it did not lessen her hatred of him by one iota. She was in a contest of survival. He obviously no longer thought of her as a threat because she was blind. He had taken the time to prove to her that he was not all bad. That meant her estimate of him had some value to him, and maybe that was a sign that he would allow her to keep her life.

As she was leaving the bedroom Eileen realized she could hold back her bladder no longer; she could not save the evidence of her assault. The scare with the knife in her throat had sharpened the pressure to urinate. There was no way she could delay voiding until the police came—until they took her to a hospital. Holding out beyond another minute or two was going to be impossible.

"Hey, I've really got to go to the bathroom" she told him, "I can't wait any longer." Her cheeks felt hot and red. If that wasn't foolish! The man had invaded her body twice and now she was embarrassed about telling him she had to urinate.

"You have to leave the door open," he said without hesitation. "I'll stand outside the door."

When Eileen returned to the living room he called to her, "I have your purse." He removed her wallet and leafed through the credit cards. When he came to her bank cash card he lifted it out and examined it closely.

"Eileen Ross. Eile-e-e-e-n Ro-s-s-s-s-s" he said, elongating her name to give it false emphasis.

He said it again, drawing out the pronunciation, and Eileen, irritated, said evenly, "Yes, that's me. Who are you?"

"Wouldn't you like to know?"

"Yes, I really would. But instead I'll give you a name to remember you by."

"What name?"

"I think Hani is a good name for you."

"Who? Hankey?"

"No, Hani."

"Hani? What kind of a name is that?"

"It used to be my boyfriend's name."

"And you want to call me that?"

She bit her lip. "It wasn't a happy relationship."

"Wow! He must have been some dude?"

Her face tensed. "Nobody can compare to him."

"Little blind girl got hurt, didn't she?" he said with mild sarcasm. "I've got your bank cash card," he chuckled. "Forget about names, I'm not telling you mine. I don't advertise. Just give me your bank card number."

Eileen looked at him with alarm.

"I . . . don't remember it."

"What do you mean you don't remember?" he said ominously.

"Well, it's new," Eileen faltered, "I don't remember it. I . . . I . . ."

In one angry stride, the man reached Eileen and dug his fingers hard into her chin. The knife pointed out of his other fist in a straight line to her throat.

"I told you not to bullshit me, and you keep trying. I've given you more slack than anybody 'cause you're blind. But you're taking advantage of me. Now, I'm going to cut you. You need a demonstration." He pushed the sharp cutting edge of the blade under the shelf of Eileen's chin.

"All I have to do," he growled, "is to saw this once and your neck will flop open like a stuck pig."

Eileen began to shake. Her voice choked as she sobbed, "I . . . Oh, God . . . the numbers are the same as the word 'beagle.' I remember that. I just have to think what numbers the letters stand for . . . Don't hurt me. I'm sorry . . . I didn't mean . . . anything."

Hot tears ran down her cheeks. She couldn't see his face; but the threat in his voice had scared her more than anything he had said, more than the screwdrivers. He was angry, furious, a vicious, controlled rage. He was going to punish her for taking advantage of his lenience with her. Eileen realized she had made a fatal mistake. Trying to fool him about the cash card may have jeopardized everything. Instinctively, Eileen understood she might not survive the next few minutes. The edge of the knife was indented so deeply into her skin that an ounce more pressure would slice her flesh open. Her tongue was parched and her mind was blank. She couldn't visualize the numbers that stood for 'beagle.' She knew she was going to die.

Chapter 4

"You got the numbers yet?" the man asked. He pushed the knife a little harder against Eileen's throat. Eileen ached to swallow but didn't dare; the wrong movement might jar the blade and cut her deeply.

"Please," she cried softly, "please. I think I remember."

He reduced the pressure on the knife but held it in position. Gratefully, she swallowed, feeling the dryness in her throat, a burning ache that throbbed.

Desperately, she had been trying to visualize "beagle"—the letters in the word that would correspond to numbers on a telephone dial. She forced her mind to identify the combination. The number corresponding to "b" was two. Thank God! They came faster and she said, "The number is two . . . three . . . two . . . eight . . . No! . . . four . . . five . . . then three. That's it. Two . . . three . . . four . . . five . . . three."

The man removed the knife, he stepped away. On her writing desk against the wall he found a postcard she had received from a friend vacationing in Oregon, and he wrote the numbers Eileen had given him on the margin. As he bent down to print the combination, Eileen, standing where he had left her, realized how weak she was. Her head was swimming; she swayed, jerked herself upright and took two deep, shuddering breaths. She had almost fainted. Her terror had overwhelmed her senses. In the last few seconds, she had come closer to death than she could ever have imagined. Never in her life had she been so frightened and so helpless to do anything about it.

The hardest thing for her to do was not to lose control, to keep her wits about her so she could eventually get even with this man. She was moaning silently for what she knew was to come. She knew she was never going to be the same again. Even if she survived, part of her trust of other human beings was going to be gone. In its place was the anger she was hiding, holding on to like a fiery beacon that made her strong.

The man strode over to her and said, "Well, its time for me to go. We'd better figure out what you're going to say to the cops when you call them." She flinched but she wasn't surprised. It was time for him to leave. *What more could he do to her?*

She listened carefully as he told her he was going to take the second-hand mink coat, which he thought was valuable, the VCR, a few dollars in change from the kitchen cupboard, her cash card, and the shrimp from her refrigerator. "That'll go good for a snack. I really like shrimp." Then he said, "Now this is what you tell the cops. You just say a man came in here and robbed you. Nothing else. Remember, I do get even and I could kill calmly. Now, we'd better rehearse this so you won't forget."

"Now I'm going to be the police," he said, drawing her across the room to her desk in the office. He picked up the telephone receiver and held it against his ear.

"Hello, pooolice," he said elongating the word with a humorous intonation in his voice. Eileen was amazed at his jocularity. He wanted her to cooperate in his comical portrayal of a desk sergeant answering an emergency call. "Now, what do you say?" he asked Eileen, indicating she should pretend that she was calling 911.

She gulped and tried to think of something. "Oh. I, uh, oh, police? I've just been robbed. I want to report it."

"Now that's not how a frightened, angry person would call the cops," he said. "You've got to sound more convincing," his voice hardened, "otherwise they won't even show up."

For the next few minutes Eileen practiced calling 911 until she got what he considered was the right sound of urgency in her voice. She felt stupid performing for the man, hearing herself promise never to reveal anything that had happened to her except the theft of a few valuables. He had threatened to come back and kill her if she talked. Twice, he had promised to return and murder her (he used the word like a club), if she reported anything more than the robbery. Did he actually believe she was going to say nothing? Didn't he understand that once he was gone he couldn't frighten her anymore? If some of his victims—and she was sure now that there had been many—had concealed their rape and lived with the memory waiting for it to fade, but never free of the agony, the terror, she knew she would not. There were many women like that. Poor, intimidated souls who convinced themselves that their shame outweighed the brutality of their rapist. But she wasn't one of them. She had survived. She would get even.

She heard the Joan Baez cassette that had been playing for ten minutes or so and realized she had been so terrified that it had been become an indistinguishable part of her ordeal. Now she focused on the lyrics. The song was "We Shall Overcome". And she realized the supreme irony of the words echoing in a room where rape had viciously stolen a woman's private sense of herself. Her bitterness surged in her throat like bile. She was going to make those words come true. Despite her current vulnerability. In the end he would pay.

When the man asked her suddenly how close was the nearest branch of her bank, Eileen told him calmly there was an automatic teller located at 86th Street and Lexington Avenue. She hoped he would go there because she would send the cops, when they came, to that location.

"Now, I'm going to tie you up," he said. Eileen protested.

"I've promised not to say anything. Don't you believe me?"

"I'm not going to take the chance you'll get your courage back before I get a head start. I don't want you talking to anybody for at least ten minutes."

He used the extra long earphone cords from her tape deck to tie her on the couch with her right hand roped to her left ankle.

As he lifted the suitcase from the floor, he said, "You're not tied too tight. You'll get loose in a little while." He walked with his booty to the office. She heard him open the window over the work station. She heard a thud. He must have pushed the suitcase through the window, then followed it into the protection of the shrubbery where he had concealed his entry into her apartment.

Eileen stayed in the awkward position in which she'd been left for a few minutes to make certain that the man was gone for good. Around her the walls seemed to reverberate like an echo of disaster. Then there was an overwhelming silence. So ominous that Eileen shivered involuntarily. She couldn't see the window where he had made his exit. There was no other sound except the last few bars of the song.

He had left her right hand free to pluck at the knots he'd made in the cord. She struggled with them but she couldn't get them to give or unravel, they were too tight. She tried standing up. The cord was too tight to allow that but it stretched a little when she partially straightened. Stooped over, she hobbled slowly into the kitchen. She sat down on the chair and with her free hand grabbed the house phone that connected to all of the extensions in the apartment building. She dialed the security desk.

"Help me!" She yelled into the phone. "Call the police. I've been raped. This is Eileen Ross in apartment one thirty-five. I've been raped. Call the cops. I've been raped."

She was trembling so hard she wasn't certain of the spoken acknowledgement that came over the intercom, but she didn't trust the results. She couldn't call 911 because she remembered the bathroom phone was off the hook. Reluctantly, she decided to call her friend David Wilson, who lived in the same building. He had a key to her apartment but, sick as he was, he would have to drag himself out to the kitchen to answer the phone.

His voice fogged with sleep finally came on the line.

"Who . . . yes. What is it?"

"David, it's Eileen. I've been raped. Listen to me! Wake up. Can you understand what I'm saying?"

"Eileen . . . you've been raped? Jesus! Are you all right?"

"I've got a bloody head and I'm tied up. Please could you come down and cut me free?"

"Eileen, oh my God. It'll take a few minutes. Have you called the cops?"

"No, but I called the building super and told him to. So far nobody's come."

"Bastards. I'll be down there as soon as I can."

She waited for what seemed an interminable time but was no more than ten minutes. Finally, David opened the door with his key. She heard him as he reached the hall outside the front door.

"I'm coming, Eileen. I'm coming," he yelled.

She was still an awkward captive of her bonds when David entered. He swayed against the door frame; as he came closer to her, she noticed how gray he looked, how he resembled a frail, tired, older man. He breathed rapidly, heavily from the physical effort it cost him to come downstairs.

"Oh, David, I'm so sorry I had to wake you." Eileen's mouth trembled. She was going to cry. The presence of her friend, the security and concern he represented, melted the last residue of strength she had clutched about her for the last two hours.

"Oh, God, David, I am glad to see you," she sobbed, unable to stop the flow of tears that ran down her cheeks.

"It's alright now, Eileen." he said. "Jesus, you look terrible. Is your head alright? Did he hurt you badly anywhere?"

Unable to speak Eileen shook her head, still overcome with the feeling of safety David gave to her.

Finally she got control of herself. "Bonnie, on the terrace, will you please get her? I don't know whether she is dead or just tied up. I hate to ask you, but please."

David nodded, got to his feet with an effort and walked to the terrace door. He was gone no more than two minutes when he returned.

"She's okay," he said, "tied to the rail. I took the rubber band off her mouth. She's fine. She licked my hand."

David sat down on the couch and worked on the knots that bound Eileen, listening as she told him what had happened. His fingers moved slowly picking at the cord and he took deep breaths to give himself the energy to complete the simple chore.

"I'll bet he came in the window with the broken latch," he said, as he finally freed Eileen's left hand.

"I'm sorry it took so long," he wheezed. "How many times have you complained about the latch?" he asked. "You ought to sue the bastards." He shook his head and wound the cord slowly around his hand in a loose circle.

Shakily Eileen got to her feet and walked to the bathroom. Her hand shaking she replaced the receiver.

Then, taking a deep breath she called the police, after which she telephoned her best friend Kay. David and Eileen were both sitting on the couch when they heard a series of knocks on the front door and a voice announced: "Police."

Eileen admitted the two uniformed policeman into her apartment. They appraised her shrewdly, looking accusingly at David, and the middle-aged one with salt and pepper hair said harshly, "Did he hit you? Are you alright? Did you guys have a fight?"

Alarmed, fuming about his assumption, Eileen retorted, "Are you crazy? No, no, he's a friend. He came down from his apartment to let me loose. The rapist tied me up."

"You were raped?" the cop asked suspiciously.

"Yes," she said softly.

"Who hit you on the head? Him?"

"No!" Hot tears stung her eyes.

"Listen," the younger policeman said, "The call we got came in as a domestic squabble. Does he have a key? Did you know he was in the apartment? We'll have to fingerprint you," he said turning to David, who sat amazed and angry on the couch.

In the next few minutes Eileen fought to control her temper as the two policemen inspected the apartment and shot a barrage of questions at her and David that clearly indicated the men were convinced that the two were lovers who had quarreled. The older cop charged

represented, not only to herself but to millions of New York City women who were at risk. As Eileen thought about making her rape public she did not once forget that her intruder had said he would kill her if she talked. What would he actually do when he read a description of himself in the daily newspapers? She was unsure. But despite this fear, her mind was made up.

David Wilson, fatigued and showing the ravages of the illness that had opened his body to virus attack, was allowed to return shakily to his apartment when Eileen persuaded the rape squad that he was the man who had freed her from the bonds attached by her rapist.

Then, courteously but insistently, they pressed her to tell them exactly what had happened during the two hours the intruder held her captive. When she told them about the fingerprints she had induced the man to leave in the kitchen on the blue drinking glass, that they could find the glass in the sink, the chief of the rape squad detectives sounded surprised. Quickly he added, "Good thinking."

She told him also that she was certain the intruder had left more fingerprints on some of the porcelain surfaces and fixtures in the bathroom. Her narrative was interrupted by the arrival of the ambulance attendant who perfunctorily examined her head and said it wasn't bleeding, but needed stitches. When police technicians came through the door to dust the apartment for fingerprints and search for evidence of the intruder's identity by insignificant things he may not have known he left behind, the sex crimes interrogators interrupted their interview with Eileen long enough to direct the evidence team to the objects in the apartment Eileen had designated.

By 6:00 A.M. "official strangers" had taken over Eileen's apartment. Officers walked in and out carrying on various aspects of the investigation.

Kay Ketchum, the close friend Eileen had called after David freed her, came into the apartment, identified herself, inspected Eileen critically, gave her a reassuring hug, then picked up Bethie and promised to take the dog by cab to a twenty-four hour animal medical clinic in mid-Manhattan. The dog was listless and sleepy, symptoms of a concussion. After delivering Bethie, Kay would meet Eileen at Lenox Hill Hospital, where she was to be taken in a few minutes after the Sex Crimes Squad completed the first round of questions.

Eileen was grateful for Kay's strong support. She was a woman who translated friendship into action.

As Eileen walked to the ambulance, dressed in her bathrobe, escorted by two members of the Manhattan Sex Crimes Squad, one of whom was the female detective, Eileen began to realize gratefully that it was probably going to be many hours before she would be able to return to this apartment. She suddenly discovered the idea of being alone here was disturbing. How could that be? She loved her home. It was her nest, her place of safety. Here she was unassailable by the world.

Then she realized all that was gone, her security, her independence. The acknowledgement was like a stone dropping. Bewildered, she blinked her eyes to stop the tears from coming again. She had always liked being alone, independent, pleased that she was confident enough to take care of herself. Now she felt afraid, a deep emptiness at the way her life was altered. It would never be the same again. "Oh, God," she said to herself, "it isn't fair! What am I going to do now?"

In the ambulance, the detectives collaborated in a stream of questions to Eileen about her state of blindness. Could she see well enough to identify a man from a mug shot? Could she recognize a man standing across a room? What was the medical name for her vision disability? In what way as a blind person could she infallibly identify an intruder? By touch? By hearing? Could she recognize the man's voice?

Eileen was still answering the questions patiently when the ambulance arrived at the Lenox Hill Hospital emergency ramp. She was helped out of the vehicle and guided through the silent doors.

She sat alone for a few minutes in an examining room which she was certain was like dozens she had seen in her career as a medical transcriptionist. There was sure to be a metal table with a thick pad covered by a crisp white sheet. Locked cabinets with rows of drawers that contained medical supplies and surgical tools. Two round, vertical stainless steel posts would be attached to the foot of the table and from their high ends would hang six-inch plastic loops, or there would be stirrups.

There was a brisk knock on the door followed by the entry of a uniformed man, who identified himself as a police photographer, in the company of the female member of the Manhattan Sex Crimes Squad.

Eileen was asked to stand and be photographed. As the photographer shot flash pictures of her from several angles and asked her to sit down for a closeup of her head wound, the female detective explained that the photographs were for the police victim's file and would form the basis for a crime action folder the Manhattan District Attorney would compile on her case. Eileen was also expected to permit herself to be fingerprinted at the 20th Precinct the following day. The detective gave her personal card to Eileen when she and the photographer departed.

Another woman who identified herself as a doctor

—no name—entered the room with a uniformed nurse who later came to be known to Eileen as Karen.

Eileen could not see the woman, but from tunnel vision glimpses of her and a general impression, she pictured the physician as a tall, spare woman in her mid-thirties who wore a stethoscope around her neck and a starched white jacket. She explained tonelessly to Eileen that she was going to conduct a "chain of evidence" examination and each part of the examination required the victim to sign a consent form giving the hospital permission to conduct the procedure. The results of the physical investigation of Eileen's body, she said, would be turned over to the NYPD's crime laboratory.

Eileen disliked the woman instantly. She was cold, imperious, without humor or personality. Moreover, the nurse standing by her side with a clip board of hospital forms showed Eileen little comfort or warmth. Eileen was angry. Here she was a rape victim, a woman who had been viciously invaded physically and emotionally, and now the signs on her body of the rapist's intrusion were going to be listed and described by medical personnel who demonstrated absolutely no interest in her welfare.

Eileen scribbled her name on the first form with a pen the nurse gave her and stood on the small white paper footpad the nurse placed on the floor.

With the doctor looking on silently, Eileen removed her bathrobe and handed it to the nurse, then drew on the flimsy white hospital gown the nurse gave to her. The paper crinkled under her toes as she shifted her weight. She was surprised when the nurse said, "The paper is to catch any body hairs or fibers the man may have transferred from his clothes to you."

She indicated another form for Eileen to sign, then the doctor touched Eileen lightly on the elbow and silently directed her to climb onto the table and lie on her back. The nurse folded the paper mat Eileen had stood on and put it into a paper bag.

"I'm going to do a vaginal examination, Eileen," the doctor icily said, lifting Eileen's left leg and sliding a plastic loop around her ankle. She repeated the procedure with Eileen's right leg and Eileen found herself lying on her back with her legs spread. She felt awkward and uncomfortable.

The doctor began to describe the steps of her examination in a calm, impersonal voice; Eileen thought she detected a degree of warmth that had not been evident before.

"I'm going to dilate you, Eileen, and examine you for penetration and injury. And I'll take some swabs." She held some kind of a long shiny instrument which Eileen could not clearly see. It was called a speculum, and vaguely resembled an elongated pair of large tweezers with flat leaf-like ends. She warned Eileen that she might feel an instant of coldness when the ends were inserted into her vagina.

"Don't tense," the doctor warned.

There was a sudden odd, cold shock when the instrument separated the labia majora, the soft, sensitive pliable lips inside the vulva. Eileen squirmed uncomfortably. She hated being poked at.

"You're not on estrogen are you?" the doctor asked. "When was your hysterectomy?"

Eileen confirmed that she was not taking estrogen and hadn't been for six years. She told the doctor the uterus had been removed in 1980.

The doctor nodded and inserted cotton swabs into Eileen's vagina. Eileen flinched as the doctor removed them and handed them to the nurse who smeared the fluid-saturated cotton on two glass slides. Paying no attention to Eileen's discomfort the doctor went on, "I've got to pull some hairs now, Eileen. You'll feel the pinch."

Eileen winced as the hairs came out. Hardly pausing the doctor said, "Now, you'll feel something in your anus, Eileen. Just a cotton swab to get a specimen."

"He didn't sodomize me," Eileen objected.

"Well, we don't want to take any chances do we?"

Eileen felt the slight pressure of the cotton probe and stiffened her back. Then she tried to relax. Another invasion, small as it was, was not going to matter after what she had been through. Despite her resolve she felt tears come into her eyes. She hid them with her arm shielding her face.

The doctor appeared not to notice and offered no words of comfort. "Now I'm going to comb your pubic area, Eileen. We're looking for any foreign debris, dried semen, anything deposited by the man who did this." Eileen felt the teeth of the comb run through the hair on her pubis. Though she hated the procedure, Eileen was glad it was being done. It was the final step toward creating evidence against her rapist.

"Sit up," the nurse motioned impatiently, disengaging Eileen's ankles from the plastic loops on the vertical posts. Eileen opened her eyes. She heard the doctor leaving the room. No word of encouragement, no consoling statement, no attempt to express the empathy of one woman for another who'd been injured. A cold bitch, Eileen thought and took the clean comb offered her by the nurse and combed parts of her hair now entangled with dried blood. She gave the comb with the loose hairs embedded in the teeth to the nurse. She put them in another envelope.

In the next few minutes, as Eileen sat on the edge of the table, the nurse released the neck tie of the hospital gown and examined Eileen's skin closely with the aid of a portable ultraviolet lamp. "I'm looking for semen stains on your skin." She said and gave the hospital gown back to Eileen and announced cheerfully, "All that remains now is to draw some blood and get a urine sample."

"What about the stitches in my head?" Eileen asked. "The doctor left so fast you'd have thought her ass was on fire."

"That's no way to talk about a doctor."

"You work for her, I don't. What about my head?"

"Well, It's not bleeding. There'll be an intern along in a little while. You'll have to be patient."

"Patient, crap, I've been raped, attacked with a hammer, kept a captive in my own home for two hours, and now I'm told I have to wait for an intern to put stitches in my head. I don't have time to sit around. I want to get hold of Crimestoppers. I want other women in this city to know about the bastard who did this to me. I want the cops to feel a little heat so they'll get moving and find the rapist before he does it to another woman."

The nurse was startled. Eileen heard her step back in surprise. "Oh, no, dear," she said. "You're just in shock. Why we couldn't let you do something like that, that you'd regret for the rest of your life."

The nurse leaned forward and said earnestly, "A rape victim often doesn't realize how deep the shock goes. You just don't want to make any important decisions until you've talked to a psychiatrist. Why I know a woman who was raped on a date and put off psychiatric treatment and six months later ended up in a mental institution. You don't want that to happen to you do you?"

Eileen turned her face in the direction of the

woman and said, "Thanks for the advice but I want to use a phone."

"I just told you that we can't allow you to do something you'll regret. It's our responsibility to tell you what your best interests are. Now, listen I'll just take your blood, and you collect your urine in the bathroom, and after that why don't you just lie down here and rest and collect yourself. After you've had a little nap, you'll see things a lot clearer. You have a right to be worked up. You've been through a terrible ordeal, but you've got to place your confidence in us. We see a lot of rape victims. The last thing you want to do is to draw attention to yourself. You don't want to do something you'd end up hating yourself for. And nobody would understand why you did it."

Eileen was about to reply when there was a knock on the door and Kay Ketchum poked her head in. "Are you decent?" she asked.

The nurse started to ask, "Who are . . ." but Eileen breathing a sigh of relief called out, "Kay, thank God you're here." She turned to the nurse and said, "This is my friend, Kay Ketchum."

"Oh, good," the nurse grimaced at Kay, "Maybe you can talk some sense into her."

Kay raised her eyebrows, arches of eloquence in a lovely face with a contrived expression of responsibility and calm, "Of course I'll help her do the right thing," she said walking over to Eileen and giving her hand a squeeze of comradery.

"You're just overwrought," she said and squeezed Eileen's right hand again to let her know she was on Eileen's side.

Kay chatted amiably with the nurse who took blood from Eileen's left arm. A few minutes later, the nurse left the room with a urine sample from Eileen and the rape evidence kit bearing the swabs and slides and permission forms.

When she closed the door Eileen urgently whispered to Kay, "They won't let me make a call. You'll have to get hold of Crimestoppers. And tell them to come to the hospital."

"The hospital's not going to like it."

"That's their problem. I won't let that stop me. I want that bastard caught. I've thought about it a lot. Keeping quiet may protect a woman's name, but it hides the man. I'll turn the city upside down to find the son-of-a-bitch."

"Good for you," Kay beamed.

It was forty-five minutes later when Kay and Eileen decided that diversionary action was necessary if Eileen was going to get her story on television. By then Kay had contacted Crimestoppers at Channel 7 as Eileen had asked, informing the news reporter, Rolanda Watts, that a rape victim who had been assaulted in her East Side apartment wanted to make a public plea for the capture of the intruder. Watts told Kay that a camera crew would start rolling toward the hospital in a few minutes and would meet Eileen in the emergency room waiting area.

Kay was waiting there when Watts, an attractive black woman with high cheek bones, snapping brown eyes and a cultivated voice, appeared and was told by a hospital guard and a nurse supervisor that she and her cameraman would be barred from the examining room where Eileen was waiting.

"We'll wait in the TV van across the street. We'll do the interview outside," she said.

"Oh, no you won't," the nurse snapped. "You have no right to be here. It's our responsibility to protect the privacy of the victim. You should be ashamed."

The news reporter shrugged, motioned her cameraman to proceed her out the door, and cast a look of inquiry at Kay, who nodded imperceptibly. She was followed by the truculent security guard who stood with his hands on his hips and waited until Watts and her companion crossed the street heading to their news van. Once Watts had retreated, the nurse turned to Kay and said in a withering tone, "If you can't behave yourself and follow hospital rules, we will have to ask you to leave. You're not doing your friend any favors by encouraging her to do something she could regret for the rest of her life."

Kay stifled the retort that was on her tongue, turned on her heel and pushed into the examining room. When she told her friend what had happened, Eileen said in a rush, "The news people won't wait forever. I've got to get out there. Damn fools. I'm not going to let them ruin my chances to nail this guy."

Eileen's fists were clenched and she was shaking slightly. She took a deep breath and gathered her thoughts for a moment. Then suddenly she smiled wickedly at Kay. "Listen," she said, "how about causing some excitement, kicking up a fuss so I can slip out of here? Will you do it? You know, raise hell with them for stalling, for not fixing my head. Yeah, that's a good idea, distract them so they'll get mad at you, so that I can slip outside in the confusion."

Kay smiled broadly. Her lovely, serene patrician face lighted with mischief. "I love it. I'll do it," she said. She started for the door, then stopped.

"What are you going to wear for God's sake? Won't you look ducky on TV in that peek-a-boo hospital gown? You could drive a truck through that slit down the back."

"Oh, don't worry about me," Eileen said. "I'm going to wrap the sheet on the examining table around me."

Eileen had removed the sheet from the table when she heard the sudden screeching tenor of Kay's voice through the examination room door. "You bastards, why don't you stitch up her head? You think you can intimidate her by keeping her waiting? And where are her clothes? Why are you hiding her clothes?"

Eileen grinned as she completed the job of reversing the hospital gown, folding the vertical halves in a long closed seam and tying the sheet firmly at her waist so that it enclosed the ends of the gown. She opened the examining room door and slipped out. Though she could not see Kay standing flushed and angry, her aristocratic chin thrust forward pugnaciously at the nurse supervisor who was lamely defending the hospital's right to preserve a patient's privacy, Eileen could imagine the scene.

She began to quickly walk in the direction of the outside door. Eileen had been at Lennox Hill Hospital on several occasions in connection with her medical transcription business. The Medical Records section was not far from the Emergency Room. A revolving glass door led onto 77th Street where she wanted to go. Across the street Rolanda Watts and her Channel 7 TV news van waited.

Eileen felt her courage rising, her resolve hardening as she found the revolving glass door and slipped out. As she left, Kay was being confronted by the nurse supervisor, the burly security guard, two wide-eyed emergency room receptionists, an irritated doctor and an amused hospital orderly.

"If you don't quit making a scene," the security guard said, "I'll have to remove you bodily."

Kay's lovely mouth tightened. "You touch me,

buster, and you'll have a lawsuit on your hands quicker than you can say I'm sorry."

"Don't you have any concern for people who are ill? Your commotion can jeopardize their recovery. You must lower your voice. Really! *I insist!*" the nurse supervisor said to Kay.

Turning her head, Kay saw Eileen gliding out the revolving door; she smiled at the nurse supervisor and shrugged. "You people have got to learn that you can't force people to . . ."

The nurse glanced in the direction Kay was looking, only to see Eileen—bareheaded, without shoes, hair tangled, pale, determined—in her inverted hospital gown and sheet-draped skirt leaving.

"Stop," the nurse shouted and rushed to the revolving door. "Stop! If you leave the hospital, we can't treat you any further."

Eileen did not even turn her head. She had reached the curb on East 77th Street. Across the thoroughfare, Rolanda Watts was waiting and an assistant was walking toward Eileen, watching for traffic from both directions.

Striding out of the building, Kay joined Eileen. As they started across the street, the nurse supervisor turned and rushed stiff-backed through the revolving door into the Emergency Room reception area. She was obviously intent on getting help to thwart her runaway patient. It was too late.

Rolanda Watts grinned at Eileen. "Where are your clothes?" she asked.

"The police took them for identification purposes. The hospital gave me a gown and I borrowed the sheet."

Watts laughed, "You're one spunky lady. Does your head hurt? Who's your friend?"

"My head's battered but okay and this is Kay Ketchum, a very good friend."

The news reporter turned to Kay and said, "You're the one I talked to on the phone?"

Kay nodded.

Eileen, intent on her purpose, rushed on, "What can I tell you that will help you find him?"

"Well, I need you to answer some questions before we start the tape rolling. You're an anomaly. A raped woman who's not ashamed to admit it. How come?"

Eileen sighed. Suddenly, she felt giddy, exalted and at the same time weary and drained. All of the resolve pent up during those agonizing hours had had some positive result. Now, she was going to tell a story that would reach an audience of millions of people. Someone would see her, hear her words and recognize her assailant. She was not a helpless, hapless woman.

She felt relieved, and triumphant. The promise she had made to herself in her kitchen when she realized the man was going to rape her was going to come true. She had made it come true by keeping her wits about her and now it was *her turn.* She couldn't stop the tears from running down her cheeks. It felt so good to cry, to let go in safety, to feel the accumulated tensions drain out of her.

She blotted her eyes with an edge of the sheet and smiled weakly at Rolanda Watts.

"I'm sorry," she said. "Everything came to a head all of a sudden." She took a deep breath, then said, "No woman should be ashamed of being raped. Hiding from what's happened doesn't do any good." She lifted her chin and her voice firmed.

"A man came into my apartment, kept me prisoner for two hours, raped me twice, stole my thrift shop mink coat, the little jewelry I own, some cash, and a bank card. I have a right to be mad. Women who keep quiet, because they are afraid people will stigmatize them are playing right into the attacker's hands. Well, I won't. I want that bastard caught. I want him punished. I want other women to know that they have to speak out if they expect any kind of action. I want to put some heat on the cops, so they'll catch the guy while he's still fresh in somebody's mind, who may have seen him."

Rolanda Watts nodded her head. "Good for you," she said.

As the interview continued Eileen stood straight and determinedly in the sunshine of a hot July day with the sound of traffic on East 77th Street in her ears, and the nostalgic, sharp smell of warmed asphalt in her nose. She answered Rolanda Watts' questions honestly and clearly, giving the terrifying facts of what happened in her apartment. Then she made her heart-felt plea that women should not shrink from publicity, that they should come forward and accuse their attackers because publicity would not only aid police in the capture of the violent men, but would act as a positive deterrent to prospective rapists, who might think twice if they thought there was a real danger of being reported and apprehended.

Eileen was practical enough to realize that probably no more than a minute of her interview would be aired, no doubt accentuating the actual details of the rape, her description of the man and the fact that he was carrying her suitcase. The parts involving her frank attitude about public disclosure by rape victims would probably be minimized, if used at all. But, poised and determined, Eileen unflinchingly told it as it was and began to bait the trap which would snare her attacker.

Chapter 5

The Seventy-First Precinct in the Crown Heights section of Brooklyn, at the corners of Empire and New York Avenues, is housed in a modern steel, glass and concrete building. Centrally located among the surrounding neighborhoods of apartments, quiet, tree-lined streets and small, busy enclaves of dry cleaners, gasoline stations, jewelers, grocers, bakers, dentists and florists, it is typical of dozens of newer police stations in New York City.

As Detective Lieutenant Jim McGeown hurried up the stairs he looked pensive, apprehensive. Arriving at his office on the second floor he felt suddenly more at ease. For fifteen months he had occupied the twenty-by-twelve-foot space. Human nature being what it is, he had endowed the room with his quiet, reflective personality and a few objects of his profession. Occasionally, he laughed at himself when he viewed his official space with the eyes of a visitor. To a stranger—a civilian—who had never been in a squad commander's office and who was unfamiliar with the trophies and emblems of police life, he supposed his room would have looked shabby, impersonal and cluttered. But he liked the faded posters on the gray walls exhibiting smudgy black photographs of "Perps," the cop term for men and women who were wanted for crimes. Many of the ones pictured in his outdated posters had long ago been caught, and were either incarcerated or had their cases relegated to the unsolved files.

There was an enlarged street map of Brooklyn on one wall. It took up an area four feet by five feet, was covered by a sheet of light green glass, which, when the light was right, displayed fingerprint smudges around its edges. There was a wooden bookcase behind his desk with hardcover copies of police procedurals, department manuals, books on criminology and case reports. He had been tempted to frame his masters degree in criminology and display it modestly on one of the walls, but decided it would earn him jibes from the other cops at the Seventy-First who may have accused him behind his back of being a show-off. He knew he was referred to as the "Professor" because of his frowning, stooped-shouldered manner and the thoughtful, soft-spoken way he insisted on choosing his words carefully before he gave an opinion on something.

Well, he'd discovered the time taken for consideration before a decision often saved hours of regrets. The habit of weighing advantages and disadvantages had saved his life dozens of times in a twenty-four year career in the NYPD. From the time he'd walked a foot post in Harlem, hating the rain and snow in winter that slipped down the collar of his black rain cape like a cold finger, he had exercised caution and balance in his thinking. *Don't act precipitously before committing to an irreversible course of action* was the watch phrase he had learned to rely on. That didn't mean holding back when action was called for. Plenty of times he had been in dangerous situations from which he had escaped because of the "cold eye" inside his head that measured the odds and gave him direction.

In short order he had risen from rookie in Harlem, to Queens and auto crimes, to uniformed sergeant in Manhattan Detectives and two years later upgraded to lieutenant. He had collected his slight stoop from a drug dealer in Queens who had dragged him sixty feet when he thrust his arm into the man's car displaying his shield. He had managed to boost himself into the driver's lap in the accelerating vehicle and subdue the man, but not before his body had sideswiped a telephone pole and he had lost his shoulder holster and gun in the wrenching collision. His sprained neck, torn muscles and abrasions healed, but the injured vertebrae reformed in a slight curve, giving his shoulders a forward cast, a stoop.

In the years that followed he had earned a reputation as a tough, no-nonsense cop, a man of steely determination who acted decisively once his mind was made up.

Now he sat down behind his desk, tilting comfortably in his chair, the color of the morning light through the window behind his desk promising another hot July day. In a few minutes, when his squad arrived, he and they would have to make an important decision. They were meeting to decide whether there was enough evidence to declare an official crime pattern for a suspected serial rapist who had been terrorizing Brooklyn women. The Sex Crimes Squad, of which he was the commander, had been investigating a half a dozen brutal rapes in Brooklyn committed, they were certain, by the same man. The squad had a reputation for success. In a remarkably short period of time—less than a year and a half—it had earned a reputation for apprehending two vicious rapists and dozens of other less violent sex offenders.

One of their arrests had been the infamous Bensonhurst Beast, Lionel Walker, who had been convicted and sentenced to forty-three years in prison. He had viciously raped women in Queens "every morning," he had told one member of the Sex Crimes Squad. An equally violent nineteen-year-old, Keith Braithwaite, who preyed on young children, was paraded in handcuffs on television after his capture by the sex crimes cops to end the fears of anxious parents who had been accompanying their children to and from school. The young rapist was sentenced to ten to thirty years for his crimes.

McGeown chewed on his lip thoughtfully. Despite the unit's success he knew that the department frowned on line cops playing up to publicity. A cop who snared a bad guy and talked about it could be seen as trying to build credit for himself—a risky reputation to get in a business where one's name should *never* be written larger than the New York Police Department itself. As he thought back over his team's remarkable arrest record, he had to admit that from the standpoint of the police brass who monitored the activities of their subordinates, their reputation had a touch of flamboyance. The team had been dubbed "The Fancy Dans", a nickname that presumably arose when two members were observed in evening clothes at a Hispanic Society dinner in Great Neck, Long Island. Actually, they were moonlighting, with permission, as waiters in formal attire.

The fact was, though, the Sex Crimes Squad was vulnerable to criticism because of its success. And that was the crazy part. Jim knew it took a special kind of detective to investigate rape cases. As a class of crime it was so low in the police rating system that cops who were assigned to "sex" squads were automatically considered to be screwups. Even Jim had once believed that being sent to a rape squad was like being demoted to Siberia. And even in New York City, with perhaps the most experienced, best trained police force in the nation, cops hated to work rapes.

Homicides were more glamorous and robbery detail was a quicker route to promotion. And not only were rapists elusive and difficult to catch but their emotionally shattered victims could give detectives a lot more grief than the silent ones left behind by the act of a simple killer.

As Jim thought about the publicity his unit had attracted as the result of the capture of the "Beast" and the ugly headlines demanding results that had preceded the arrest, he realized that the brass didn't like the way he handled sex crimes. Already, he had heard rumors in the Old-Boys-In-Blue Network that his team was in disfavor with the chiefs in power. The brass despised the limelight; they preferred that their cops operate in the shadows. Mayhem that wasn't managed in an orderly fashion, with a minimum of publicity, was treated suspiciously. The cops involved were scrutinized in an insidious fashion and quickly, quietly, and ruthlessly ostracized. And that was the real trouble with rape from the detectives' standpoint: it attracted the attention of the cops in power to the men and women at the squad level. There was nothing worse to them than sex crimes cops who become transient newspaper heroes.

Jim sighed. The brutal acts of the criminal his squad would be scrutinizing in a few minutes indicated a personality weirder than any they had yet encountered. He wondered if the brass who criticized his unit's tactics understood that special methods had to be used to catch the strange gallery of warped, vicious, sadistic men who preyed on women. The criticisms by those higher up was a shame because the members of his squad were probably better at their jobs than any cops assigned elsewhere.

He tapped his pen on the papers in front of him and waited impatiently for his team to arrive.

Catching this particular weirdo might be the unit's

last hurrah, but they would go out with a bang, not a whimper.

"This guy's nuts," murmured McGeown. He got up and walked over to the conference table, sitting down on the wooden slot chair at the table's head.

Bob Merz was the detective who thought up the euphemism for the rapist who, monkey-like, had rappeled fearlessly down the sheer side of a Brooklyn brick building, supported only by a flimsy television antenna wire. Merz, a member of the sex team who dutifully recorded appropriate police reports into the squad's crime pattern book, a vigorous chunky man with white blond hair who wasn't easily impressed, had looked over the roof wall of an eight-story building and shuddered. Wrapped around the stand pipe near where he was standing was one end of the TV antenna; it had been severed from the portion that led down into the apartments below, then attached to the pipe. The free end had been dropped over the coping and the rapist had descended more than fifty feet holding on to the wire.

"Who in his right mind," Merz had said yesterday, "would trust his life to a flat rope made of two thin wires pressed into a ribbon of plastic?" It was obvious that the rope had stretched like a string of chewing gum pulled to the breaking point. Yet the "Perp" had descended four stories and climbed into a fourth floor apartment through a bathroom window. Merz looked down again at the antenna descending like a long slim finger pointing out the path of the intruder, and despite his detestation of a man who would rape without compunction, he grudgingly admired the recklessness, or sureness—he was not sure which—of the "Perp" who had made Spiderman look plausible. That was the name that stuck in Merz's mind. Spiderman, the character who scaled walls, climbed sheer faces and teetered on the edge of space with impunity. Merz thought up the name, but it was the newspapers that later applied the euphemism officially and gave the rapist substance and fearful form.

Merz walked in now and exchanged pleasantries with Jim McGeown. Then he poured himself coffee from a pot on a hot plate resting on a small table. He had the crime pattern book under his left arm. He sat down next to McGeown and placed the book in front of him near his coffee cup. In the center of the table were three large cartons. They contained cards on hundreds of sex offenders, parolees and other suspects. Merz had joined the New York Police Department in 1966, spent five years in uniform, switched to vice for eleven years, specializing in undercover gambling probes, earned a masters degree like his boss, Jim, in criminology and was one of the ten detectives who had been assigned to the notorious Palm Sunday Massacre.

The next officer to appear, Bruce Milau, sat down quickly, his elbows extending about halfway across the table. A barrel-chested former athlete who stood about six feet three and weighed close to two hundred eighty pounds, loved fancy jewelry and liked plain talk, the big cop had earned a chest full of medals and had the best reason to be a member of the Sex Crimes Squad. Catching the dirtbags who raped was a personal triumph every time an arrest was made. It was one more payment on the rage he had felt when a member of his own family had been the victim of a rape attempt.

He had never mistreated a prisoner, but he had been honest when Jim McGeown interviewed him originally. "I don't know what I'll do the first time I have to arrest one of these scumbags," he had said to McGeown.

Jim admired his honesty and was glad to have a

man who cared so deeply. He wasn't worried about his uncertainty. Milau was a professional and would be extra cautious about handling rape suspects because of his feelings.

Patti Kehoe, the only female member of the team, came in calling out, "Hello." Blonde and tiny, she was bright, wisecracking, and smart as a whip, a cop through and through. Her pert-looking femininity never got in the way of her job and she quickly set straight any male cop who questioned her ability to perform. Patti had graduated from police matron status midway through her training and became a full-fledged cop in 1973 when the New York Police Department reversed its policy of not putting women on the street. Before joining the sex crimes unit in the Seventy-First Precinct, she had amassed an outstanding record on the vice squad as a confidential undercover informant in kiddy-porn rackets, and earned her detective shield. Three years later she was pulled from the Seventieth Precinct and placed in sex crimes. She was furious at first; for a real cop, sex crimes weren't what a fast-tracked detective did. She thought she had been set back in her career.

As usual the last to appear was Sal Catalfumo. "Late again," Patti said, quickly ribbing him.

"Saving the best for last," Sal grinned, pulling out a chair and plunking himself down on it. Sal was a dedicated cop and they all knew it. As lead investigator on the Flatbush Rapist Task Force, assembled to capture the thug who savagely sodomized and robbed seven women in Brooklyn, he brought a broader point of view to the sex crimes unit when it was formed late in 1984 following the arrest of the Flatbush rapist.

He had been the cop who had run twenty-six year old Gregory Pought through a police line-up after the man had been apprehended by a routine traffic patrol on a gun-carrying charge. Ballistics identified the gun as the .25 caliber automatic that had been used in connection with the rape-robberies. He was sentenced to five hundred forty-six years by New York Supreme Court Justice Sybil Hart, who characterized him as "a menace to the women of Brooklyn."

Sal, a six foot-two Italian with an operatic look enhanced by his full black moustache, understood immediately the significance of the Sex Crimes Squad. By setting up a separate unit that would become expert at rape investigation in the same fundamental way that cops became experienced in auto theft or murder, a master team could be organized that could operate with maximum efficiency based on the concept of specialization. The key to the squad's efficiency would lie in its adherence to a set practice of sifting and recording and judging rape complaints that flowed in from precincts all over Brooklyn.

The team, actually designated Pattern Crimes and Special Investigation Squad, would be looking for repetitive behavior. Jim McGeown, also a veteran of the Flatbush Rapist Task Force, knew rapists were guys who did one rape, then another, then another, and another until they got caught. They were predictable as dirty streets before a rain. The strategy of catching them was simple: study the pattern of their behavior. They were cunning creatures of habit. They enjoyed hurting women, bloodying them, dominating them. The frenzied act of intercourse was often anticlimactic for them.

Now, on this hot summer morning, the Brooklyn Sex Crimes Squad was assembled for the purpose of making a final decision about the rapist they now called Spiderman. All of the squad members understood that by declaring Spiderman a serial rapist they would be creating misery in thousands of Brooklyn homes when radio and TV news reporters described the acrobatic agility with which the man entered windows thought to be burglar-proof far above the pavement. And who ever heard of a rapist that deftly bridged the wide gap between two facing buildings on a wobbly, cracked two-by-four in the dark early morning hours like some bat-eyed, high-wire aerialist, then made his entry through a kitchen window that had no outside hand grips other than the half-inch wooden frame that surrounded the square hole in the wall?

The misery in store for Brooklyners would happen when they locked their windows against the threat of Spiderman. Thousands of apartments were not air conditioned. They depended on cooling from night breezes that dropped temperatures as much as fifteen to twenty degrees. Windows were thrown wide open when the sun went down. Apartment dwellers who had to lock themselves in their unrefreshed, boxy rooms on hot summer nights to avoid being molested were going to get irritated. Tempers were going to fray and frazzle, disputes were going to break out, arguments flare, and fights were going to result in hundreds of nuisance calls to cops.

Jim McGeown sighed. "Okay," he said, taking in the three men and Patti at the table, "We'd better get started. Who's first? Sal?"

Sal Catalfumo straightened the edges of a stack of complaint forms and tapped them on the table to even them out. "As far as I can determine there's no question about a pattern. Bob has the book. We've all studied it. The guy's a goddamned, fucking squirrel. It beats me how he gets in and out like he does, but he does.

"Okay, we know this much. He's black, not shoeshine black, but mahogany. Probably weighs in at about one hundred seventy to one hundred seventy-five. Not muscular looking but strong. Has to be, to be able to get around buildings the way he does. Hair, according to four witnesses, is curly and short, close to his head like a fuzzy cap or a short Afro. He wears dirty jeans, sneakers, polo shirts. Sleeves to mid-arm.

"Some of the women insist he had a short goatee like a wad of black cotton on his chin. Others say no, he's clean shaven. Three of the women said he wore a moustache with the goatee. That's about all as far as the description is concerned. Oh, one woman said he smelled like he hadn't bathed for three or four days. Fingerprints. We've got some but so far we've got no valid suspect to match against them. That's the next step," Sal said gesturing at the overflowing cartons of suspect cards.

"Bob," Jim McGeown said, looking at Merz expectantly, "You've got the book."

Merz studiously put on his reading glasses, opened the sturdy cloth-bound crime pattern book, and unhurriedly examined several entries on a page before he spoke.

"We think this guy has raped six Brooklyn women, at least those are the ones we know about. He pops in a window in the early morning hours, between 1:00 and 3:00 A.M. I think he checks the place out first before going into the bedroom. That's my opinion because several of the victims have said he seemed familiar with where things are. Sort of tested them with little trick questions like, 'Where do you keep your cassette record player?' or 'Do you have any rings worth anything?' Does this to see if they are telling him the truth. If he thinks they are lying he waves a knife in their face. or points it at their throat.

"Before he rapes the women, he invariably orders

them to cook breakfast for him. Some of the victims have been lulled into a false sense of safety by this behavior. The guy's strange, they say. Likes to talk, likes women to talk about themselves. At the beginning maybe he's basically harmless. Maybe he won't do anything, they think. After all, whoever heard of a rapist who wasn't in a hurry? Maybe he's just after my valuables, they've reasoned. But they're wrong.

"After his chatty breakfast, he gets down to business. Actually, I think the guy was a burglar first, then turned rapist. Probably hit on some woman for her money and jewelry and decided to rape her for dessert. She didn't report it. A lot of them don't, as we know, and he figures he's got a good thing going. One thing for sure, my guess is that he cases his victims first. I think he's cagey as hell about that. Gets their routine down, checks to see who they are living with, then makes up his mind. Doesn't seem to matter to him if there is a husband involved. In some respects, it might make things easier. We've got two cases where he slipped in, jumped on the sleeping husband beside his wife and sticks a knife in the guy's throat, promising to cut it wide open if she doesn't cooperate. He gets her to tie the husband securely, then takes her in the kitchen for the breakfast scene. Then after he's eaten, he rapes her with the helpless husband looking on."

Patti Kehoe sat with her fingers clasped on the table in front of her. She shook her head as she envisioned the woman's fear and humiliation.

"Any chance," Jim McGeown asked, "that this guy is the same "Perp" they've got on the East Side, the one the newspapers are calling the Silver Gun Rapist? He's a bandit also."

"I don't think so," Bruce Milau replied.

"I talked to Manhattan Sex Crimes today. According to the cop I talked to, his guy gains entry on the street side of a building by climbing the ironworks to the first floor. He rapes and sodomizes, then steals from the victims, but no breakfast business, no chatty stuff and he doesn't linger like our boy here.

"I agree, there is a lot of similarity between the two men. About the same build and color. Dress about the same. So far their man has scored four times that they know about. But I think, from what we know, our man is more of an actor. He takes pleasure in leading the victims on, getting them to think that if they play up to his strange conversational curiosity, he won't hurt them or force them to have intercourse. Also, the Manhattan guy has never demonstrated the agility of Spiderman."

"That is right," Sal interrupted. "Bob and I have seen some of the stunts this guy pulls. He's incredible. In one case on Ocean Avenue, the son of a bitch laid a plank from the coping of one apartment house at a downward angle of about forty degrees to the open window frame in an adjacent building about ten feet away. This is on the seventh floor! Eighty fucking feet to the pavement. And this guy walks down this incline like he was strolling on Fifth Avenue. He's nuts! No, climbing a wrought-iron fence is one thing, practically walking on air is something else. Maybe we should look for a guy who has had circus or acrobatic training."

Patti Kehoe, who had been unusually quiet, was obviously burning with a contribution she had been holding back. She said, "I think we've overlooked something about this man. One of the cases shows the depth of violence I think is indicative of what we can look forward to with this 'Perp'."

Patti turned her perceptive brown eyes on Sal and said, "Remember what that kitchen looked like on Rogers Avenue?"

Sal nodded. He had a strong idea where Patti was leading.

"And remember," she said, flashing her eyes at the three other men at the table, "this was the one case where the victim got away? The woman's dog, a sort of mix between a lab and a shepherd, attacked the guy when he came in through the kitchen window. She heard the commotion and ran out the front door of her apartment. And he not only killed that dog with a knife after she left, he eviscerated it, then smeared blood and guts all over the kitchen. Christ, that place looked like a slaughter house.

"That guy was mad." Patti said. "He was furious that the woman had escaped. And to show her what happens to people who don't do what he wants, he not only killed her dog, he cut it to pieces. It was a demonstration of his frustration. And I think it was a clear warning of what we can expect from this man the next time he meets a woman who resists him, or who tries to get away. This guy is carrying a load of rage. He's going to get more violent and he's going to kill somebody. And when that happens, when he realizes how good it feels, I think he's going to continue killing.

"We've got a real bad one on our hands," Patti said in a hard low voice. "Maybe the worst one we've ever had. I think we'd better find him damn quickly. If we don't he's going to go all the way."

Jim McGeown nodded his head. He looked into the faces of Bob and Sal and Bruce and saw reflected in their grimness the deep concern Patti had expressed.

"Well," he said, "there's no question about declaring a pattern on this guy. Nothing on the TIPS line I suppose? No good citizen with a lead to the identity of Spiderman?" He smiled. "It was too much to hope for. Well, I'll go to Nicastro and tell him we want to name the Spiderman as a definite pattern rapist. He won't like it."

"He'll like it a lot less," Patti said firmly, "if some woman's killed by this guy and the newspapers find out he had a pattern of violence and the public wasn't warned. I think that's what you should do, Jim, ask him to include in a news release that this guy is crazy when he's crossed."

Jim McGeown shook his head. With mild sarcasm, he said to Patti, "Can't you just see that happening? Richard Nicastro, Chief of Detectives, condoning a press release that practically advises women to hold still for rape? That'll be a cold day in Hell."

The four detectives pushed back their chairs and wadded up their empty paper cups. They had collectively agreed to advise their superiors that a vicious serial rapist was preying on women and that every indication was that the intensity of his rape attacks would increase, eventually accelerating to rape-murder—which would elevate him into a more savagely elaborate cycle of predation on women.

Bob, Sal, Bruce and Patti left Jim McGeown struggling with the wording of his notification to the chief of detectives. They picked up the bulging cartons of police suspect cards from the table and carried them to their desks in the squad room. There were hours of checking and cross-checking of the cards to do to sift a plausible list of possibles from the discouragingly large number of twisted men who preyed on women. It was going to be like finding a crow in a swarm of cowbirds.

Chapter 6

When the Channel 7 news reporter, Rolanda Watts, shook Eileen's hand and wished her luck, Eileen smiled, placed her hand on Kay's forearm and crossed the street to go back to the hospital.

It was obvious when she and her friend stepped into the Emergency Room reception area that the hospital personnel had witnessed the filming of the news interview.

The nurse, Karen, who had been present during Eileen's sexual assault evidence examination, stopped Eileen and Kay and said sternly to Kay, "You will not be permitted in the hospital. You have to leave. *Now.*"

Kay took in the woman's determined expression and the fierce resentment in her eyes.

"I'll wait for you outside, Eileen," she said.

The nurse escorted Eileen to a different examining room.

"An intern will arrive soon to stitch your head," she said coldly.

After that the woman said nothing to Eileen. Her disapproval was evident in her glare and in her starchy movements.

Just a few minutes after the nurse silently left the examination room, a young blond-haired intern entered.

"You're Eileen Ross," he said smiling and reaching out his hand to shake hers. "I'm glad to meet you. You've had a bad time I hear, I'm very sorry."

"It's nice of you to say that," she replied. "You're the first friendly voice I've heard."

"Some of the people around here get pretty jaded. Don't let it upset you," he shook his head.

Directing her to sit on a metal stool, he explained that he was going to stitch the wound in her head. As he found scissors, sutures, medicinal swabs and antiseptic in a locked metal cupboard he observed, "You know Eileen, that rapist sounded like the one who terrorized five women and tied up a man in an East Side household."

She listened more intently, "Go on."

"He forced some women to clean their houses, scolding them because they were untidy and dirty. Can you beat that? Then he raped two of the women at gun point. They brought them to Lenox Hill Hospital and they had to submit to the same sexual assault examination that you endured."

Eileen nodded, "Those women's descriptions of the man sound like mine," she paused, "and the man's actions resemble those of the man who raped me." She frowned. "In fact, he bragged about tying up the husband of one of his victims after the man pointed a gun at him. Also, he made a point of telling me that he thought I was an inferior cook."

The intern finished sewing up her stitches and, wishing her luck, bade her goodbye. Though there were intriguing points of similarity between the two rapists, Eileen could not be certain they were the same man.

It was almost 2:00 P.M. The head nurse tried to get her to agree to stay in the hospital overnight for observation.

"It's for your own good," the nurse said in a saccharine-soaked voice.

"I think not," Eileen answered determinedly.

She left the hospital feeling liberated from an oppressive experience. Kay and Eileen hailed a taxi and went to Eileen's apartment.

"I need the opportunity to collect myself, to be alone with my thoughts, and to put my feelings in focus with the events of the past twelve hours," Eileen said wearily.

That opportunity was delayed when *New York Daily News* reporter, John Randazzo, hailed her as she and Kay entered the Navereign. A silver-haired sixtyish man, he was thorough, skillful and painstaking as he began to slowly record Eileen's account of her rape. Impressed by his diligence in getting every detail, Eileen invited him upstairs. By the time he and the photographer, Clarence Davis, left Eileen's apartment it was almost 5:00 P.M. and Eileen began to perceive that her story had caught the imagination of New York's Fourth Estate, as well as scores of people whose telephone calls kept her phone ringing.

The redoubtable Kay Ketchum dutifully took messages and listened with growing amazement at the odd conglomerate of telephone calls: some expressed sympathy, others morbid curiosity, and still others, opportunism. Eileen, involved with the *Daily News* interview, was not aware of the wide variety of the calls and some of their peculiar substance, until later when Kay could report on them and Eileen herself began to answer the telephone.

Meanwhile, interviews with the *Daily News*, a subsequent call from the *New York Post* requesting an interview, and other demands from radio and television stations for her cooperation convinced Eileen that her plan to get the media notice and enlist their aid in finding her attacker was working. In a few hours she had become a minor celebrity and curiosity. And she began to realize that she now had an opportunity to benefit thousands of women by representing herself to be atypical of the average rape victim. She recognized that most raped women, shocked, shamed and disoriented, fled from publicity, but if she could prove by her own example that quick retribution could result from public disclosure, then she could be responsible for the prevention of many rapes by men who would be frightened by the idea that they might be reported by their victims.

In truth, for Eileen, the issue went far deeper than deterrence. She was convinced that intrinsically predatory males took advantage of females because of social taboos that placed the onus on the victim to prove her innocence and lack of complicity. *That was wrong.*

Worse was the fact that women hid behind silence because they didn't believe they deserved the same sexual equality as men. She had the chance to champion the rights of raped women; if she stood up for herself and for her sex maybe other women would take courage from her example and stand up for themselves. The notion that her thinking was idealistic never really occurred to Eileen. The idea of defending the sexual rights of women everywhere was practical if she could focus her grievance as typical of theirs.

If Eileen needed additional proof about the stir of sympathy and admiration she had created, it was evident in the calls she answered when she relieved Kay at the telephone. Her growing conviction that the course she had adopted of encouraging publicity was substantiated when she listened to people congratulate her on her courage and commiserate with her for the harm she had suffered.

The voice of Louise Broadley, the hospital administrator at Flower Fifth Avenue Hospital, where Eileen had worked years before as a medical transcriptionist, surprised her.

"Eileen, I just called to tell you how sorry I was

when I heard what happened. Are you all right? Is there anything I can do for you . . . ?"

Eileen thanked her, embarrassed by her own emotion at hearing the gentle words of regret expressed by her old boss.

Louise Broadley's call was only one of dozens of surprises:

Anita Moallen, a radiologist, called offering to lend Eileen the money to buy and install a burglar alarm in her apartment. It was a sweet offer and Eileen was touched.

Adele Noppe, the demanding, crotchety chief of transcription services at St. Vincent's Catholic Hospital, who was never satisfied with the turn-around time of transcribed medical cassettes Eileen delivered to her, offered genuine sympathy and showed a different side of her personality saying, "Anything at all I can do to help. Please call."

Eileen was especially amazed by the many who called to congratulate her for reporting her rapist and having the courage to stand up to his threats of retribution if she talked.

People with whom she had only a nodding acquaintance, or those she had met walking her dogs or at hospitals that hired her transcription services, registered their distress and pledged their support. One woman offered to run errands for her if she needed her. Another offered to come for healing talks and quiet listening. She'd had a daughter who had been raped.

A transcriptionist who typed freelance reports for Eileen offered companionship and cooking services.

By the time Eileen had conversed with eleven or twelve people, she experienced that strange revision of her own sense of worth that can happen when a person is showered with attention. Other calls were not as inspiring. Eileen and Kay compared notes about all the oily lawyers who called asking to represent Eileen.

One was typical. "I am an attorney who practices in New York, and while professional ethics prevent me from soliciting your business, I will be glad to help you in any way I can. It's terrible that you were raped in your own bed. You should sue for damages."

There was always a pause after the name and advice had been given as they waited for Eileen to jump into the conversational breach and hire their services. She declined the offers.

A rude caller who identified himself as "Mike," a sophomore at Brooklyn College, said that he had seen Eileen on television. "You are certainly attractive and I don't mind blindness at all. I'm good looking with a forty-six inch chest expansion, a thirty-two inch waist and I am well hung. The girls like the way I do it and I would like to be your companion." Without replying, Eileen hung up immediately.

Another man told Eileen in broken English that he wanted to live with her and said she should send a taxi for him. She and Kay could not suppress their laughter.

Finally, after Eileen had talked with her own relatives who had heard about the rape on an early television broadcast, and assured them she was all right, she and Kay blocked incoming calls by turning on the telephone answering machine. They switched on the television and Eileen, sitting barely six inches away from the screen, studied the image of herself and Rolanda Watts. She realized she looked poignant, distressed and startled answering the reporter's questions. The last statement Watts made was: "Anyone having any information on the Ross rape should contact our hotline number." The number flashed on the screen.

It was after 8:00 P.M. when Eileen, certain of surcease at that hour from nuisance calls, picked up the ringing telephone to discover that Channel 5 TV wanted to interview her in her apartment in the next half hour. Weary, tired to the bone, numb from the emotional drain of the day, Eileen nevertheless assented. She was asked to examine artists' composites of the man police called the "Silver Gun bandit." A sketch of his face had been flashed on Channel 5 several times. A news editor wanted corroboration from Eileen, and hopefully her affirmative response that the man they had captured in drawings was the one who had raped her.

She sat on the couch and conscientiously studied the composites with the closeup vision of her right eye. But she was soon certain that the man in the sketches was not the one who had assaulted her. The reporter and camera crew thanked her and left. She heard her denials that same night on the ten o'clock news and listened to her own voice describe her intruder as a man with a moustache and a goatee.

After turning off the television, Eileen and Kay made a discovery that proved sad and disconcerting for Eileen. The woman found a hole above the beagle, Bonnie's, right eye. Eileen and Kay, who was spending the night, fondled the dog, who had spent the day with Eileen's friend David Wilson.

It dawned on Eileen as she cuddled the dog later in her bed that the intruder had lied. He had told Eileen that he had tied the animal to a railing on the terrace and had not harmed her. The hole in Bonnie's skin over her right eye and the small lump Eileen could feel with her fingers were proof of his treachery. The little dog, bewildered and in pain, shivered as she was touched. Eileen began to shake as well.

Somehow, the discovery of the wound was especially frightening to Eileen. Like other victims of violent people who come into their lives, Eileen had created in her mind a psychological map of the man who had attacked her. She thought she understood his thinking processes. And that was important to her because the accuracy of her own sense of judgment depended on the correctness of her assumptions.

She was shaken when she realized how badly she had misjudged the man. She had been wrong about him. He was far more devious, and therefore more dangerous, than she had imagined. He had threatened to come back and kill her if she told the police about the rape. She hadn't believed him. She looked at Bonnie resting against her breasts and hugged the little dog. The fear that had left her when the man slipped out the window returned and she shuddered.

As she fell into a troubled sleep, it was a comfort to know she was not alone. Rick Rivera, who worked as a messenger for Eileen, had immediately volunteered to act as a temporary bodyguard and was there sleeping on the spare bed in her office. Sammi, Kay's husband, was bunking restlessly on the couch. They were good people, a counterbalance to the terror that had come into her life.

Chapter 7

Jim McGeown stretched out on his living room couch to watch the nightly Channel 7 television news. He swore softly to himself when Eileen Ross, a rape victim, began to talk about her attacker. At first he resisted the idea, but his gut instinct told him the man the woman was describing had to be the same one his unit had been studying all day, the man who had been raping women and burglarizing them in their apartments in the Crown Heights section of Brooklyn.

What had made him momentarily resist the thought was the fact that the man his squad was after—who had been publicized as Spiderman by the newspapers—had never been known to stray from Brooklyn. All of the women he had assaulted were Crown Heights residents. Rapists were just like any other criminals when it came down to the way they operated. They confined their activities to a defined area. The reason was simple. On their own turf, they were familiar with the area. They knew where to hide and dodge and hole up when it was necessary. They knew what to expect and they planned their crimes accordingly.

Stepping outside their stomping grounds meant increasing the risks. Even rapists, who were motivated differently, by a compulsion to dominate, felt safer in their own back yards. But Spiderman's behavior was more complex than any of the rapists Jim and his squad had investigated before. Apparently he was a burglar who had turned rapist. It had happened before to break-in thieves who, attracted by the vulnerability of a woman living alone, suddenly, impulsively, attacked her.

Slowly he walked back to the living room and Jim McGeown turned off the television, stood sipping his cold coffee and thought that what Patti Kehoe had said had come true. Spiderman had showed up where he was never expected to be. That was disturbing because it indicated versatility in the man's thinking. But the sign that was even more portentous was the bloody blow he had struck against Eileen Ross. When she had screamed, he had hit her with a mallet.

McGeown could not help but remember Patti's account of the woman who had sicced her dog on Spiderman. He had gone crazy. He mutilated her dog. If she had not escaped would he have mutilated her? If what he had done to Eileen Ross was an example of the way his rage was intensifying, the answer was yes.

He picked up the telephone to call Sal Catalfumo. He and Patti Kehoe made a good team. He would send them to interview Eileen Ross and find out what else they could on her rape from the Manhattan cops.

But no matter what the circumstances were that created the opportunity for rape, it was always a discharge of anger or rage. Usually, the anger was so deeply hidden in the rapist that he did not understand he was transferring it to the hapless woman he had chosen. The rapist always thought he assaulted a woman because an overpowering need for sex drove him to it. That was an acceptable honcho male explanation. Of course McGeown knew the impetus was intense anger. Buried deep in the man, it surfaced like a monster released. And almost inevitably the second rape was more violent than the first. Each rape was a progression in violence.

As he looked at Eileen Ross on the television

screen, standing on a street in Manhattan on a hot July day, blood-spattered, her hair in snarls, clutching a skimpy hospital gown, telling her story of the man who forced her to fix breakfast for him, then raped her twice, McGeown realized that maybe she represented the "break" his squad was looking for. He decided to call Sal Catalfumo and Patti Kehoe—alert them to the Ross rape in Manhattan and let them follow through with the Manhattan Sex Crimes Unit that had investigated her case.

McGeown made a wry face. He had a low opinion of some Manhattan sex crimes detectives. He believed that most were chosen, not for their exceptional qualities, but just the reverse. Many were screw-ups, hardheads, bunglers. The worst cops often got assigned to rape squads. It was a clear indication that the brass did not regard rape as a serious crime, even though it was one of the fastest growing classes of crimes in the five boroughs of New York City.

McGeown pushed himself out of his chair and walked into the kitchen to pour himself a cup of lukewarm coffee. His own squad was a different story, the one exception to the riffraff that was usually chosen for rape duty.

Sal Catalfumo caught Eileen Ross on the Monday night eleven o'clock version of the Channel 7 television news, after he had been alerted to watch her by his boss, Jim McGeown.

After listening to Eileen describe her assailant's demand that she cook eggs for him, he had the strong feeling that McGeown was correct about suggesting that Spiderman may have changed the venue of his operation. Apparently the man was becoming more ambitious, enlarging the range of his predatory activities. That wasn't a good sign, Sal knew, for it meant the man had an ego that was expanding, demanding more emotional nourishment, more vicious delight from his encounters with the women he raped.

That was the frightening thing about the criminals who used sex as the expression of their rage. Predictably they got worse. He had never forgotten one of the victims of the Brooklyn college rapist, Derrick Hamilton, who he had helped to jail.

The girl was an eighteen-year-old, whose partially nude body had been found with her hands bound. Marks on her body indicated that she had been strangled and stabbed. Her body had been dumped in a closet at the President Street IRT Subway Station and set on fire.

Sal immediately called Patti Kehoe, the only female member of the Brooklyn Sex Crimes Squad, and she made an appointment to meet with Eileen Ross on Wednesday. She and Sal would go over the woman's story. Together, they hoped they could piece together from what she told them enough information to decide conclusively whether Ross's rapist was the same man who had attacked several Brooklyn women. On the surface, everything seemed to fit.

Sal admired Patti Kehoe. He grinned to himself as he thought about the feisty Irish temper of the blonde, petite thirty-nine year old "fireplug" with great legs and a strong determination not to be treated as a woman by her associates.

Sal's mind spun back to the way she had demonstrated her intelligence and spunk on the Brooklyn College rapist case when, after checking stolen jewelry she and her partners had gathered during the rape investigation, she discovered among the items a gold fortune-cookie charm the rapist had given a friend. It resembled one described as belonging to the girl he had killed.

Kehoe passed the information to homicide cops. When the charm was shown to relatives, they identified it as the one the girl had been wearing on the day of her death. In June, a homicide indictment charged Derrick Hamilton with the slaying of Monica Crichlow.

Kehoe's alertness had cinched the case.

Right after talking to Patti, Sal dialed a second number. He reached a detective who was a member of the Manhattan Sex Crimes Squad. When Sal identified himself, reported the Color of the Day (a police identification sign used before privileged information could be transferred by telephone), and told the man that he and his boss believed the man who had raped Eileen Ross might be the same person who had attacked at least four Brooklyn women, the man said, "Hey, don't get your water hot about that idea. We think the victim may be lying. A lot of things don't check out."

"Like what?" Sal asked.

"Well, for one thing the call came in as a domestic squabble. The security guard at the apartment house said that the woman's a trouble maker. He reported it as a fuss and said she had caused trouble before. His story was that "a black boyfriend was in her apartment when our guys from the Twentieth Precinct arrived.

"According to the guard, they had an argument. She got sore, he banged her on the head and there's blood all over the place. She gets hysterical and calls the security guard yelling rape. Well, she doesn't want to call herself a liar; so she goes along with the story when the detective shows up. Then, she gets the bright idea that maybe she can make some dough out of this thing, sue the apartment building, so she calls Channel 7.

"Next thing you know she's on the 5:00 o'clock

news. The security guard says she was always belly-aching about something. So, if I were you, I'd take her story with a grain of salt."

Sal Catalfumo thanked the detective and broke the phone connection. He wasn't convinced that Eileen Ross was lying. The rapist's insistence that she cook breakfast for him was too familiar to ignore. He had pulled that game on the four Brooklyn women.

Sal decided to withhold judgment about whether she was telling the truth until he spoke to the woman personally. He knew cops were as impressionable as anybody else. If the security guard didn't like the woman, had had a run-in with her, his report would have been biased. There were a dozen things that could affect the way a victim's story was evaluated. Sal would wait and see but, reflecting on her television appearance, there was something about the young blind woman's strength and determination that impressed him.

Officer Richie Harker, who had also watched the rebroadcast of Eileen Ross's interview on the Channel 7 news, had a hunch. The problem was that since he was not a police detective but a "Latent Print Man" in the New York Police Department, he didn't have the authority to follow it as far as he would have liked. He had seen Eileen Ross on television during the news Monday night and now the next morning, he was rushing out to buy a *New York Daily News* and read a printed version of her story. For, he always said, mulling over details, there was never any substitute for the printed word.

Now, at 8:00 A.M., he was drinking a cup of coffee in a little Crown Heights delicatessen where nobody bothered him and he could think. It was a neighborhood hangout with a few tables and a kitchen from which came marvelous cooking odors. Nobody tried to mind your business here and that, plus the good coffee and danish, was something he really appreciated. It was also convenient and safe for cops who wanted to talk informally with street people who liked a discreet place on neutral ground when they had some important information to impart.

Right now, he was thinking about an informant who did not like to be thought of as a snitch. His tidbits of information reflected his "good citizenship." The ten dollars or twenty dollars Harker occasionally passed over to him was certainly not payment for anything. The amounts were too small for that. Reimbursements were, the man insisted, for expenses.

The last time Harker had seen his informant had been several weeks earlier when he had passed on a tip about a burglar. When he first heard Eileen Ross on television the night before, something had rung a bell. And that's why the *Daily News* story he was now reading intrigued him. The newspaper account, written in sparse journalese, reported the fact that the rapist had insisted that Eileen cook breakfast for him:

"Ross said she tried to make scrambled eggs, toast and bacon as the man searched her apartment. As the eggs cooked, he forced her into her bedroom and raped her. He then nibbled some food and raped her again in the living room."

The breakfast scene was what fascinated Richie Harker. It was *distinctive* behavior. It marked the man who had assaulted Eileen almost as thoroughly as a legible fingerprint. What he wished he could do, but he didn't have the authority, was to call Eileen Ross and ask her if the rapist had demanded fruit juice with his breakfast.

That was the hunch he wanted to prove. As a Latent Fingerprint man for the Seventy-Seventh Precinct in Crown Heights, Brooklyn, he and his partner, Jack Baker, were among the first on the scene after a major crime had been committed. Among the hundreds of prints they had lifted in the past year was a man, yet to be identified, whose profession was burglary. But he was a burglar with a difference. Either he was stupid, didn't care, or was on dope when he was on the job.

He had left his fingerprints on fruit juice bottles at two burglaries. At least four or five other burglaries bore witness to his habit of drinking juice, or a soft drink if he couldn't get fruit juice, before he left the scene. That's why Harker was interested in the *Daily News* story, the part about the rapist forcing Eileen Ross to scramble eggs for him. What did he drink with his breakfast? Or had he requested a drink afterwards? That's what Harker wanted to know.

The answer to that question contained implications that could be crucial to the Brooklyn Sex Crimes Squad which was investigating the Crown Heights rapist, who also forced his victims to cook breakfast for him after swinging like Tarzan into their top floor apartments.

In Harker's mind were several diverse pieces of information. If he could bring them together, when united they might provide the information to find out the identity of Spiderman. Harker ticked them off, one by one.

Of course, first out of the starting gate was the fact that there was absolutely no proof that the burglar who had been ransacking apartments in Brooklyn's Crown Heights was the same person as the rapist who climbed down sheer walls to enter inaccessible apartments in Crown Heights and raped the female occupants. But there was reason to believe he might be, Harker thought, scratching his chin.

The next fact to consider was that six weeks earlier Harker's snitch had fingered a man who might be doing the burglaries. Harker had discovered the man was an ex-convict with a burglary rap sheet that was impressive. There had been no reason for Harker to connect him to any rape burglary attacks until Eileen Ross had gone public with her story of an assailant who liked women to cook for him before he raped them.

Richie's idea of matching the Brooklyn burglar who liked fruit juice with the rape burglar might have come earlier if he could have been sure that the four other Brooklyn rape victims prior to Ross in Manhattan had cooked breakfast for their assailant. This information, if it had been recorded, would be in the police reports filed by the cops who first investigated the rapes. And that was the next hitch.

You didn't go barging into a detective's case with an unsubstantiated theory unless you wanted to be reprimanded for sticking your nose in somebody else's business. Also, you couldn't very well ask a detective if you could see his case report on a rape unless you were prepared to tell him what you suspected.

In a way, Harker mused, the system helped to defeat itself. Valuable information like the piece which had come from Eileen Ross was available in other cases, but shame and fear in rape cases encouraged victims to keep quiet.

Another limiting factor was the archaic precinct system of fingerprint identification. A Latent Print man in a typical New York Police Department precinct had on hand hundreds of prints which related to criminals who were thought to be operating within the general jurisdiction boundaries of the precinct. If a burglar, whose prints were unknown to the precinct, was active he might remain unidentified for weeks until he became really troublesome. Then, the precinct print man would take his prints from a crime scene over to BCI (the Bureau of Criminal Identification) in downtown Manhattan and search among the thousands on file.

The comparison checking had to be done manually, an unbelievably tiresome process open to serious errors because of the tedium involved. There was talk about computerizing the fingerprint system, but until that happened the biggest police force in the world was hampered by horse and buggy methods comparable to handcranking a car to start it in the electronic age of reving up the engines of the turbo jet.

The result was that dozens of crimes waited for solution or were pushed back in priority by more headline-catching offenses that demanded quick action. In the Seventy-Seventh Precinct, there were seven men in Latent Prints: Harker and his partner, Jack Baker, two other two-man teams, and Frank Pagnucci who was the fingerprint technician, the inside man. His job was to search the precinct's fingerprint file for matchups with new prints taken from a crime scene by Harker and Baker and the others. The seven men were pressed to keep up with the work load. Despite the pressure, Harker and his partner had done such a thorough job of dusting for prints at a crime scene that almost singlehandedly, for a memorable period of time, they had produced evidence that matched dozens of suspects to their crimes. The result was fewer plea bargains, more punitive sentences, and a general warning to burglars. Reported burglaries in Crown Heights fell in one year from an average of three thousand to twenty-one hundred. The police brass was impressed.

When Harker's informant gave him the name of Tyrone Graham, he described the man as "a dude who likes to hurt people." He was fresh out of Attica and was a professional thief whose specialty was burglaries and break-ins.

At that point, Harker had no special feelings about Graham. He was just another "mutt" who broke into places for a living. He certainly didn't associate Graham with the baffling robberies of certain top-floor apartments in Crown Heights buildings. He was mystified by them and at first confided to his partner, Jack Baker, that he thought they had been performed by a family member of the victim. He said the same thing to Frank Pagnucci.

"Listen, Frank, I think these burglaries are inside jobs. A son or daughter-in-law. You know, stealing from the folks. Hell, there's no way for a mutt to get in. No fire escapes, nothing."

As the number of top-floor burglaries increased, the percentages alone ruled out the idea of thieves in the family stealing from their own premises. It was then that Harker noticed that empty juice bottles or soft drink containers were reported by tenants who invariably found them in the kitchen, although one white-haired lady who lived on Eastern Parkway was furious to discover two empty Coke cans and dried rings on her grand piano. She was helpless with rage and threatened by the idea that someone so thoughtless could have entered her home at night while she slept.

Harker shared his information with his partner and both men decided it was another piece of evidence in the crime pattern of a window man who had the agility of a monkey. Later, with the name furnished by his informant to go on, Harker called BCI in Manhattan and spelled Tyrone Graham's name carefully to the administrative aide in the Latent Print Section of police headquarters at Number One Police Plaza.

Although the New York Police Department did not

then have a computerized fingerprint comparison system in effect, it did furnish computer searches in its criminal name file. Tyrone Graham was revealed as a repeat burglar offender who had been paroled from Attica State Penitentiary in March of 1986. New York Police Department gives every convict a serial identification number. It was this number, with Tyrone's name, that Harker turned over to Frank Pagnucci with a written note requesting a search of the precinct files for copies of his prints.

A few days later, Harker received a call from Pagnucci. "Hey, Richie, how hot is this guy, Tyrone Graham?"

"Well, the word is he's a bad dude doing burglaries."

"Well, we don't have his fingerprint card. I'll have to go to Manhattan and get it. I called BCI. This guy hasn't been arrested for years. He's been away. So what's the big deal?"

"I call it gut instinct," Harker said. "Go to BCI. Get his card. I think he's doing his thing over here. If I'm right you'll probably get him on a couple of hits and put him back inside for a couple years."

That was the last time Harker thought about Tyrone Graham until the day he watched Eileen Ross on television describing her rape in Manhattan.

Chapter 8

For a few moments after Eileen awakened late Tuesday morning her mind was clear of the events of the previous thirty hours. It was a hot July day, and sunlight flooded her room in rich yellow colors. Bonnie and Bethie were cuddled in small mounds near her left hip. Bethie was still sluggish from the concussion wound in her head, and Bonnie, who'd also been struck, was still moping around. The veterinarian, to whom Kay had taken both dogs for examination, had said they could mend at home.

Eileen sat up in bed, separating herself from the dogs and eliciting a groaning complaint from Bonnie. God, she thought, was it only yesterday the rape had occurred? *Yesterday* seemed like a memory from the distant past. As she sat there thinking, Kay Ketchum's words about how fortunate it had been that Eileen had stayed "cool" and had boldly planned a strategy of submission to stay alive filtered back to her. Eileen reflected on the fact that strength and violence seemed to always have been part of her life.

The Queensbridge Housing Project in middle-class Queens, New York, was where she had first learned about life. Her earliest memory, a fond recollection, was the one of Christmas in 1951 when she was almost two. She could still remember her father hoisting her on his shoulders and taking her to the hall closet where she could reach for candy kisses wrapped in silver foil hidden on the shelf. It was a delightful discovery. Under the tree that year was a lovely doll her mother had chosen for her. Eileen promptly named it Lulu from the nonsensical children's song, "Little Lulu." Thirty-five years later, Lulu was still a comfort to Eileen, a surviving childhood companion who always reminded her of the best years in her life.

It was Eileen's father who had taught her to play the guitar and later it was he who had run interference for Eileen with her mother.

Ross (Rosario) Musumeci, blind since he was ten years old from spinal meningitis, had originally opposed Dorothy Musumeci's decision to have a baby. A history of congenital cataracts in her family practically assured that any children from the union of Ross and Dorothy were going to be blind. But Ross loved their only child unstintingly.

Unlike his daughter, Eileen, who had some vision in her right eye, Ross Musumeci was totally blind. Yet he was a mechanical magician, his ability to repair almost anything and his mastery of the piano, organ and accordion were indicative of the independent spirit which he passed on to his only daughter.

There was much similarity and sympathy between them. They had the same slight build, and a stranger who didn't know their relationship would have guessed in an instant by the similarity of their features that they were father and daughter. It was from her father, in feminine form, that Eileen inherited the shape of her head, her straight nose, dark eyes and clear brow. And it was first from him that she had learned to be effective as a human being, not to be overwhelmed by the setbacks nor conquered by the challenges of being blind.

Her mother was still warm and loving until Eileen was three. In her memory there were two women, a good mother and a bad mother. It was strange, when she thought about it, how the two images never merged. One was the patient, caring woman who had shown amazing tact and insight into the fears of a neighbor's child who was blind, deaf and retarded. Dorothy Musumeci became the caretaker for the two-year-old when her mother was too drunk to care.

Eileen, only a little girl herself at the time, was afraid of Delores who threw things and, with strange, uncoordinated movements, wildly crawled and bumped into furniture, bruising herself as she cried with anger and frustration. She lived in a frightening world. Delores had nothing. Her parents, who could see perfectly well, ignored her or treated her with contempt. They fed her like a little animal. She lived in a hostile darkness, unable to express her terror and bewilderment.

Dorothy taught the child to walk, how to feed herself, and to tap on the table, creating sounds she could connect to herself, to an act of her own volition.

What progress Delores made under the supervision of Dorothy Musumeci would disappear in the long chaotic intervals when the parents would take her back home. When she reappeared, she would be wild and uncontrollable again, a small human trapped in an inefficient body, unable to express her anguish except through undecipherable noises, erratic motions and banging with her fists.

Eileen didn't like Delores coming over. She didn't understand her. She wished she would go away but her mother had been patient and tender with the child.

Her mother seldom spoke of her own childhood. Eileen learned about it years later and it helped in a small way for her to understand the woman who brought her into the world.

Dorothy had been orphaned early, abandoned by a father who was a drunk and a mother who suffered from the eye disease that Eileen would inherit. She left

Dorothy to be raised by Catholic nuns. Her upbringing was strict and loveless. Housed with other children in a dormitory, the nuns made a fetish of obedience and reinforced their authority with coat hanger beatings of young flesh that left red welts and shaking fear of blackhooded figures who crept in the dark to discover children talking after lights out.

When Dorothy wet her bed at night she was punished in a singular way. The next morning she was forced to drag her soiled mattress across the street onto the lawn in front of a public high school. There she sat, the object of scorn and ridicule from the students, until the nuns thought she had learned her lesson. Eileen never forgot that story of her mother's humiliation.

Marriage for Dorothy was like a sentence being lifted. She met Ross Musumeci in a photographic film processing plant, where they both worked in the dark room. Ross loved music; he played the piano beautifully. He represented freedom and a cultural bridge to Dorothy. Ross, though at twenty-three, only a year older than she, married her barely five months after they met. For her, his musical talent was a tangible connection to the exciting world of movies and plays and effervescent stars whose names were like beacons of light to her.

She liked his voice most of all. It was rich and had the texture of a person whose horizons were expanding.

Disturbing signs of the other woman in Eileen's mother began to surface when Eileen was three. Eileen was left-handed and naturally favored that hand when she fed herself or brushed her hair. Dorothy felt that left-handedness somehow denoted weakness or inferiority or an insidious difference in her child. And she insisted that Eileen use her right hand. If she gave her daughter a glass of milk she would not release it unless Eileen took it in her right hand.

When Eileen persistently demonstrated stubborn adherence to her left hand, Dorothy resorted to cruelty. On one occasion when Eileen reached out for an object with her left hand, her mother grabbed her fingers and wrenched them painfully. Another time because her elbows were on the table, Dorothy whirled at Eileen and growled like a dog. The guttural, snarling sounds coming out of her mother's mouth frightened Eileen. Dorothy never conceded the battle of left-hand preference to her daughter.

School was more of a trauma for Eileen at five than for her classmates with whom she eventually made friends. But then her mother wanted to completely control the thoughts and actions of her daughter. Eileen was too young to understand her mother was repeating the stern control on her own daughter that the nuns had imposed on *her*. All Eileen understood was that her once loving mother had become a tyrant. As long as Eileen acted out her childhood within the prescribed limits of her mother's approval, there was harmony between the two of them. But whenever Eileen expressed ideas of her own, Dorothy thought she was being a traitor to her mother's love.

Eileen learned braille in a school in which only part of the student body was blind. In the first grade she met Pat Logan who was to become a longtime friend. For years their paths crossed. Eileen also met Richard Wingard, Allan Oringer and Denise Decker who, with Pat Logan and Eileen, formed a group of five who hung out together.

Denise's mother died when she was six; it was Eileen's introduction to death. She sympathized with her friend and regretted the loss of her mother whom Eileen had thought was beautiful and kind.

Fortunate to spend the first year or so of her schooling with Miss Sullivan (who had taught Helen Keller), Eileen discovered in her replacement, Miss Roman, a woman who played favorites and who took a firm dislike to Eileen and her four friends. She displayed her disapproval of Eileen one day when Eileen showed up in class with dirty knees and a soiled dress. She had left home clean and bright, but got involved in a game with other kids and was soon playing on the floor of the bus.

Miss Roman waited until Eileen, wearing the blue and red striped sailor dress that had been immaculate when she left home, came to the front of the class with other children. It was her turn to proudly hold the flag in a patriotic pledge of allegiance ceremony.

When Eileen was in position with the flag, the teacher stepped to her side and took the standard out of her hands.

"Go sit down," she ordered. "You're filthy. Dirty little girls can't hold the flag. I guess your parents don't know when you're filthy!"

Eileen never forgot Miss Roman's cruel, unfair words. What kind of world was it, she later pondered, that would create a sighted woman blind enough to think that people without sight could not keep their children clean? For as long as she was a pupil in Miss Roman's class, Eileen never, after the flag incident, received a satisfactory mark for hygiene on her report card.

Eileen discovered when she was seven that she was a natural at roller skating. She soon became a familiar figure on the sidewalks of the Queensbridge Housing Project. Her keyhole vision gave her the confidence to spot obstacles immediately in front of her and her ambient vision of indistinct shapes was sufficient to give her a sense of daring as she whizzed on the straight concrete surfaces. Roller skates constituted a freedom that was exhilarating to Eileen. She could escape from the cloying supervision of her mother for hours at a time, lost in a feeling of physical and emotional release.

An event that was to change Eileen's life profoundly and to sharpen her sense of her mother's instability with other people was an invitation that came by letter from the Lighthouse for the Blind for Eileen to audition for a small part in the Broadway production of *The Miracle Worker.* It came about because on Saturdays, Eileen's mother would take her by train from Queens for activities at the Lighthouse, which was located in Manhattan.

For Dorothy Musumeci it meant sitting for four hours on a Saturday to wait while her eight-year-old enjoyed the activities the Lighthouse offered blind children. It illustrated Dorothy's intention to keep a short string between her and Eileen. Eileen was going to be the child in Dorothy that had never had a chance to flower. There was no sacrifice of hers too great to achieve that objective. She refused to understand that her dominance of Eileen was inexorably driving her daughter away from her.

Other blind children traveled together from Queens to the Lighthouse by bus. It was an interval of freedom from their parents that the kids looked forward to. But Dorothy insisted on the tiresome train trip. It extended her influence over Eileen. For Eileen, it increased the hard core of resentment for her mother that was growing larger every year.

The Lighthouse was a wonderful place for Eileen. There were a lot of marvelous activities. There was bowling, roller skating, game room, pottery making, drama classes, dozens of things to do. She signed up for drama, but found it too dull and switched to the game room after two weeks and divided her time between that activity, roller skating and bowling.

Roller skating brought her in contact with Richard Swanson, a boy a few years older who found the dark-eyed, dark-haired Eileen fanciful and exuberant. They were soon skating hand in hand and talking about the skaters they admired on TV's Roller Derby. Eileen refused to be swayed by derogatory comments from her friends about Richard's having to repeat a grade in school. He was thirteen. They said they loved one another and for the first time, Eileen was smitten.

Eileen also met a young man who sat in the lobby of the Lighthouse and played the guitar. She admired the sounds he could coax from the strings and his beautiful music stirred longings in her heart to learn to play. The man was Jose Feliciano, who many years later achieved international recognition and fame for his artistry.

Another person Eileen never forgot was a strange, gentle man named Malcom Parkhurst who was a volunteer at the Lighthouse. He was especially kind to the blind little girls and bought gifts for them. Always, however, courteously asking the parents for their permission. He was a compassionate, indulgent, kind man, affluent, apparently, for he spent money extravagantly. Once he asked Dorothy for permission to buy Eileen her own roller skates and he accompanied Eileen and her mother to a posh sporting goods store in Manhattan where Eileen chose skates "just like the ones they wear on Roller Derby."

The pair the clerk placed on her feet felt like gloves. They had round bumpers, just like the professionals', hard rubber balls that extended from the front of each shoe. They were a dream. They cost $125. Dorothy was astonished. Eileen's father only earned $73 per week. Eileen was delirious with joy.

An exciting happenstance came into Eileen's life at that time. The letter came from the Lighthouse to her parents about the audition for *The Miracle Worker.* It was the result of a contact made by the producers of the play. An important scene in the play occurred when Annie Sullivan, played by Anne Bancroft, was leaving the Perkins School for the Blind in Massachusetts to teach Helen Keller in Alabama. It was a tearful good-bye in which the children at the school made their farewells and embraced their teacher.

Eileen was among twenty-four children about her age whose parents were attracted to the idea of their participation in the play for several reasons. The Musumecis, especially Eileen's mother, wanted her to do it. One reason was that each child who had a part in the play would earn $135 per week. The second inducement was unspoken. There was the opportunity to be close to the glamour of the stage, to rub elbows with people whose names were framed in lights. Dorothy Musumeci was star struck.

The audition took place at the Playhouse Theatre on 48th Street and 7th Avenue. Seated in the audience were the principals of the play, Peter Van Zandit, Dick Via, William Penn. The lines Eileen was asked to recite were: "I'm sorry you're going away, Annie." On the day of the audition, Dorothy dressed Eileen in a lovely, pale yellow dress; her hair was softly curled; there was a blush in her cheeks.

When she met Anne Bancroft, the actress said, "Oh, what a lovely child."

Eileen herself was not impressed. Miss Bancroft was a nice lady but her mother acted as if the actress was a goddess. Eileen would have preferred being on roller skates or skylarking with her friends. At that age, she was thoroughly a tomboy and enjoyed activities that were physical, noisy, and exciting.

When her mother gushed at her on the way home that she was sure Anne Bancroft would put in a good word with the casting director for Eileen, Eileen said, "Oh, Mom, she was just being polite." Her overexcited mother's tremendous need for her to get a part in the play was almost pathetic, she decided.

Four children from the Lighthouse for the Blind were selected. Eileen was among them, and was chosen to be understudy for the others. Donna Pastore was chosen, a child who had been a poster model for the Lighthouse. The others from the Lighthouse were Lynn Schoenfeld and Rita Levy. Two sighted children were selected, Candy Culkin (Bonnie Bedilia's sister), and Dale Bethea.

Almost from the beginning of rehearsals for the play the parents tried to develop strategies to advance the course of their children. Eileen discovered from other children actors that her mother was not the only one who had gone "crazy", acting like a stage mother whose own fantastical dreams of lucky stardom were rekindled in her daughter.

"You've got to show yourself off to best advantage, Eileen," Dorothy kept advising her. "You never know where this one part will lead."

Eileen was glad for her father's sake that the money she earned, far more than his own salary, was going into the household to improve the Musumeci standard of living, but Eileen, always practical and down to earth even as a child, didn't subscribe to any of her mother's flights of fancy concerning her future on the stage. She was grateful for Miss Bancroft's attention to her and she realized she seemed to be a favorite of the actress. But she didn't know how to reciprocate Miss Bancroft's subtle display of preference.

When a new phonograph came in the mail for Eileen from the actress, Eileen was proud but nervous telling her friends of the gift, but she could not have anticipated the furor among the parents of the other blind children that the gift caused. They demanded that Miss Bancroft discontinue showing favored treatment to Eileen. The actress was astonished at how a gesture of approval could be so exaggerated out of proportion. Afterward, obviously annoyed by the parental attitudes, she kept her distance. When the actress abruptly turned her back on Eileen as if she didn't exist, Eileen became hurt and disappointed and commented on it to her mother, expecting sympathy.

Eileen's mother could find no fault with Anne Bancroft. To friends and acquaintances she spoke of her "friendship" with the actress, making polite conversational exchanges between her and the actress as more than the civility of one person to another when they are confined with a group in a small place of work.

Dorothy's determination to squeeze every ounce of value out of the tiniest compliment from the actress made Eileen feel physically sick. She was dismayed hearing her mother make up things that never happened between her and Anne Bancroft. She was embarrassed for her and sorry that she had to depend on the reflected glow of another person to put light into her life.

After the opening of *The Miracle Worker* in Philadelphia and the return of the play to Broadway, the bickering between the parents and their constant maneuvering to get one child a stage advantage over another grew from bad to worse. Finally, curtain calls for the children were discontinued, because the parents argued so violently about which child should stand where to take applause after the curtain was raised for them.

Eileen was not unhappy when her role in *The Miracle Worker* stopped. The play ended its run on Broadway after nineteen months. Half of the original cast had already been replaced by other actors, including Suzanne Pleschette, who took over Anne Bancroft's role as Annie Sullivan. Eileen stayed to the end, but had grown too tall to be considered for a part in the movie version of the play.

She would miss some of the people she had met, Patricia Neal, Patti Duke, Torin Thatcher, Michael Constantine and James Cogdon, women and men who delivered a quality performance night after night. There was a richness in their personalities she would regret losing contact with. And, of course, she would particularly miss watching Anne Bancroft, an actress whose range of emotion was stunning. She would never forget her and would always be sad about how their relationship had been ended by the jealousy of others.

When Eileen changed from public school to Lavell School For the Blind, the event brought into her life a seventy-year-old laundry owner whose small establishment fronted on the street where Eileen, accompanied by her mother, waited for a school bus station wagon to pick her up at 7:15 A.M. every morning.

It was winter. Snow was on the ground, temperatures dropped below freezing. To keep herself warm, Eileen stamped her feet and huddled in her coat while she waited. She hated winter; she hated snow; she hated cold.

When Mr. Hyde, the laundry owner, who came to his place every morning about half an hour before Eileen and her mother arrived at the bus stop, invited Eileen into the store to warm herself, she was grateful and only vaguely puzzled that he did not include her mother. Dorothy Musumeci thought it was a fine idea for Eileen to get warm in the old man's laundry. She was not unhappy to remain outside in the cold by herself.

It was cozy in the laundry; it smelled of cleaning fluid, detergent and oil. Eileen didn't mind when the old man patted her head and chucked her under the chin with his hand. He didn't smell too good, and he had long hair. She hated the idea of having to go back outside, so she was willing to be admired. Mr. Hyde always pulled down the door shade so no one could see in after he had escorted Eileen into the laundry room. He was mindful of time, though. He always opened the door for her a minute or so before the station wagon school bus arrived.

At first, Mr. Hyde touched her like any older adult would with hugs of grandfatherly affection, then he began to kiss her on the mouth. After that things deteriorated rapidly. Soon, when she came in holding his hand, he would push her against laundry sacks full of clothes and run his hands over her body under her clothes.

She hated for him to kiss her, but endured it because she liked being warm. Still, his wet mouth made her want to gag and when he put his tongue in her mouth she wanted to spit. It was detestable. Eileen was not sure what was wrong with Mr. Hyde. When she asked her mother, "Why does the laundry man kiss me all the time?"

Dorothy always answered, "Because he loves you."

If her mother did not object to the old man's behavior, Eileen reasoned, then it must be all right. But she was not satisfied. In the back of her mind something nagged at her when she thought about how excited he got, how his hands shook sometimes and how his breath was hot on her face.

For two years, in the winter when it was cold, Eileen marched into the old man's store and suffered him to push her against the laundry sacks and press his body against hers while her mother shivered outside. When she changed schools in the fifth grade, her school bus pick-up was in a different place and she never saw the old man again. Sometimes though, she dreamed about him and shivered under her sheets. And sometimes when she thought about him kissing her, her revulsion was so great that she had to wash out her mouth, as if by the action she could expunge the memory of his thick lips.

At home, as Eileen grew into her pre-teens and sought the company of friends outside of her family, Dorothy Musumeci became more demanding of Eileen, more strident and abusive as she became convinced that her daughter's independence was a deliberate attempt to abandon her mother. The idea that she was losing control of her daughter terrified her and she became vicious and constantly harassed Eileen. Nothing the child could do was right. For years Dorothy had used her hands on Eileen to enforce her ideas. Now, the slapping got worse. It became a habit. If Eileen walked past her mother in the kitchen it was not unusual for her to whirl suddenly and slap Eileen's face without explanation. Any disagreement was an excuse for her to raise her hand to Eileen.

"If you cry, I'll slap you some more."

The abuse got so bad that tiny veins in Eileen's thighs, a favorite mark for her mother's hands, became enlarged. Often she carried black and blue marks from repeated open-handed blows from her mother. If Ross Musumeci tried to interfere in the random punishment, it got worse. Once, exasperated beyond endurance with Dorothy's haranguing Eileen for not drinking all of her milk, he grabbed the glass and threw the contents in a wild swing that splattered milk on the ceiling. Furious, Dorothy attacked him and they rolled on the couch as she pummeled him with her tightened fists. The couple had long ago given up sleeping together. They fought like cats and dogs.

Dorothy had always been suspicious of Eileen's friends; she approved of few and one in particular, Pat Logan, drew her ire because Pat refused to paint her own parents in a favorable light. Pat and Eileen were playing in the bathtub one day, got carried away, and flooded the bathroom. Dorothy stepped into the overflowing puddles, became greatly enraged, and started beating Eileen furiously. Pat started screaming and when Dorothy realized that her secret abuse of Eileen had been discovered, she left the room. From that day forward, her hatred of Pat Logan knew no bounds. She took every opportunity to berate the child to Eileen.

When Eileen's menstrual periods began, her emotions were intense. When she started dating and boys kissed her she trembled and got upset and mouth sores also appeared, erupting in a day or two. She was nineteen before she understood that she had not escaped from the delayed influence on her mind of the laundryman's slobbery kisses when she was ten. And that the effects caused physical and emotional repercussions. She had known then that something was wrong but she could never put it into words. Though Eileen endured her mother's abuse, her response to her mother grew more bitter as Eileen got older. She avoided her as much as possible. By then Dorothy had grown more vitriolic and accusative of people she thought wanted to do her wrong. And she slyly put them into lyrics she composed from popular songs:

"I'm in love with you, you, you."

(Left) Eileen Ross and dad, Rosario Musumeci.

(Above) Christmas 1988; Eileen, Rick Rivera, and their dogs.

(Above) Scene from Broadway play, *The Miracle Worker.* Anne Bancroft *(seated)* and Eileen *(behind Anne)* are among the cast.

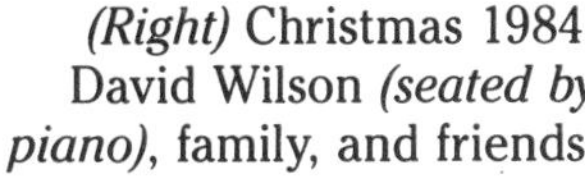

(Right) Christmas 1984; David Wilson *(seated by piano)*, family, and friends.

PHOTO FROM DAILY NEWS

(*Above*) Former members of the Brooklyn Sex Crimes Unit. (*Background*) Bruce Milau. (*Foreground, l to r*): Jim McGeown, Bob Merz, Patti Kehoe, and Sal Catalfumo.

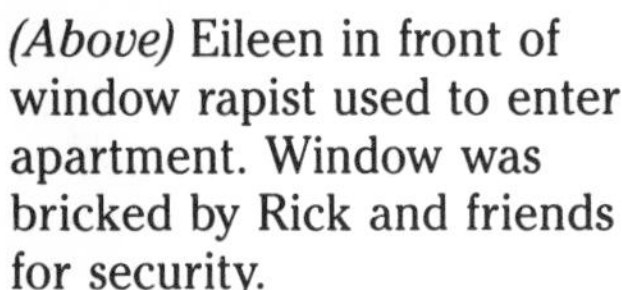

(*Above*) Eileen in front of window rapist used to enter apartment. Window was bricked by Rick and friends for security.

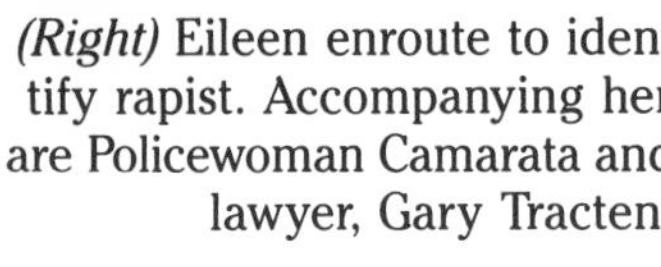

(*Right*) Eileen enroute to identify rapist. Accompanying her are Policewoman Camarata and lawyer, Gary Tracten.

PHOTO BY JOHN PENDIN, *DAILY NEWS*

Rapist, Tyrone Graham, being processed by police after his arrest.

PHOTO BY JOHN PENDIN, *DAILY NEWS*

"I'll beat you with my shoe, shoe, shoe."

By the time Eileen was sixteen the abuse and disparagement from her mother had become so bad that it was like a litany: "You're no good. Bad, bad, bad." An argument over a boy, Roberto Arroyo, whom Eileen liked, turned out to be the climatic event that resulted in Eileen running away from home for two days and returning to a confrontation that was inevitable.

Even if Robert had been everything Dorothy wanted a friend of Eileen's to be, (actually he was idealistic, religious, a boy who didn't drink or smoke) the conflict between Dorothy and her daughter would still have been intense. It came to a breaking point a year later. By that time, despite her guilt over wishing her own mother harm, Eileen could not stop dreaming of her mother dying violently; falling from a window and hitting her head.

Eileen could never remember exactly the nature of the particular incident that prompted the violent argument between herself and her mother. They were in the kitchen and Dorothy slapped Eileen hard for a reason even she may not have known. But the cruel blow was the final straw to Eileen. The years of her mother's craziness, her rigid control, the constant slurs and condemnations, the raw insults, the tears and screaming and the unfairness of her criticisms, welled up in Eileen and for the first time, she stood up for herself, furious at being unfairly attacked, "Don't you ever hit me again," Eileen screamed. "If you hit me again I'm going to hit you back."

Eileen didn't realize as she yelled that she held her arm across her forehead in a protective fashion. Livid, Dorothy reached out and grabbed Eileen's fingers and twisted them.

Hurt, angry beyond control, Eileen grabbed her

mother and shook her. The two women struggled, grappling with one another. They locked and circled and Dorothy pushed Eileen against the kitchen window.

With a hard wrench, Eileen reversed her position with her mother. The mother's wild-eyed face was next to Eileen, and Eileen could perceive over Dorothy's shoulder the window pane and she knew the street was far below.

She thought: I'm going to push her out. She heard herself yelling, screaming, "I'm going to kill you. I'm going to kill you."

"You might as well," her mother grunted as they struggled. "I might have cancer so you won't have to worry about killing me."

Shocked, Eileen pushed her mother away and the women stood apart, sobbing, their chests heaving. Eileen felt she would not have pushed her mother through the window, but she would never know definitely. She had wanted to. She had come *very* close.

Eileen backed away from her mother. "Just leave me alone," she said.

When her mother's cancer diagnosis was confirmed, Eileen knew she had once again been manipulated by her mother's jealousy of her, her need to control and to instill guilt. After that, her mother accused Eileen of causing her to worry, bringing on the disease. She was an ungrateful child who wanted to see her mother dead. But then Eileen had become so inured to her mother's threats and promises of harm that she just pushed her mother's accusations away.

What love there might have been between the two had long ago perished in the hateful punishment of Dorothy Musumeci. The slaps and abuse had left Eileen a hardened survivor who viewed her female parent as a wretched woman who had no sense of her own worth and tried to live through her daughter. But despite her sense of detachment from her mother, Eileen lived with a sense of dread and resignation during the next two years as Dorothy slowly died from cancer of the breast.

If Ross Musumeci had not insisted, Eileen would not have gone to her mother's funeral. Many of her relatives were scandalized when Eileen didn't cry at the funeral, but few knew the truth about the long years of abuse.

Reflecting on her mother from the vantage point of her thirty-seven years, Eileen thought there should have been some mellowing of her anger toward the woman who gave her life, but the honest truth was that her mother had destroyed their relationship, leaving her only a few memories of those early years when her family had been intact. Still, her mother had caused her to become strong and resilient in order to survive the slaps and cruel disparagements. In a real sense, Dorothy Musumeci had forced her daughter to create a courageous woman from the child of despair. In the strangest way, that strength had come to her aid when she was raped. And it would aid her in her trials to come.

Chapter 9

Kay Ketchum walked into Eileen's bedroom and gasped.

"Jesus, Eileen, it looks terrible in here," she shuddered.

Suddenly, not only did blood-tinged images flash through Eileen's mind as she sat up in bed, but she remembered the aftermath and having to change the blood-stained sheets on her bed the night before, stuffing them in a laundry bag. She remembered the awe in Kay's voice, and the anger in Rick's, when they saw her disheveled bedroom.

Kay continued. "There's blood everywhere. How did it get on the ceiling? On the lamp shade? They're even splotches on the closet door," she sighed. "Your bedspread is probably ruined."

Looking around, Rick was more pointed, "You are lucky," he said in a hard, small voice. "He could have killed you."

Kay touched Rick's shoulder and said to Eileen. "We'll leave you alone for a few minutes. Call out if you need anything. We'll be in the next room."

Rick nodded his agreement and waved goodbye.

Eileen touched the bandage on her head and thought about the man who had struck her so brutally with the kitchen mallet, then with apologetic arrogance to prove he was a "decent person", washed the bloody wound and patted it dry with a towel. Tears of anger sprang to her eyes. Quickly they were replaced by the ominous thought of AIDS. Could her attacker have the fatal disease? Her stomach turned over and she felt giddy. AIDS. Could he have infected her? She'd have to have a blood test, but they told her at the hospital that the disease often didn't show up for months or even years.

How long would it be before she really knew if she was in danger of the slow death? For a moment she thought of her friend, David, upstairs who was dying of the disease, and his dear, wasted face and body leaped into her mind.

Then her thoughts turned back to her attacker.

Bastard! She thought. Damn the bastard who'd broken into her life. *Bastard! Bastard! Bastard!* Anger made her blood quicken. What would she do if she found out that she had AIDS? She pushed the thought out of her mind.

The first thing to concentrate on was finding him. That was where she had to place all her energy and fortitude. The television coverage ought to help. She shivered, suddenly recalling his threat to kill her if she exposed the rape. He had been described on the program as a Jekyll and Hyde then ridiculed for stealing five pounds of shrimp which he had placed in the same suitcase with her video recorder and mink coat. She bet he didn't like that, remembering his ego. She couldn't suppress a smile when she thought of that coat. She had bought it in a second-hand store for $50. He was going to be furious when he found out it wasn't the expensive treasure he'd expected.

Slowly, Eileen got out of bed. She was certain of one fact: Her life would never be the same. Even though it gave her a small sense of satisfaction to realize the Birchwood Corporation, which owned the Navereign Apartment House, was going to suffer financially for the neglect that had permitted a burglar who raped his victims to enter Eileen's apartment through a window with a broken latch.

Her attorney and friend, Gary Trachten, was bringing a personal injury attorney, Norman Pearlmen, to the apartment in the afternoon to discuss his legal representation of her in a suit against the building. She shook her head over the stupidity, greed and carelessness of people. By refusing to repair the broken latch, callously ignoring her entreaties, letters, telephone calls, the apartment owners had become a party to her attack. There was a sense of justice in the civil suit that would demand reparation for their negligence.

Eileen entered her bathroom and started to touch her things, everything was out of place. She saw smudges everywhere of the powder the police had brushed over surfaces to trap fingerprints. She shook her head, suddenly feeling depressed, miserable. There were dirty trails in dozens of places in her apartment. In her bathroom, they were on the wall telephone, the laundry hamper, the cabinet mirror, the shelves inside, the wash basin and the light switch panel near the door.

Snatches of conversation seeped through the wall —Sammi, Kay's husband, speaking in the living room. She sighed. She was so thankful they'd stayed with her. Though she remembered the night with amused exasperation. Once, when she had arisen to go to the bathroom and heard Sammi wandering about, she called out, "What's the matter? Can't you sleep?" Unable to see his face, she had had to imagine the anxious expression matching the trepidation in his voice.

"What if he comes back?" he whispered. "What'll we do?"

"There are four of us, Sammi," she said, emphasizing the number.

"Yeah, but he might surprise us, like he did you."

"Well, try not to worry about it. There are more of us than him."

She was irritated with herself for reflecting on the possibility of the intruder's reappearance as she got back into bed. Damn Sammi for his fretfulness. Tired as she was, she lay awake for some time before she was able to fall back to sleep.

By nine o'clock, Sammi and Kay had breakfasted and left the apartment. Eileen was returning telephone calls to people who had called and Rick Rivera, who had stayed close, dependable, and protective, was laying out his day's work of errand running and planning assignments for free-lance transcriptionists whom he would contact.

By ten o'clock, Eileen had received a call from one of the doormen on duty at the Navereign Apartment asking if she wanted him to admit a religious group who had come to pray for her and wanted to deliver a message of spiritual healing. Eileen told him to thank them but say no.

A few minutes later Rick answered a call from the lobby desk, where he was advised that the morning mail was extra heavy. He took the laundry bag for the extra letters, Eileen was amazed when she counted ninety-one sympathy envelopes from strangers who wrote to share their feelings about her rape.

As Rick read her the letters, Eileen realized the majority were from women who did not sign their names; many explained they wished to remain anonymous, because they were afraid to identify themselves as rape victims. Yet each one of the writers congratulated Eileen for her bravery, for speaking out, for being their vocal champion.

It was distressing for Eileen to absorb the pain that came to her through the handwritten lines. These were women who admitted that the worst thing they could have imagined happened to them was their own rape. The next worst thing was their own cowardice. Sadly she realized that shame of secrecy in which they lived was wrenching and insidious. It destroyed their self-confidence. One letter postmarked from New Jersey was especially touching:

> Dear Miss Ross,
>
> I am a raped woman who cried when I read about your ordeal. I'm writing because I share your grief and your sense of shock. If you are like me, it is a memory that won't go away easily. I was attacked three years ago and I'm still not over it. But it does help to share, and at least I can tell you my feelings, knowing that you will appreciate and understand them.
>
> I'm proud of you. If I had a sister I would want her to be like you are. I wish I had had the courage to tell people what had happened to me, but I didn't. Nobody knows, except my husband and the police who came. They acted as if it was my fault when I said I just wanted to forget what happened.
>
> The worst part for me was that I let them make me feel guilty. I wish I'd gotten mad. I wish I'd stuck up for myself like you did, but I didn't.
>
> I just wanted to tell you how much I admire you. I think you may have a easier time recovering from what happened to you than I did. If I had spoken up for myself I know I would have liked myself better.
>
> Good luck to you Eileen.
>
> A Silent Friend

A one-hundred-dollar bill floated out of another letter Eileen opened. The note accompanying it was brief:

> Dear Miss Ross,
> I'm not rich, but this might help you to restore some of the things you lost. I hope you feel better soon.
> There was no signature

Eileen felt a wave of warmth flood over her as she read the note. A donation from a stranger who wanted no thanks, nor acknowledgement. It was an expression of common humanity. Tears sprang to Eileen's eyes.

A mother whose daughter was raped wrote a thought-provoking letter that conveyed many women's sentiments about keeping rape shrouded in secrecy and her ambivalence about Eileen's decision to tell her story to the newspapers.

> Dear Eileen,
> I'm reaching out to you with the hope that somehow I can say something that will help. Sexual assault is a profoundly shocking experience. You might be feeling very helpless and alone right now. There are others of us who have experienced these feelings.
> When my daughter was assaulted, the pain I felt was deeper than I could have anticipated. I felt overwhelmed, afraid and filled with a sense of loss beyond what I could understand. My daughter and I had counseling as part of a healing process. The shock is over but there will always be a certain sadness that she had to endure that trauma. Rape seems like a secret crime and it usually isn't discussed.

I had mixed feelings about your decision to tell the newspapers. I admit your courage; I'm not sure it was appropriate. Rape is a subject that makes many people uncomfortable. I understand some of what you're feeling and my heart goes out to you. Please believe that you have the love and support of a lot of women. You will come through this crisis. My daughter did. So will you.

An Anguished Mother

From the Clinton Correctional Facility at Danemora, New York, an inmate wrote offering hundreds of dollars reward toward recovery of some of Eileen's stolen articles. From his words, Eileen sensed his motive was to help someone who had been victimized. She promised herself to thank him by letter for his sentiments. Among the letters were three other missives from inmates, lonely men who found her predicament a reason to express their longing for outside human contact in the form of sympathy for her.

The letter she liked the most was from a man who praised her reasons for speaking out about the crime against her:

Dear Miss Ross,

I would like to thank you for your brave and selfless act of speaking to the public about the crime that was committed against you. The most effective kind of leadership is leadership by example; and I think that your example, through its effect on others, will make our city safer for all of us.

I hope you and your beagle make a complete recovery as quick as possible.

By the time Rick had read most of the letters to her, she was convinced that her plan to search out and punish her attacker, the plan she had put into effect by having represented a wish for righteous revenge that most woman who had been savagely attacked felt, was the correct thing to do. And she realized that rape was much more than forceful intercourse. It was brutalization. The shattering of a woman's self-image of herself as competent and independent. When that was shattered, a woman's total self-confidence, her pride, her absolute sense of self, was destroyed, and it required a valiant effort for her to put the pieces of her life back together.

The last letter was from a female psychologist. She expressed her own unspoken fear of the rape's repercussions:

Dear Miss Ross,

I am a woman about your age. I was raped by an intruder while my husband was gone on a business trip. It happened four years ago and I'm almost recovered. By that I mean I have made my peace with what happened and I don't jump at shadows anymore. I'm still worried about creating any opportunities for someone to take advantage of me. In other words I live in a world of locks and bars and precautions. I am a psychologist by profession so what I am writing to you may help in the weeks to come.

Unless you are very different than most rape victims, you are going to experience a "rape trauma syndrome." This involves short term, intermediate, and long term reactions. The acute phase is characterized by sleep disturbances, fear, suspiciousness, anxiety, major depressive symptoms, and difficulties in social function. It took me about three months to get through this.

Based on what you done by coming out and identifying your attacker I can believe you are a tough lady. But don't be surprised if you suffer some or all of the symptoms I've described. I didn't write them down to present you with a list of things to worry about, but simply to warn you that when they happen have faith in yourself that they will pass. You can't go through an experience like we have without injury. It will take a while for scar tissue to form in your heart.

Because you have created an example, I thought you, especially, needed to know some of what's ahead of you. It also may be helpful to locate a qualified rape crisis counselor. Someone you can talk to.

I wish I were that person, but I don't have the guts or the wisdom for that kind of communication. This letter is the best I can do.

Best wishes to you. For obvious reasons I am not signing my name.

Eileen shivered. The voice of the woman sounded in Eileen's ears as if she herself had whispered the words the woman had written. Eileen had been avoiding confronting the idea of being alone. Rick and Kay and Sammi had been the temporary wall separating her from the repercussions of the rape. Well, she couldn't have the armor of their presence forever. What was she going to do when they left her alone? In less than an hour Rick had errands to run. Her transcription business could not stop because she'd been terrorized and was suffering post-rape trauma. She would be alone until he returned from picking up audio cassettes with doctor's dictation from several hospitals.

As she looked at the dark-haired young man bending conscientiously over her work desk in the spare bedroom-office, suddenly she felt a surge of affection for him. She had hired him as a messenger. He had a quick grasp of what was needed to transact her business at the hospitals. And now she was touched by his loyalty, sensitivity and protective silence. She knew he admired her and liked the forthright manner with which she dealt with issues as they came up. He actually watched over her in a subtle, unobtrusive fashion as if he had made up his mind that she was somebody valuable who needed a quiet, undemanding companion.

He was not a big man, a few inches over five feet, with a slender frame, deep brown eyes and an ascetic face. He spoke very little, keeping his opinion to himself. His origin was Puerto Rican. He came from New York's West Side. He had a dry sense of humor, a strong sense of family, and a deep dedication to her. The feeling between them was growing. He had become, in a brief period, almost indispensable.

The telephone rang as she was about to join Rick at her desk. It was her father. Immediately she felt better—she always liked speaking to him. In answer to his questions, she assured him that she was feeling well and there was no trouble with the head wound, although the bandage was a bother.

Her father had talked with the manager of the Navereign Apartment Building, who promised her father that by no later than 5:00 P.M., the maintenance crew would arrive at Eileen's apartment to install bars across the window with the broken latch. He absolutely assured Ross Musumeci the job would be done.

"Better late than never," Eileen said. She chatted about ordinary things a minute longer with her father, then hung up. She was surprised to find Rick ready to start his errands as she turned from the phone.

"Are you going? Is it that time already?"

"Yep. Are you going to be all right?"

"Oh, sure, I've got correspondence to catch up with and this place is a mess. There is print powder everywhere. God, the police were messy."

"Well, then I guess I'll get going."

Rick made an uncertain false start, stopped glanced at Eileen again.

"It's all right," she reassured him and, despite his apparent qualms, he quickly left.

It felt strange to be alone in the apartment. The silence was disturbing, as if it, like her, was waiting for something to happen.

"Oh, damn," Eileen said to herself sternly, "Quit it! You will make yourself panic. Stupid!"

She fussed in the kitchen, making noise on purpose, getting a Pepsi out of the refrigerator, cracking the ice cube tray, some of the cubes bouncing into the sink. She emptied them into a glass and poured from the bottle. Then she carefully replaced the bottle in the refrigerator, taking time to feel for the label and turned it front. Suddenly she realized she wasn't winning. The skin at the back of her neck felt prickly; she was apprehensive.

"I have to stop this nonsense," she whispered determinedly. She walked firmly to her desk and sat at her computer. Her father had built her work station. It faced the outside wall of the apartment building. Sitting in her chair, her back was exposed to the wall behind her and the door leading into the living room.

Eileen straightened her shoulders and turned on her computer, bending forward when the screen flooded with green light. She pushed a file access button. Uneasiness was like an insistent warning cloud in the back of her mind.

She moved her chair slightly to one side so that she was seated at a slight angle to the computer. It was a foolish strategy to alter the position of her body. To put it into a more defensive posture.

"If you try to type this way, you will have a crick in your side in ten minutes," she said to herself.

But she felt herself trembling despite her entries.

"What am I going to do?" she murmured.

She turned away from her desk and leaned back, feeling defeated. She heard the quiet hissing of the air conditioner. A sudden low whirring sound came out of the kitchen to her left. She started and then momentarily relaxed. The refrigerator, of course. It had turned itself on. She took a deep breath and let it out.

What am I going to do?

She remembered the prediction of the psychologist who had written to her. During the acute post-rape phase she was going to be fearful, suspicious and anxious. Well, she thought, that lady hit it right on the button. I'm sitting here afraid to turn my back to the room. Eileen tried to gain control of herself, breathing in slowly, regularly. What am I afraid of? That he'll come back in broad daylight at one o'clock in the afternoon? Don't be silly, she chided herself. The next thing you'll be imagining is that the walls have a memory of violence and the air holds echoes of cruelty.

Shakily Eileen got to her feet and rubbed her arms. She was chilled, irresolute and uncertain. She knew she was avoiding facing the truth. It terrified her. She was afraid to be alone. As the admission passed through her it was like opening a window to let in black, frightening thoughts. Her pleasant work room, the one she had once enjoyed so much, was suddenly too small. She felt trapped, panicky; she wanted to run.

"Bonnie," she called in a husky hesitant tone, her voice startled her.

"Bonnie, Bethie, come on, pups, we're going for a walk."

She hurried into the kitchen and the dogs came into her small tunnel of vision; she heard their sharp little claws scrape on the linoleum tile floor. She scooped them into her arms and cuddled the warm animals. Bonnie licked her nose. Eileen felt better. Grabbing their walking leashes, she fastened them in place, chucked to the beagles with her tongue and locked the apartment door behind her. Her decision to leave wasn't cowardly, or weak. Her admission of fear was *honest*. She had to face it. The attack had made being alone terrifying. She would have to find someone to stay here with her until the fear faded away, until her sense of vulnerability was replaced with new confidence.

She wondered if that would ever happen? She felt a sudden, wrenching sense of loss that was far deeper than the hurt she remembered from yesterday. She began to understand how deeply the wound of her rape cut into inner regions of her being she had never explored. The aftermath of the violence she had endured was going to be more demoralizing than the attack. She could understand that now and she was shaken with dread.

Eileen walked slowly through the park trying to enjoy the warmth of the sun. She encouraged Bethie who was lagging a little, which Eileen attributed to fatigue stemming from the dog's concussion. As Eileen sat down on a bench she sighed again, realizing it was not only the summer day but fear of going back which held her outside. Rick would not have finished his work. There would not be anyone in the apartment and she knew she did not want to be alone.

Getting up again, walking beneath the green trees and the dappled sidewalks reflecting shadows of leaves refreshed her, dispelled some of her feelings of anxiety. Feeling the heat now she moved into the shady spots where the patches of coolness were fragrant with mixed scents of mowed grass, manicured shrubs, and wet cement, drying from the afternoon sprinklers of park caretakers intent on keeping long stretches of lawn watered and green.

As she approached the entrance to the apartment Eileen thought about her dilemma. Her independence had meant so much to her. A combination of pride and achievement. She didn't want to acknowledge that that freedom was gone. It meant giving up her strong sense of individual competence and personal security. It went against everything she had striven to create for herself as a woman who was proud of her ability to manage her own life. Eileen seldom thought that her lack of sight as a handicap. Now, having to depend on other people for her safety put her in a category of "damaged humans." Those who had lost control of their lives. Her rape had handicapped her more than her blindness, and anger within her surged up. She wasn't going to let that damned animal destroy all she had created. Purposefully, her back straight, head high, she walked inside.

It wasn't until Eileen had locked the door to her apartment and had reached the center of the living room that Bethie and Bonnie started barking. It was the sudden hysterical intensity of the beagle's voices that alarmed Eileen. They were obviously frightened. They barked shrilly, then they ran in frantic circles around her. Bethie growled viciously, pushing herself beneath

Eileen's skirt, between her legs. Eileen could feel the tension and fear in the terrified animal and she began to shake.

Within seconds absolute terror clutched at her. Her heart beat frantically, her breathing rapid and short. She was paralyzed by the rushing emptiness of the room that surrounded her. She could not scream or move her lips, or take air into her empty lungs. Frozen, stiff, she stood trembling, convinced someone was in the apartment waiting to maim her, to attack her again, this time to kill her. In her petrified state, she listened to the dogs yapping and screaming, like her, they sensed something in the room. Finally, she found the will to move. She ran into her office-bedroom. Just then, the phone rang. Eileen snatched the cordless phone from her desk and burst through the door to the terrace. It was Kay. Unaware, Eileen began screaming. Eileen could not stop the high shrieks of terror that came piercingly out of her mouth, cries like punctuated cries of pain.

"Kay! Kay! Kay!" she sobbed, "Please, please answer. Help! Help! He's here. He's here."

She was hardly aware of Kay's voice, startled, comprehending, insisting on information. "What's happening? He's there? Hold on. I'm calling 911 on the other line."

"Yes, Yes." Eileen confirmed and rushed to the iron railing that formed a barrier between the elevated terrace and the sidewalk eight feet below. Her frantic voice reached passers by on the sidewalk.

She could hear their shouts, "What's wrong? Are you hurt? Do you want help?"

She almost wept when she identified the familiar voices of Sammi and Louis, two friendly, pet-owning hair stylists she had met while walking her beagles.

"What's wrong Eileen? Is somebody there?"

Sammi shouted. "Louis is phoning the cops. Be calm. Keep talking. Who are the dogs barking at?"

"I don't know," Eileen said, clutching the phone, aware that Kay's voice was pleading for her to speak to her again. Eileen was talking incoherently, not even aware of what she was saying to Kay when the first of the uniformed cops climbed up the tree growing close to the terrace wall and dropped off into her patio.

"Lady, you all right? Where is he?"

Unable to speak, confused, grateful, relieved, she pointed at her apartment, "In there. Somebody. The dogs were going crazy." Eileen was crouching, holding the beagles against her legs, petting and soothing them, soothing herself with her comforting words.

More uniformed policemen clamored onto the terrace. Two men entered her apartment, warily crossing the patio with drawn revolvers and entered her office-bedroom. A minute later they opened the locked front entrance, admitting a score of police officers who were banging on the door.

Slumped in a patio chair, consoling the beagles, the phone silent in her lap, Eileen could only nod her head when a tall, dark-haired policeman said to her, "Whoever it was is gone, ma'm. Are you alright?"

She heard herself apologizing when she was informed a few minutes later that no evidence of an intruder could be found in her apartment.

"That doesn't mean somebody wasn't here, Miss Ross," a stocky, husky-voiced policeman said. "You and your dogs may have frightened him away."

Eileen answered in a shaky voice, "I'm worried my friend won't get here soon. Can somebody stay until she arrives?" The policeman nodded. Even when Kay appeared, Eileen was still shaking. She felt confused, awkward, convinced that someone had been in her apartment.

As the balding police sergeant started to gather up his things, "Don't feel foolish. Strange things happen in Manhattan. Never think twice about calling the cops even if it turns out to be a false alarm. You never know. You could be saving your life. It's our job to be here." Eileen clasped his hand gratefully.

Later, when Eileen and Kay sat in the kitchen of Eileen's apartment drinking Pepsi, and marveling that fourteen policemen had answered the two 911 calls so quickly, Eileen confided to her friend, "I thought I was scared when that guy pressed a knife into my throat and I thought he was going to push it in. That doesn't compare with what happened to me today. Kay, I was paralyzed. I couldn't move. I couldn't scream. My voice was gone. It was terrible. I don't even remember running out on the terrace. I got there, but I don't know how."

She took a deep breath and let it out slowly.

"God, the cops must have been here in five minutes. They were really quick but it felt like forever. I know you called them," Eileen paused and Kay nodded, "and Louis must have also. I felt helpless."

She sighed. "Somebody must have been here. Or why would the dogs have barked? They were going crazy. Out of their minds. Poor little pups, something scared the daylight out of them," Eileen concluded.

"Kay, I know you're not going to believe this," Eileen hastily added, "but I think the guy who raped me came back. The dogs have never acted like that before. He surprised them and me the first time. They could have remembered his particular smell. I'm not saying he was actually here when we came back from our walk, but I'll bet he was here while we were gone.

"You know, Kay, he swore he'd come back if I told

the cops about the rape. And if he did come back, he came back to kill me."

When Rick Rivera returned to the apartment shortly after 5:00 P.M. and learned about the dogs and the scare, he asked Eileen's permission to call some friends of his.

"We'll form a team of guards who will take turns sleeping in the apartment; three at a time." According to Rick, his friends were young, tough, didn't frighten easily and could protect Eileen.

Eileen didn't have to think twice about the idea. "Rick, I don't know how to thank you," she said softly, tears leapt to her eyes.

"Your friends can bunk on the floor and in sleeping bags."

"Have they come to fix that window and latch yet?" Rick said glancing around. Eileen shook her head reactively. "Damnit," Rick murmured.

The apartment owners had failed to honor their promise of placing bars on the window in the apartment through which the rapist had made his entry. Not only had no maintenance crew appeared at her door, but the manager had even failed to notify Eileen that the job would not be done.

Angry, Rick said, "Let's brick up the window."

"Good idea," Eileen answered.

Quickly, Rick called three of his friends who, like him, had sturdy utility bikes with heavy-duty baskets.

The four met at a brick yard that stayed open late on Manhattan's West Side and loaded their baskets with bricks and mortar. By midnight the window was solidly encased with a wall of hard red bricks and Rick and his three friends, Alex Holmes, Rodney Holems, and David Alisea were bedding down for the night.

It was 1:00 A.M. when Eileen, ready for bed, and

Kay, who'd stayed late and was on the verge of departing, heard the phone ring. Puzzled and a little apprehensive about the identity of a person who would call so late, Eileen answered the phone tentatively.

The voice she heard was high-pitched, drawling and whiny.

"Do you know who this is, Eileen?"

Eileen faltered, then realized it was not the voice of the man who had raped her.

"No! Who is it?" she said.

"You mean you haven't heard about me in the newspapers? I'm surprised. I've got a reputation. I've read about you. I've read a lot about you. I'm Calvin and I think I should come over and visit you . . ."

Eileen slammed the phone down. She turned to Kay.

"A guy named Calvin just called and invited himself over. I'm supposed to recognize his name. He's been in the newspapers. Do you know who he is?"

Kay's "no" reflected her own puzzlement. A week later, Kay resolved the issue.

"Eileen," she called on the phone horrified. "Remember that guy Calvin, who phoned you? He's the Silver Gun rapist. They just caught him."

Chapter 10

There were three laundry rooms in the Navereign. All of them were located on the first floor of the building. If the one that Eileen favored had not been closed for maintenance work, she probably never would have pushed her cart into laundry room B and heard the conversation between one of the building's security guards and a woman who was waiting for her washing machine to complete its spin cycle.

The thin, gray-haired woman was saying, "I wish I could dream up something like the Ross woman is doing to get money," she said. *"Easy money. Easy money.* She must have been convincing for the police to swallow it. Have you met her?"

"No," the heavy-jowled sixtyish guard said, "I've just seen her from time to time and she doesn't look blind to me. You're right though, I've got a wife and kids. I wish I could find a way to get some easy money."

Eileen's face burned. She had half a mind to push her cart up to the pair and spit in their faces. She tried to cool her temper and rolled her cart down a row of glistening white machines two aisles away from the man and woman who had taken no notice of her. Then she silently loaded her clothes into a vacant automatic washer.

"Is that what they really think?" she asked herself. They had no knowledge of the lawsuit that had been prepared in her behalf against the Navereign, yet if their gossip was typical, then a lot of people thought she was faking.

Eileen felt chagrined and angry. Where did they get

the idea that she had made up the rape? How did they think she got the wound in her head? By inflicting it on herself? Did they think she'd taken a hammer and cracked her skull open to provide the bloody evidence of assault? How did she spray her bedroom with splotches of her own blood? There were so many stains on the ceiling and walls that Rick and his friends were going to repaint the room as soon as the Brooklyn cops, who were coming in a couple of hours, had viewed the display of violence. *Damn small-minded people who always blamed the victim. Damn them for cheapening someone who defended herself.*

Eileen forced herself to calm down. She had learned to stand up for her rights. Stand up or be trampled. She frowned and thought about the origin of the slander she had heard between the guard and the old woman.

Gossip had to start somewhere and, of course, the source had to be with the management of the Navereign. They had to be aware that one of her attorneys, Norman Pearlman, had quickly circulated a questionnaire among the building's tenants asking for written complaints about lax security in the sprawling apartment building. And they couldn't ignore the photographer he had brought around to shoot dozens of pictures of the exterior of the apartment building, her terrace, and the window through which the intruder had entered.

She had to hand it to Pearlman; he hadn't wasted any time in getting proof of negligence. She remembered his words on the telephone earlier.

"Yes, Eileen, the suit's going to be filed this afternoon. For $11,000,000. That should get their attention. You wanted fast? Well, you got fast. Also, I've circulated a questionnaire to the tenants asking about security problems in the building. We'll get a lot of routine bitching, but we'll also get some genuine complaints we can use as ammunition to prove general negligence."

Eileen removed her spin-dried clothes from the washer and placed them in a dryer. She sat down again and began to think about the fact that the apartment owner had considered her to be a thorn in his side before—because of her letters insisting on the repair of the window latch in her apartment and her friendship with a black man, they must think of her as a giant pain now.

She knew from her own experience that big rental corporations in New York were irritated by tenants who threatened the placid inefficiency of their corporate operations. Their philosophy of management was to ignore the requests of apartment tenants that represented any deviation from prescribed policies of service inadequacy. Eileen was a fly in the ointment at the apartment building, a wave in the even flow of inferior service.

As she methodically folded her clothes into the basket of her laundry cart, her mind darted to other things. Suddenly she had to smile as she recalled her previous day's telephone call from Lisa. Lisa Sliwa who, with her husband Curtis, had started New York's subway vigilantes, a flamboyant, militant group known as the "Guardian Angels." The Angels were volunteers who patrolled the subways, looking for muggers who preyed on passengers. Lisa told Eileen that after reading Eileen's story in the newspaper, they wanted to send a group of fifty or more Angels to patrol the Navereign for rapists. Eileen was delighted. Her principal attorney and friend, Gary Trachten, was horrified.

"Jesus, Eileen, what do you want to do, create more notoriety? That's not good for our case. You've got to keep it cool. People don't appreciate being put in the spotlight. Don't encourage these vigilantes. It will backfire."

Accepting Gary's advice, Eileen had called the Sliwas back and regretfully declined their offer. Now she tightened her lips purposefully. If Gary or anyone else thought she was going to retreat from her determination to keep New York's newspapers interested in her case, they were wrong. Still, she realized that were the Guardian Angels to set up a vigilance in the apartment building, the resulting "high profile" could harm the way people perceived her reasons for making her rape public. She wouldn't take that chance because she really wanted to gain support for her cause of changing the public focus from the raped woman's response to the crime against her.

Still, the gossip was troubling, especially the statement the older woman had made: "She must have been convincing for the police to swallow it."

Eileen thought about the nasty implications in the woman's comment as she wheeled the laundry cart back to her apartment. She couldn't forget the cop who had blundered into her living room, accusing David of hitting her on the head, and told Eileen the 911 call that alerted the police had come in as a "domestic squabble." Twice yesterday the Manhattan cops had telephoned her, insisting that she have David Wilson come down to the Twentieth Precinct to be fingerprinted.

"He's too ill to go down there," she told the cop on the phone. "Can't you send a fingerprint team up to him?" That suggestion seemed to confuse the policeman.

"He's too sick?" the officer said questioningly. "I don't know about sending somebody."

The next time the call came it was a different cop, and Eileen patiently explained again about David's illness and his weakened condition. She wondered why they didn't call David directly.

It was evident to her that the police suspected David had played a part in the rape and that was why she was so concerned about what the old woman had said. But when she tried to figure out the cop's actions she became confused. If they were convinced that he was the rapist, why didn't they fingerprint him in his apartment, as she suggested, and talk to him? Why were they playing hot and cool about his fingerprints? Could it be that they were undecided about her story of the rape, yet did not want a confrontation?

She thought about the suspicion in the cop's voice when he had asked her if David had hit her. He was the first one into the apartment, the same one who ran outside and yanked three frightened black men off the street and urged her to identify one of them as the rapist.

Eileen's doubts about the cops's belief in her story had been increased by four other events that made her even more anxious about the direction of the police investigation.

Gary Trachten had reported that Norman Pearlman had learned from a contact in the Twentieth Precinct that the aluminum and wood kitchen mallet the intruder had used to strike Eileen had not yielded a vestige of evidence.

She was shocked when Gary relayed the information. "I don't believe it," she said, astonished and skeptical. "What about blood and hair embedded in the striking face of the mallet? It had sawtooth ridges and grooves. Surely, blood and hair would have been trapped. What about dog hairs? He hit Bethie, and Bonnie too. I can't believe it."

Gary assured her that his information was correct.

The second blow came when Gary reported negative results in her rape examination. No foreign hair had been found in combing her pubis. Additionally, no semen, no saliva, no blood, nothing had been found in any of the openings of her body. Aside from the indelible memory of his presence, the man had apparently left no other discernable trace of himself upon her.

The third event had occurred when she told the Manhattan Sex Crimes Squad detectives, the man and woman who interviewed her, that she had narrowly escaped being raped once and her coat had been slashed by the perpetrator. She realized now that her frankness might have been misconstrued. She remembered the detectives' unbelieving voices and wondered if they had characterized her either as a fool who walked home alone through a dark construction neighborhood just asking for it, or a secret sexual fantasizer who took dangerous chances to act out her strange yearnings.

The fourth blow that disturbed Eileen resounded like a slap in the face.

Norman Pearlman had called to warn Eileen to watch what she said over her own telephone, "Because it might be tapped."

"Tapped? Why?" she demanded.

"Oh, they do that, I'm told in cases like this. I can't say for sure that it's true, but don't be surprised if it turns out that way."

"I think you're paranoid," Eileen said, but after she finished the conversation with the personal injury lawyer she began to have misgivings.

What if what Pearlman said was true? What if the cops had tapped her phone line? Wouldn't that be a conclusive fact to add to the others to prove that they were not convinced that she was telling the truth?

God, what did they need to believe in her? Her dead, mutilated body?

As Eileen closed her apartment door behind her and pushed the laundry cart into the bedroom, she heard the buzzing of the intercom in the kitchen, reminding her that it must be 11:00 A.M. That was the time a police officer from the Twentieth Precinct would be calling with photographs of suspects for her to look at.

When Eileen opened her door for her visitor, she discovered it was a small intense-voiced dark woman who introduced herself as "Officer Cruz." She refused to sit down, saying, "I have four photos for you to examine. It will only take a minute."

Eileen stood next to her and put the photographs up to her right eye as the woman handed them to her, one by one.

"Do any of these people look familiar?" Officer Cruz asked.

Eileen shook her head, disappointed. Not one of the men resembled the description she had given to the police. Doesn't anybody listen? she wondered. The man who raped her was mahogany-skinned. The men in the photos were light-skinned with curly, straight, or long hair.

"Would you look at them again?" the woman entreated.

Again, Eileen held each one of the photographs close to her right eye, shaking her head as she scrutinized the faces captured in the squares of slick paper.

"You are sure none of these men look like the one who attacked you?"

"I don't think so," Eileen said.

The woman shrugged, placed the photos in a file and the file into a large flat purse with a shoulder strap. She asked to be shown out two minutes later, leaving behind an impression of a cold, efficient woman who cared little about Eileen's ordeal.

One more impression lingered, however. Eileen was sure that her failure to identify one of the men as her assailant somehow was a mark against her.

But as Eileen wearily closed the door, she was glad she had not positively rejected the photos. She wasn't going to identify anybody until she was absolutely certain the suspect she was viewing was the man who had raped her. She had tried to convey her determination to the woman. Even if Officer Cruz was merely a messenger in uniform, Eileen suspected the officer was going to be asked her impression of the blind victim with keyhole vision in one eye, who claimed she was raped after a bizarre breakfast dialogue with a phantom intruder. Someone who was so ephemeral, that no evidence of himself could be found in the sexual examination procedures.

"What kind of woman is this Ross?" Officer Cruz would be asked. Eileen wondered if Cruz's answer would be:

"Well she didn't fall for that old trap. She was disappointed that none of the suspects I showed her were black. If she's lying, we're not going to find out with phony skels (police slang word for "low lives") to show her."

Eileen realized she could be way off base thinking Officer Cruz had brought her fake suspects' pictures, but as she reflected on the woman's demeanor Eileen was convinced that it had betrayed suspicion. And more than ever, Eileen suspected that the police wanted to believe that David was the rapist. It was *convenient*. He had been present in the apartment when the cops arrived. The call they said they had answered was the one that reported her rape as a domestic squabble. Eileen had discovered it had been made by the security guard who answered the intercom when she yelled, "Help! Help! Call the police. I've been raped." The cops never mentioned Eileen's own call to 911.

Why, in the name of God, had the security guard on duty reported her plea for help as a *domestic squabble?* Now that she thought about it, he had never called her back, or sent anyone to check on her safety. That would have been the vigilant, sensible thing to do. Common sense told her that whoever the guard was, he had believed her early morning call was the hysterical voice of a woman who had been a participant in a family scene and he had called it in that way.

That's why when the first police in the apartment had seen David—sitting tired and subdued, and she, bloody and disheveled in her blue robe—they had perceived them as wary combatants who had taken a breather from their fighting. Prepared to deal with a nasty family crisis, the cops had seen Eileen and David, a black man and white woman whose presence together at four o'clock in the morning was evidence enough. And it was the paramount impression on the middle-aged patrolman who took charge when he entered the apartment. Instantly, he "read" the scene as violence between interracial lovers. His first impression was the one that stuck with him, the one that influenced his superior when later the mallet and the rap examinations proved inconclusive.

When Eileen, acting uncharacteristically vocally for a rape victim, appealed to the media for help and the cops felt the sudden pressure of page one headlines, they began to view her as a clever opportunist who orchestrated the publicity for the benefit of a law suit. Manhattan's East Side played right into her fantasy story of a two-hour ordeal with a black intruder who thoughtfully cleaned the wound he had made in her head as a gesture of gallant kindness before he left with her possessions.

Whoever heard of such a generous act of mercy from a serial burglar-rapist who viciously preyed on women and raped them?

Eileen felt a stab of fear. She could understand the cops' faulty reasoning, but she could not forgive them for their stupidity and arrogance. Nor could she allow their bad judgement of her to influence her decision to find her attacker and bring him to justice. She had to do something. If they had taken the trouble to ask her, or to investigate her past, they would have discovered immediately what kind of person she was. There was nothing mysterious or fantastical about her dreams and hopes. If they'd looked they would have found out that all of her life she had been involved in causes and ideas and pursuits. In fact, she was once a folk singer and it was in this period that she adopted her father's first name as her last name. She had become a champion roller skater, so adept and daring on flashing wheels that no one ever felt she had a handicap.

She had marched in the sixties in civil rights parades. Arm in arm with other idealistic flower children, she was swept up in the cadence of personal freedom that was as potent as sweet wine. To the lyrics of Bob Dylan, the exhortations of Timothy O'Leary, the moving words of Martin Luther King, Jr., and the haunting perfection of folk singer Joan Baez, Eileen's consciousness as a young adult was motivated to action and results. Through twenty years of ferment culminating with the disillusionment of Vietnam, she was proud to be a protester, involved in life, in the excitement of change, and armed with the conviction that, blind or not, she could make a difference.

Perhaps the best indicator of Eileen's character, which was to form the one central core of the strong, independent personality of the adult woman, was her discovery when she was nineteen of "Dial a Demonstration", a mercurial service in New York that acted as a clearing house for information on the times and places of public protests. It was right down Eileen's alley. Her independence as a blind person, and her belief in the rights of other blind people to grow to their potential, became a cause for her early in life. Her refusal to have her life quenched, limited, by a handicap was typical of her decisiveness. She mastered roller skating, she learned the guitar, she inspired others by her songs of love and courage. She was not going to be put down, or pigeonholed as helpless, or allow anybody to victimize her.

She was Eileen Ross, a vital, loving woman who had made a success of her life with a history of protest and a strong sense of activism. She was her own employer, independent, asking no favors which she could not return, and when she was raped, her response to the assault was to draw on her experiences in protest and militance. It was natural for her to create a cause of her rape. It became her obsession, her responsibility to herself and to other raped women who were not as outspoken as she was.

It was three o'clock when detectives Sal Catalfumo and Patti Kehoe knocked on Eileen's door. She told them to come in and seated them on the couch across from the chair she occupied.

Despite her deep anger, her strong feeling that the police would love to close her case because it was an irritation that could become a headache, Eileen was determined not only to cooperate with the Brooklyn cops but get them to understand the real story. She hoped they would not be as ineffective as the ones from Manhattan.

It was Sal, dark, smooth, splendid-looking with his full, black moustache, who put Eileen at ease immediately with his insightful comment, "We know you've told your story several times and must be tired of repeating it. But listen, we've got a man in Brooklyn who's raped several women. Rapes then steals from them. From what we've heard and read on the media and in the papers about the man who attacked you, he might be the same one."

Eileen breathed a heavy sigh of relief. Here was someone alert to the truth.

"Do you know who he is?" Eileen asked.

"No, not yet, except that he can climb around buildings like a damned monkey.

"The man that raped me was black," Eileen slowly said. "He bragged about being a burglar. He said he took a gun from a woman's husband and tied him up."

Patti Kehoe shot a knowing glance at Sal Catalfumo, who acknowledged her silent message with a nod.

"What else can I tell you?" Eileen asked.

Patti said, "According to what we've read, the man made you cook breakfast for him. Was this before or after the rape?"

"Before," Eileen answered. She added, "I don't want to sound stupid or anything, but haven't you read the reports from the cops who came here and interviewed me? I told them everything I know. Don't misunderstand me, I don't mind going over it again, but the details were fresher in my mind right after it happened."

Patti chuckled. If Eileen could have seen her

crooked, almost sardonic grin, she would have approved of it.

"We're from Brooklyn, Miss Ross. We're lucky to get the time of day from Manhattan. I know that sounds ridiculous, but there's always . . . a . . . rivalry between boroughs, particularly if it's a celebrity case."

"You think I'm a celebrity?"

"The way the papers are handling you, it seems that way and I don't mean that in a derogatory way."

Eileen warmed to the woman detective. She had stood close enough to her as she came through the door to see the strong features and determined look on her face. She was a sunny blonde, wore her hair styled in a loose shag, was small and compact, had a trim figure, a friendly mouth and a pugnacious chin. She spoke with a pronounced Brooklyn accent.

"Well, I'm not a celebrity," Eileen said. "I'm an ordinary person, but I want people to know about this guy—how brutal he is. I know enough about the way things work in New York to know you get action quicker if you've got the newspapers on your side."

"I agree," Patti said emphatically.

"You do?"

"Yes," Sal interjected, "and so do I."

"God, I wish I'd talked to you first."

"Why?" Patti asked.

"Well . . . because I think the cops from Manhattan resent publicity. Not only that, but I can't understand how they could show me pictures of white men, Italians, and Hispanics, when I've specifically told them the guy who raped me had black skin. After all, it's not a matter of prejudice. I was close enough to him to see his skin color. Just a few hours ago, a woman officer showed me some pictures. None of them were anything like the man who broke in, the man I described. I just don't get it."

Sal nodded and Patti frowned. "Sometimes when the cops are under pressure," she said, "they jump at straws.

Eileen got the strong feeling that there was a lot more Detective Patti Kehoe wanted to say about jumping at straws, but that she was restrained by her own sense of duty. She went onto another tack.

"Also, you'd be surprised . . . ," Eileen abruptly broke off the sentence.

"Look," Patti said, "could you reenact what happened Monday morning?"

"Sure," Eileen said, "please follow me into the bedroom." She pointed to the walls and the ceiling, then touched the bandage on top of her head.

"I was asleep when my dog, Bethie, started barking. He hit her and then he hit me. I learned today from my attorney that the kitchen mallet that he used to hit me, one out of my own kitchen, had no traces of blood or hair. Nothing. I don't understand it. With all that blood you'd think some of it would have transferred to the mallet."

"Perhaps he washed it off," Sal said thoughtfully.

"You just can't tell what happened." Patti interjected.

For the next half hour, Eileen retraced the movements of the man who had raped her, culminating with his departure after he tied her to a chair with the long cords of her stereo head phones. When the detectives and she resumed their seats, Patti Kehoe said softly but forcefully, "You say you touched the man when you deliberately fell against him. That took guts. Did he have facial hair?"

Eileen nodded and went on, a thoughtful expression appearing on her face.

"Yes. Scruffy hair on his chin and sort of a wispy moustache. The hair on his head was short, close to his skull."

Patti turned to Sal. It was plain by his nods and silence that he did not have any questions. Eileen took advantage of the lull and said, "How do I find out if the cops here found the man's fingerprints where I told them to look?"

"What do you mean?" Sal asked. There was sudden strong interest in his tone. He looked over at his partner, "Patti?" he said his voice rising.

Eileen picked up on the inflection.

"Oh, I guess you don't know about that. I keep forgetting you haven't read any of the reports. Before I fell against the man, I handed him a glass with which to drink the 7-Up. I know my fingers touched his when he took the glass from my hand. So I know his fingerprints were on it. The police who were here took the glass with them. I'm sure they also took fingerprints from the extension phone in the bathroom."

Eileen hesitated, then focused her limited gaze at the two figures on the couch and said, "It is the same man, isn't it? There are too many similarities for it to be anybody else. The man who was here is the one you are looking for? He's called Spiderman, isn't he?"

Patti glanced at Sal, then said to Eileen, "Eileen, it looks that way, but I've got to get something clear in my head. You're saying you deliberately tricked the man into taking the glass?"

"Sure. I had to do something. I had to figure some way to get a record of him, to trap him. That's why I'm anxious about the prints. They will prove he was here."

"You're very sure about this?" Patti asked.

"Yes, I am," Eileen said firmly. "I gave him the glass very carefully and I'm sure he held it in his hand. He drank from it. He handled the telephone in the bathroom. I didn't plan that but I was very aware of it."

Patti grinned and got to her feet, followed by Sal Catalfumo. Patti leaned forward slightly and touched Eileen's shoulder; "That was a hell of a thing to do. Off the record, I think the man who raped you *is* the same one we're looking for, the one they're calling Spiderman. I think what you did just might help us nail him."

"I hope so," Eileen said vehemently.

Eileen was cheered by the visit from the two Brooklyn police officers. They had promised nothing, but they had been friendly, honest about the lack of communication between police boroughs in New York. Though they hadn't come right out and said the man who had assaulted at least four women in the Crown Heights section of Brooklyn was the same one who had raped her, they had left her with the definite impression that they thought the man might be one and the same.

She especially liked Patti Kehoe. Her impression was that Patti had spirit just like she did. Some would call her a firecracker about to go off. Eileen smiled to herself. That was okay, Patti looked like a woman who had trained herself to keep her vivacious enthusiasm and outspoken opinions under enough control to channel them in the right directions, just as Eileen herself did. And Eileen had received a message from Patti that she approved of Eileen's campaign to pressure the police through publicity about her case. It was the detective's warm responses and her parting squeeze of Eileen's hand that had said more than words.

Eileen had learned a lot about what was going on in her case from what the detectives didn't say. It was apparent that the Manhattan Sex Crimes Squad had volunteered no information to their Brooklyn counterparts. They might even be hoarding crime facts they had accumulated. One thing was certain: She was convinced she had to increase the pressure on the Manhattan cops and she had to do it before the newsworthiness of her case lost momentum. She knew honest complaints to the police often died from inattention, or simply got lost among the half a million New York's finest processed each year. If her rapist was going to be caught, she was going to have to make his apprehension an absolute priority for the cops.

During the next few days, Eileen instigated a telephone campaign. Among the organizations whose aid she enlisted were the National Organization of Women, New York Women Against Rape, The Rape Crisis Center at Mt. Sinai Hospital, and her own apartment house neighbor, Gail Turner, who was delighted to call her friends and conspire with them to institute a steady barrage of telephone calls streaming into police switchboards. Hundreds of phone calls poured into Manhattan's Sex Crimes Squad at the Twentieth Precinct and the District Attorney's office on Center Street. Meanwhile, New York television, radio and newspapers had been struck by Eileen's "plucky" story and her determination to catch her attacker. They were eager for details about her life, her attitudes on rape and on women's rights.

Eileen gladly answered their questions and with one reporter, Anne Creason from the *New York Post,* she established a special rapport. Anne had even come over to meet Eileen's special protectors, the dozen or so young male friends of Rick, who had volunteered to stay at Eileen's apartment through the night.

Anne had interviewed and photographed them and was doing a story on them.

By 4:00 P.M. Wednesday afternoon, Eileen was having a Pepsi with Rodney, one of the youths who stayed with her at night, and taking stock of her accomplishments. "I think we finally have a good chance of getting him," she was saying when the telephone rang.

Rodney passed the phone to her.

When she heard the terse question from Anne, the *Post* reporter with whom she had established a friendly relationship, Eileen was stunned.

"Eileen, did you accuse somebody of sexually molesting you a few years back?"

"Why, yes," Eileen said matter of factly. "A guy attacked me near a construction sight in 1979. I . . ."

"Eileen," the woman interrupted in a rebuking tone, "We've killed the story in the evening edition on the kids who are guarding you. I'm sorry . . . goodbye."

Chapter 11

Eileen was stunned by the announcement from the *New York Post* reporter. "Did you accuse somebody of sexually molesting you a few years back, Eileen?" The hard cynicism in the woman's voice made it plain that she believed Eileen had misled the media as to her motives by failing to mention the crazy who had ejaculated on her coat, after slashing it with his knife in the dark. As if it were an indictment of Eileen to have been attacked twice.

The reporter's "I'm sorry" was an insincere verdict of dismissal, following her announcement that the story on the young men guarding Eileen in her apartment had been killed.

Wearily, Eileen put the phone in its cradle. She wondered if the reporter could have gotten her information, and the interpretation of it, from the Manhattan Police. Eileen had been told not to talk about the rape attempt six years before by her friends and by both of her attorneys. Therefore, she had not mentioned it to the Manhattan Sex Crimes Squad when they questioned her on Monday morning. Had they asked whether or not she had been attacked before, she certainly would have told them. She had nothing to hide. But she had accepted her attorney's advice that there was no reason for her to reiterate the event of six years past, because it had no bearing on the man who had held her captive for two hours.

Suddenly Eileen's mind whirled back through the intervening years and she remembered the two blue-suited cops who had interviewed her after she had reported the frenzied slasher. They had obviously been influenced by their perceptions about blind people. They had told her that if she couldn't definitively and positively identify the man who had jumped out of the dark and grabbed her there was nothing they could do, and they didn't think she could do that. She knew they had filed a perfunctory report on the incident, a complaint upon which no action had been taken.

When she had told Norman Pearlman the story of what happened in 1979, he had frowned and warned her, "Eileen, nothing can be accomplished by stirring up old ashes. We don't want anything to prejudice your case, do we?"

Gary Trachten's advice had been couched in much the same terms, but with more vehemence: "Keep your mouth shut, don't volunteer information."

Well, it was obvious that the old complaint had prejudiced the *New York Post* reporter. Anne had found it, or somebody had brought it to her attention and suddenly the newspaper's confidence in Eileen had disappeared. The feature the newspaper was planning to run on Eileen's guardians had been killed. It wasn't farfetched for Eileen to assume that the Manhattan cops, already apparently suspicious of David being in her apartment, her being too vocal, uncharacteristic of rape victims, had stumbled on the old report and had shared it with the newspaper reporter. Questions would have come up: What are the chances of a woman being sexually assaulted twice in her lifetime? And the real corker: What had a blind woman been doing walking home in the dark at 2:30 in the morning? That was just *asking* for it.

Eileen sighed. She was angry and resentful. Why did some people always think the worst about others?

She had been squarely facing unfair perceptions all her life. Damn, they made her furious.

Though Eileen saw very little of her physical self, she had enough vision to know that she was an attractive woman. When she stood directly in front of the mirror the image reflected back was of an intelligent woman who showed the world an oval face supported by a lovely neck and skin with a fresh creamy texture. Luxurious, dark auburn hair framed her face and her eyes were large and deep brown. Her full black eyebrows, curving accents on a smooth, white forehead, gave strong definition to her cheekbones. Her mouth was the most attractive feature in her face. It was a mouth with full lips that curved provocatively to the corners. She needed no lipstick to give her mouth color. Her lips were naturally red and pouty and they drew attention to the dark Italian mystery of her face. Usually, she parted her hair in the middle of her forehead, an effect that imparted an old world demureness to her face. Combined with an habitual expression of inquiry—the only influence of blindness that provided a clue to her disability—the total effect was to give her an aspect of strong personal identity, of being somebody. She was often mistaken for an actress, the name of whom the observer could never remember.

She never thought of herself as ordinary. She knew she was smart, reliable, a little pugnacious about her "rights as a person." She did not feel deprived by her lack of sight or that God and an imperfect world had been unfair to her.

Life to Eileen had been a challenge to get where she was, to have friends who were compatible and did not feel burdened by her disability, or duty bound to entertain her because she was *unfortunate.* Whenever she detected pity in the voice or in the actions of a person she quickly let him or her know she did not want sympathy. For relationships to be valid they had to be built on mature respect. If people's estimate of her was influenced by the exceptions they made because of her condition, then their friendship wasn't worth having. She expected her friends and associates to demonstrate grace and patience and she tried to do the same. She depended upon them to accompany, not lead her.

She carried a white cane whenever she was in unfamiliar territory. She did not want to deny her blindness. She simply didn't think it was of paramount importance. Her independence was not overwhelmed by the world.

At three feet, she could see the fingers of her hand. At five feet, she could accurately describe the basic color of a woman's dress or a man's sport jacket, but she couldn't see the buttons. Up to ten feet, people were shapes, with the density of clouds or fog. She knew when someone was coming toward her or leaving. A cloud moved away or drifted closer.

People who met her for the first time marveled that she would suggest lunch in downtown Manhattan, arrive by subway alone and walk unaided to her destination on the mezzanine floor at Rockefeller Center, "where we can sit and you can see the ice skaters if we can't get a table early enough."

The subway did not daunt her, nor did the streets of New York. She often said, "Well now, listen, New York is easy to get around in. All the avenues go one way and all the streets the other."

There were times when she had to make certain where she was and she was grateful for the ubiquitous crowds of people, individuals of whom could be stopped for directions. She was not a woman who panicked easily. She had a strong sense of direction and a strong sense of self-worth. If she was in doubt she asked questions.

Still this new rejection was more than just another disappointment.

It was more apparent than ever that the Manhattan cops did not believe she had been raped by an intruder. Their suspicions still centered on David. He was so *convenient,* the black man who had been sitting on her couch when the patrolmen arrived.

She remembered what the feisty little Brooklyn detective, Patti Kehoe, had said to her: "Sometimes when cops are under pressure they jump at straws." When Eileen thought about it, Kehoe's statement conveyed a whole bagful of unspoken accusations. Eileen believed from what she had read and heard that rape in many police jurisdictions was the lowest among all the major crimes in the estimation of cops. Rape, among many police officers, was an event to be described in a prurient joke, a lewd remark, a suggestive comment. A raped woman eavesdropping on the locker room banter of the boys in blue might discover jockstrap humor that placed rape on the same basement level as sweaty socks, girly magazines, and porno flicks.

Eileen turned to Rodney, who had been looking on, confused by the whole scene.

"They've killed the article about you guys," she said, exasperatedly.

"But why?" he asked.

Quickly, she filled in the story of her previous attack.

"It reminds me of my father's encounter with cops," said Eileen.

"In 1978, he was attacked in his small apartment in the Queensbridge Housing Project. The intruder was a woman who forced Dad into a closet and stabbed him in the face repeatedly with a small knife when he tried to get out. She walked away with his accordion, which he had scrimped for years to buy, and a Social Security check.

"When he reported the violent invasion of his living quarters by a 'crazy woman, who beat me up, stabbed me and stole from me,' the housing authority cop who listened to his complaint refused to believe him."

" 'I haven't got time for weird shit like that.' the man said and told Dad that a more plausible story was that he had had a woman in his apartment, they'd argued, and she'd stolen his stuff because she was mad at him.

"Nothing Dad said could convince the man that he had been the victim of a pugnacious female rip-off artist who was strong enough to throw him to the floor when he had tried to subdue her."

Disillusioned, Eileen bit her lip pensively, "A lot of people, especially some cops and reporters, believe what they want to believe, facts to the contrary," she said.

Then she looked up and set her chin determinedly. "But I'm not going to let this get swept under the rug. Not this time. I'm going to keep on making noise until they listen."

Chapter 12

Patti Kehoe had always admired the imperturbability of Sal Catalfumo behind the wheel of a squad car in traffic. Before getting to know Sal, she had thought of Italians as hot-headed, quick to burst into temper, ready with an explosive argument or a threatening fist if they thought someone had crossed them.

Not Sal. In traffic he was a model of patience, expert at guiding the vehicle he was driving to the shortest route between two points. He was a natural behind the wheel, economical with his motions, smooth on accelerator and brakes. He enjoyed driving; he knew Brooklyn and Manhattan by heart. He was familiar with the major landmarks, the ethnic neighborhoods, composition of the people, and he had learned short cuts between the boroughs that only a person who had roamed their streets could appreciate.

As he pointed the car toward Brooklyn, Sal said, "I like Ross. She's got spunk."

Patti smiled. Coming from Sal, the compliment was like a benediction. It proved that Sal didn't regret his decision to suspend his judgment on Eileen Ross, to listen openly to her side of the story, even after having been told by a Manhattan detective that she was probably lying. It reflected his maturity and good police practice. Sal had described his conversation with the other cop to Patti and like Sal, she had refused to enter the interview with Eileen in a biased frame of mind.

"I think she's telling the truth," Sal nodded.

Patti was glad she and Sal shared the same opinion

about Eileen Ross. She liked Sal. Dark, competent, thoughtful he was a thorough professional who could be relied on in a pinch. He made a good partner. Patti and he worked so well together that it wasn't even necessary for them to define the relationship. On interviews he knew that the witness always set the tone and the character, and smart cops adapted to the personality of the witness. With Ross, as with other victims, he had sensed immediately the rhythm necessary to establish rapport and, taking note of her ability to communicate with Patti, he had taken on a supportive role without ego interference.

Patti's tone had been instinctively right.

"I liked her from the beginning," Patti continued. "And when she told me how she'd gotten his fingerprints on the 7-Up glass, I began to really admire her."

"God, that took guts," Patti said pausing. "I'm a little uncomfortable with the necessity for having withheld information from Eileen."

Sal broke in, "I know, but it's safer. Almost from the minute Eileen described her attacker I thought the man was a dead ringer for the Brooklyn suspect in those burglary rapes. Everything Ross said about the man fit, even down to her description of his thirst."

"Yeah, I think so too," Patti shook her head purposefully.

"In the six burglary rapes we've investigated, the unknown perpetrator has unerringly made a beeline for the refrigerator in an apartment as soon as he broke in."

"It was the first thing he did," Sal mused.

"A trademark of his crime pattern," Patti picked up his train of thought.

"Long before the sleeping inhabitants of the apartment discovered a predator on their premises, he had taken long draughts of fruit juice if it was present. His preference for fruit juice, orange juice, over a carbonated beverage was a strong signal, don't you think?"

"Yup," Sal concurred. "Juice is a soothing palliative to a junkie who is slowly withdrawing from a cocaine high."

"It's the high sugar content," Patti said thinking out loud.

"The juice-drinking habit of the Brooklyn rapist, whether it's drug-related or merely the habit of a man who likes juice, is also the ritual that might trap him."

"If you remember," Sal said rushing on, "he left his fingerprints on emptied juice bottles in two or three apartments he had broken into. That's another indication that the man was probably a drug user. Carelessness traps more criminals than any other piece of evidence. A perp on coke is acting under a handicap. The drug affects judgment; it gives the user a false sense of security."

"We have Richie Harker, the Latent Print Officer from the Seventy-Seventh Precinct, to thank for his alertness in picking up that clue about the fruit juice," Patti observed. "He was the one, as the 'Print man on the scene,' who saw the significance of the burglar's habit." Patti knew that more humble evidence than juice cans had trapped brutal criminals.

Patti leaned back against her seat and smoothed her skirt under her tight seat belt. She giggled half to herself and realized Sal had caught her smothered amusement.

"What's so funny?" he asked, glancing over.

"I was just thinking about the crime rate in the Seventy-Seventh."

Sal grunted and refocused his eyes on the road, "The crime rate at the Seventy-Seventh—the thickly populated Brooklyn Crown Heights area where Spiderman concentrated the majority of his attacks—is not only a joke, it's a damned shame. It's a fact of life New York Police Department officials don't like to talk about."

"And it's the best reason," Patti interrupted, "that skels like the rapist-burglar we're after are careless about the surfaces on which they place their hands in a burglary. They know cops hate to go into the neighborhoods of "Brooklyn's Harlem" to dust for fingerprints."

"True enough," Sal sighed heavily.

They both knew the crime statistics of the Seventy-Seventh by heart. There were three thousand or four thousand burglaries a year in the precinct, a police jurisdiction composed of only two square miles. And that didn't count the murders, rapes, robberies and taxi cab hold-ups.

The Seventy-Seventh was where Patti and Sal were headed now to talk to a quiet little cop who represented the kind of policemen their supervisors liked to point to with pride.

Suddenly, a call came in on the police car speaker, instructing Patti to call her boss at the Seventy-Seventh Precinct.

Sal obediently aimed the car at a phone booth half a block ahead and parked, leaving the motor running while Patti made the phone call.

She returned five minutes later with a grin on her face. "Jim says for us to come on in. It looks like a burglar—that cop in Latent Prints, Richie Harker, was wise to—may be the same guy who we've been looking for, for raping women."

Sal smiled. "We're on our way."

While he drove, Patti poured out the rest of what Jim McGeown had said on the telephone.

"According to the chief, Frank Paganucci, working with Richie Harker, first matched fresh burglary prints taken from two different Crown Heights crime scenes by Harker. But they struck pay dirt when they identified the burglar as operating in the same vicinity as the most recent Crown Heights rape on Sterling Place.

"On the surface, it appeared that the burglar's method of operation was strikingly similar to Spiderman's. His spectacular entry into victims' apartments, disdaining heights, strongly resembled the rapist's. Jim wants the Sex Crime Squad to meet and pool our information. He thinks we might discover we're closer to uncovering the identity of Spiderman than we know."

"Let's hope so," Sal said thoughtfully. "When did they find all this out?"

"The events started to unroll Tuesday afternoon when Richie Harker was stopped near his office by his precinct captain, Ralph Dumond."

According to McGeown, Dumond said, "Hey, I've got to talk to you. These burglaries, we've got a lot of problems. This guy's coming in open windows. People are hot. Have you got anything?"

Harker responded, "No, but we're working on it. We're getting prints and we're sending them in. If Paganucci can hook them up to somebody, I'm sure we'll close the cast out."

Captain Dumond grunted. "Well, keep at it."

After leaving the captain, Harker was stopped by a detective who said, "Have you seen Frank Paganucci? Well, he's got something real important for you."

Curious, Harker called the fingerprint technician who said, "Hey, Richie, remember that lady on Eastern Parkway, the one you said was so mad about those prints, prints you found on the cans, and prints you located at the Park Place job? This puts the guy in the same vicinity as some of the rapes. Do you suppose we're talking about the same mutt? Could *our* burglar be Spiderman?"

"Everything I know about this guy makes me think so, Frank. I'll make you a bet right now. The ex-con whose name I gave you a while back, Tyrone Graham. You remember, the one I told you I had a hunch about? The guy, one of my snitches said liked to hurt people? I'll bet you he and the guy you're searching for are one in the same. I'll bet my fucking shirt that you'll get a positive match with his prints and the ones you've matched on Eastern Parkway and Park Place. Did you get his prints from BCI like I suggested?"

"Got too busy, but I'll head over there tomorrow. Thanks, Richie. I'll let you know what happens."

Richie Harker ran into Captain Dumond again in the hall after he finished his conversation with Frank Paganucci. He reported what he'd found out from Paganucci and related his hunch about Tyrone Graham.

"Jesus, Mary and Joseph," Dumond said. "You think the burglar and the sex thief are the same guy, huh? Well, it makes sense. Juice bottles at the scenes of the rapes and the burglaries. The same hair-raising style of choosing break-in targets and rape targets located on the top floors of buildings. Hell, we've got to pull the guy's prints quickly. Do a comparison. Have you called Lieutenant McGeown yet? He needs to know about this. Shit, I'd better call Manhattan Sex Crimes. Tell them it looks almost certain that the man who did Eileen Ross is the same guy who's been hitting on women over here."

Harker watched the captain's broad back recede as he bustled toward his office. He felt a sudden rush of pride. Damn, it felt good to have things come together, to know you were right.

Richie Harker thought about his hunch about Tyrone Graham being Spiderman. As a veteran cop, he'd learned to trust his own "gut feeling" about a suspect. Often it was almost uncanny how accurate it could be. Sometimes, when he had been on a crime scene, he had experienced the sensation that if the walls could speak they would have confirmed his hunch about a suspect.

He had learned to respect his intuition, and he truly felt that Graham was the man they wanted. The characteristics Spiderman had displayed, of stealing from his victims after assaulting them sexually, sounded like an old thief who had gone bad. Once a thief, always a thief was his motto, but sometimes they turned from thievery to something worse.

The thinking part of his job was behind him now. He had inspected hundreds of precinct prints before he had come up with the first match on the two burglaries. It was a job that gave you a stiff neck from holding your head at the right distance from the portable fingerprint magnifier and sweeping it over card after card taken from a pile of suspects.

Your eyes got blurry and you could get a backache easily. Of course, that was a result of inactivity—sitting for hours every day looking at the lines and whorls and ridges and hills that made up the contours and patterns embedded in the finger pads of each subject. It was always amazing that not one was ever the same.

Now it was up to Paganucci. Everything seemed to indicate Harker was right though it could turn out he'd been wrong. That could certainly happen, but he didn't think so.

It was time for him to call Lieutenant Jim McGeown at the Seventy-First Precinct. It was his duty to advise McGeown of what he'd discovered. The next step would be up to McGeown. If he was the Lieutenant, he'd tell Paganucci to take the two matched prints to the Latent Prints Department at the Bureau of Criminal Identification in downtown Manhattan right away. He had Graham's NYSIS number. He had given it to him. If Graham's prints didn't match, them Paganucci was going to have to pull through hundreds of cards to find fingerprints to coincide with the crucial three.

But if there was a three-way match, bingo! The next step would be to try to match Graham's fingerprints against prints found at the rape scenes. If they could do that, Tyrone Graham would be facing far more serious charges than burglary. Harker hoped he was right. It was a good feeling to hit a bullseye. Especially in a case that involved a rapist, a criminal who inflicted physical and emotional pain on his victims. It was what it meant to be a cop. To be able to put your finger irrevocably on a suspect and say, "This is him."

In the case of Spiderman, Harker was particularly satisfied. He had a wife whom he loved deeply. He could imagine her terror and pain if she were to be raped by a man who broke into her bedroom on a dark night. Spiderman had even raped some of his victims after he had tied up their husbands. He had forced the women to submit with their helpless mates watching.

Harker called the chief of the Brooklyn Sex Crimes Squad.

"McGeown here."

"Lieutenant, this is Richie Harker. You know I told you earlier that I had a hunch about Spiderman. Well, I think I know who he is."

"You do?" McGeown breathed a sigh of relief. "Who is he?"

"Well, Paganucci's got to do final comparisons at Latent Prints tomorrow, but I think he's a burglary repeater named Tyrone Graham."

"How sure are you?" McGeown interjected.

"Not absolutely, until Frank does the comparisons. But I'm sure enough to call you."

"Good thinking. Good work. I'm going to keep my fingers crossed. This could be the break we've been waiting for, and thanks," McGeown's voice lighted in gleeful contemplation.

"My pleasure," Harker said in response.

"Let's catch the bastard."

The meeting at the Seventy-First Precinct took less than an hour. Jim McGeown wanted concurrence from the five members of the Brooklyn Sex Crimes Squad, including himself, that the man who had been indisputably linked to the two burglaries in Crown Heights was the same person who had raped at least four women in Brooklyn, and probably a fifth in Manhattan.

Eight copies of victim's complaints rested on the conference table in front of McGeown as he looked at the faces of the detectives he knew so well. One by one, he picked up the copies for emphasis and then dropped them, saying, "These are the reports on burglaries the Seventy-Seventh guys have been working on. We know for sure the same guy did two of them and according to Richie Harker, he thinks Spiderman has done them all, including the two rape-burglaries. Before you commit, listen to this. It's from the complaint taken from Julie Matthews of 233 Northern Parkway. It happened about a month ago."

McGeown lifted one of the reports and read from it: "According to two women who were in the apartment, the perp used a rope to lower himself from the roof into an open window. The apartment was on the third floor. He ransacked the frig, snooped around the apartment as if he owned it, then had something to drink, juice, and generally terrorized the occupants with a knife and threats before he left with a steam iron, a VCR, a scarf and some cash. He was described as a young man, mid-twenties with bushy eyebrows, black skin, medium moustache, and long sideburns."

"The women couldn't describe the knife accurately. Sound familiar to you?"

The detectives who were listening intently were silent but nodding. McGeown went on.

"Okay," he said. "That was on June 11th, just about five weeks ago. About a month before that an occupant at 223 Oak Place, not far from Northern Parkway, was robbed when an unknown person forced open a living room window on a top floor apartment and stole two hundred dollars in cash."

McGeown raised his eyes and stared significantly at the other cops one by one. "The occupant of the apartment was a seventy-four year old woman with a grand piano in her living room. The burglar left a can of pop on the piano and it made a ring. He also left his fingerprints."

"According to Harker, at first he thought the old lady must have been lying. Like some other burglaries, there was no normal way for a guy to get in. Harker finally figured out he had to come down from the roof."

Murmurs of approval sounded throughout the room.

"Sounds like our guy," Sal interjected.

McGeown cleared his throat to get order. "Okay, so what have we got?" McGeown fingered the reports on the table in front of him.

"There are seven burglaries of an unusual entry nature, all concentrated within a five or six block area—all close together. He hit Northern Parkway, the same apartment house two times, and then sauntered across the street to Number 225 and hit there."

McGeown paused, took a sip of water and said, "Coincidentally, Number 225 is in the same neighborhood where Spiderman committed rape the last time. It's also in the same vicinity as the burglaries and another Spiderman rape on Ocean Avenue. The one on Rogers Place happened just about fourteen hours after Eileen Ross was raped in Manhattan."

McGeown stared intently for a moment at Patti Kehoe and Sal Catalfumo. "As soon as I'm finished, you guys can tell us if you think it's the same guy."

McGeown sat down, placed his hands flat on the table and said, "Are you thinking the same thing I am?" There were murmurs of assent. McGeown went on.

"Spiderman seems to be tied to the burglaries by three factors. One is his penchant for fruit juices or soft drinks. Empty bottles or cans have been found at every one of the rape locations and at most of the burglary locations. In one burglary, the perp acted just like Spiderman, forcing two women to feed him. He didn't rape them, but the breakfast business, the threats, the knife, and the same spectacular method of entry make this burglary seem a match with the characteristics of Spiderman."

"I think Spiderman and the burglar are the same guy." McGeown turned to Patti Kehoe. "How about it, Patti? What conclusion did you and Sal come up with?"

Patti Kehoe gave Sal Catalfumo a confirming look and said, "There isn't any question about it. And there isn't any question that the Ross woman was raped, despite what the Sex Crimes cops in Manhattan think. I didn't have to ask Eileen Ross whether or not her guy demanded juice or a soft drink, she said he drank 7-Up from a glass she gave to him to trap his fingerprints." There were gasps.

"That's right! Gutsy woman! We checked, she's legally blind, but the rest of her senses are damned acute and she can see enough real close up to hand him a fresh glass for his soda pop. He takes it, drinks from it and she picks it up casually, later, and drops it in the sink, pretending to run water over it. Not a bad plan, eh. We ought to hire her." There was a round of laughter.

"Anyway, the problem with the Manhattan cops is the ones who first got to her apartment found a black guy in there. And as you know, the security guard for the apartment building called in the rape as a domestic squabble. The cops added up the biased report and their own first impression and came up with the wrong conclusion. She was not trying to cover up a love nest quarrel with a black lover calling it rape. Hell, the man is dying! He had to drag himself out of bed to get to her apartment and untie her. It took him almost ten minutes to come downstairs by elevator. A trip a healthy man could make in less than three minutes at the outside. Any thinking person would know he couldn't strike, much less rape her."

Sal Catalfumo leaned forward and said quietly but intently, "I'm with Patti. Another reason the Manhattan guys have been dubious about Ross is because of the way she's acted since the rape. Going public, I mean. It's uncharacteristic of a raped woman, but so is trapping an intruder by his fingerprints. Just because Ross is spunky doesn't mean she's lying. She's impressed me, and," he paused, "I think the robberies were done by Spiderman also. They were done before he got rape on his mind."

McGeown looked over at Bob Merz and Bruce Milau. Both nodded and Merz said, "I think the Seventy-Seventh has got a lot to thank Richie Harker for."

McGeown nodded, "You're right and now we've got something solid to tell the newspapers. They've been bugging me for a break in the case. First, we'll describe Spiderman. The next step is to see if Harker's hunch is right. He said Paganucci was going to BCI tomorrow to make a comparison between Tyrone Graham and the two prints he's already matched. I think tomorrow is too long to wait. I'll call him now, at home. We need to have him run a make on the prints from the Sterling Street rape. He can do that at the same time he's making the burglary comparison. If all three match, then bingo, we've got our man."

McGeown paused, then glanced at the four members of his team.

"Why don't we plan to meet back here in an hour or so? Say by six o'clock. Get a bite to eat, then stick around after we meet with the reporters. I've got a hunch that something just might break for us tonight."

Patti Kehoe, as did the others, looked at McGeown with approval. She started to say something, then changed her mind. There was a small, hard grin of satisfaction on her face.

At seven o'clock, as a bunch of print and TV reporters gathered in his office at the Seventy-First Precinct, McGeown read his statement. It was short and precise:

"The rape of a woman in the Crown Heights area of Brooklyn early Tuesday morning is the latest in a pattern of sexual assaults and burglaries which we are attributing to the Spiderman rapist. During several of the burglaries sexual attacks were threatened on apartment dwellers. This fact, and other similarities in the behavior of the burglar, has convinced us that the person known as Spiderman may be responsible for several burglaries without sexual assault, and at least two burglaries in which the female apartment dweller was raped.

"Anybody with information who might help us identify this man is urged to call the Seventy-First Precinct."

McGeown knew that the news reporters would embellish his sparse press release with information recapitulating Spiderman's daring acrobatic descents from tops of roofs into vulnerable apartments. But he was satisfied that the morsel he had offered would help blunt inquisitive snooping into the movements of the Brooklyn Sex Crimes Squad for the next few hours.

Then McGeown met with Frank Paganucci. By this time a plan was forming in McGeown's mind, one he thought might lead to the apprehension of Spiderman. He reached the Latent Prints officer at his home and the studious little man agreed to put his family life on hold and go directly to BCI at Police Plaza. His assignment was to pull the NYSIS file on Tyrone Graham and compare Graham's fingerprints against the "hits" he had made by matching identical prints left at the two different burglary crime scenes.

The officer's next chore was to compare the three prints—if they coincided—with fingerprints found at the most recent rape scene in Brooklyn, 222 Rogers Place in Crown Heights. That was Spiderman's last known sexual assault. It had happened less than fourteen hours after Eileen Ross had been attacked in her apartment.

If there was a four-way match, then the cops would know the identity of the elusive figure who seemed able to crawl down vertical walls, slip through inaccessible windows, then suddenly change in personality from a swift, cunning, sure-footed thief into a cruel, mean rapist who took delight in humiliating his victims before finally assaulting them.

McGeown asked Paganucci for one final print comparison: If it unequivocally matched the burglary and the burglary-rape prints with those of Graham, then he wanted Graham's prints compared with those left on the scene at Eileen Ross's apartment.

"Terrific idea," Paganucci concurred.

The last call McGeown made was to Lieutenant George Duke, the commanding officer of the anti-crime unit of detectives attached to the Seventy-Seventh Precinct.

McGeown identified himself, exchanged greetings with Duke—whom he knew well—then explained the events involving Spiderman leading up to his call, including the crucial performance of Richie Harker, the Latent Prints cop. "Frank Paganucci is at this moment probably arriving at Police Plaza. It won't take him very long to make the print studies since he has Graham's name and NYSIS number. Within the hour the verdict can be in," McGeown speculated. "We'll know if Tyrone Graham is Spiderman or not." If the latter was the case, then Paganucci was going to have a hell of a long night trying to find an unknown sex offender who did burglaries, or an unknown burglar who had turned rapist.

"My hunch, George, is that Graham is our guy. If he is, what do you say to a joint arrest action? We need to get this guy into custody as soon as possible. The way he's going, he's hitting on women more frequently and the signs of progressive violence are clear.

"Harker's got an address on Graham from his NYSIS card. It's on Park Place. Since the guy's a combination burglar-rapist you'll want him for break-ins and we want him for the sex assaults. We get him first. You could verify the Park Place address with his parole officer. What do you say?"

Lieutenant Duke said, "Sounds like a winner, but how did Harker get into this case?"

McGeown explained how Harker had discovered the repeat evidence on juice bottles at the scene of burglaries and rapes and how a street informant had fingered Tyrone Graham for the burglaries, calling him a "mean dude who liked to hurt people."

"Sounds like Harker should be a detective," Duke said.

"Yeah, I'd probably endorse him," McGeown said. "Listen, I'm going to take my team down to BCI and sit on this until Paganucci either confirms Graham or rules him out. If it is Graham, I'll get duplicates of the prints and meet you at the Seventy-Seventh. We can head out from there."

"Okay, my guys and I will be ready," Duke said. "I'll verify Graham's address with Harker and see if Graham's parole officer has any more recent address, or whether Park Place stands up. Call me from BCI as soon as you get the news."

"You've got it," McGeown said.

Frank Paganucci made himself comfortable at a desk in the Latent Print section of the Bureau of Criminal Identification. As usual, he waited impatiently. His role in the forensic process of identification was always the last link in the chain of evidence cops followed to apprehend a criminal. Of course, the coroner was the final cog in the police investigative process, but in his mind medical examiners came after the fact. That didn't lessen their importance, but it did relegate their place in the hierarchy of investigation to *ex post facto*.

On the other hand, his job fingerprint identification encompassed both the quick and the dead. That made it, for him, a science that bridged the gulf between the known and the unknown. He laughed at his own momentary feeling of self-importance. But he knew that feeling kept him committed to his work.

He looked now at the police photo of Tyrone Graham imprisoned on the NYSIS card number 401 75990 he held in his hand. He saw a young man with the characteristic closed face of the repeat offender who has learned that the easiest way to survive incarceration is to present a neutral face and a blank personality. Paganucci delayed making the print comparison until he had read the convict's arrest history. He wanted to make damn sure he had a match.

Two years after his first arrest, Graham was convicted of second-degree burglary and received three months probation. A month later he was apprehended on a charge of criminal trespass and spent sixty days in jail. In March of 1979, again he was charged with second-degree burglary and received a sentence of thirty months to five years. In February of 1980, to May of 1981, he was in Elmira State Prison and was then released on parole. A few months after he was given his freedom, he was sentenced in October of 1981 for second-degree burglary and got a thirty month to five year sentence. In August of 1982, after only a few months behind bars, he was caught trying to escape from prison and his sentence was augmented by eighteen months for his break-out attempt.

Finally, in June of 1983, he was confined to Attica State Prison and released on parole in February of 1986.

There was no question in Paganucci's mind that the man whose face was pictured on the NYSIS card was a veteran thief whose repetitive history of break-ins indicated that "crude burglary" was a choice he'd made for his life. He was a window man with no great subtlety or finesse and, based on the jobs he'd done, he'd made a vocation of petty crime, living on the edge as a ritual burglar.

As he read on, the man's face stuck in Paganucci's mind. It was an interesting thing about some mutts. You couldn't put your finger on it, but you could look at a police picture and certain guys raised warning flags. Graham was one of these people. It was almost as if he was whispering in Paganucci's ear: "Now listen, you watch out for me. I may not be much now, but look out for my smoke. One of these days I'll surprise you."

If Paganucci was right, Graham had made good on the promise. He'd bridged the gap from mere thief to brutal rapist. Carefully, he projected a photo of Tyrone Graham's thumb print on the comparison screen. In the opposite slide holder he placed the thumb print from the Bergen Street burglary. When he pushed the holder sideways the top film was superimposed exactly on the bottom one. *It was a perfect match.*

He sat back and sighed.

The rest was easy. With a sense of growing satisfaction, he next compared, in the same mechanical sequence, the right thumb and left middle fingers of Graham with the same sequence of prints found on a juice bottle in the dining room of an apartment on Northern Parkway.

The result was positive! He also obtained matches with the crucial print left by Spiderman at 225 Rogers Place in Crown Heights. His crowning feeling of accomplishment came when he viewed the perfect alignment between the master print and the right middle finger captured on the water glass in Eileen Ross's kitchen. Now all the evidence was present to charge the man. He felt good, vindicated.

He was fascinated and repulsed by the compulsion that drove men like Graham into an accelerating pattern of violence. Graham had been released from Attica in February of 1986, just five months previously. Yet in that time he had sexually assaulted at least five women. The dates of his attacks were witness to the increasing pressure of his compulsion—each attack more brutal than the last.

It was Paganucci's fondness for details that caused his decision to keep a record of Spiderman's attacks. He had written down the dates of the major ones on women and had pinned the list to the file he had made for the rapist. He'd wanted to discover for himself if there was a periodic frequency to Spiderman's appearances. He was watching to see whether the man's violence would escalate with each assault. He guessed it would. And he'd been right.

The first woman the cops knew about had been raped in Crown Heights on May 15th. That time he had stolen cash, jewelry and a camera worth about fifteen hundred dollars after leaving the woman in a state of hysteria. The second rape was on June 22nd, about three weeks later. On that occasion he left teeth marks on the breasts of the victim and, after raping her in the presence of her husband who was bound with cords, he escaped with cash, a VCR, a shopping cart, jewelry, and a stereo.

On July 14th, almost a month later to the day, Graham had raped and brutally beaten Eileen Ross. Less than fourteen hours later on July 15th, he struck again, tying up a man while he raped and mauled his wife and then stole from the couple.

These were the rapes the cops knew about.

Frank Paganucci was beginning to place mechanical copies of the evidence on Tyrone Graham in a file when Sal Catalfumo, Patti Kehoe, Lieutenant Jim McGeown, Bob Merz and Bruce Milau walked up to his desk with expressions of grave expectancy.

He grinned at the officers and said simply, "We've got him. On four cases. I was just about to call you, Lieutenant McGeown." He looked at Patti. "Also I've made him for the Ross rape on the East Side. We got his fingerprints there."

"Where did they show up?" Patti asked.

"I thought you would ask me that," Paganucci glanced at the print forms in his hand. "The number three finger, which is the right middle, showed up on the glass that was located in the kitchen sink, and . . ."

Patti interrupted, "That's the one I was waiting to hear confirmed."

As the detectives piled into the two cars that had brought them, and headed for the Seventy-Seventh Precinct rendezvous with George Duke and his detectives, Patti Kehoe thought how gratifying it was going to be to to call Eileen Ross and tell the blind woman that her strategy had been right. Ross's brave plan to trap the fingerprints of an intruder who had terrorized her night had succeeded.

Chapter 13

It was close to eight o'clock before the Sex Crimes detectives had arrived at the Seventy-Seventh Precinct and dropped a copy of Frank Paganucci's fingerprint report on George Duke's desk. Duke immediately informed McGeown that Richie Harker had vouched for the Park Place address for Tyrone Graham. This was verified by a phone call to Graham's parole officer. The address turned out to be the residence of Tyrone Graham's sister, who lived in Crown Heights.

Duke wanted Graham on burglary charges as a result of the conclusive fingerprint information developed by Frank Paganucci. Both lieutenants understood that the Brooklyn Sex Crimes Squad had first claim on Graham because the burglar's rape offenses were major crimes. He would be charged with any of the burglaries he could be tied to as part of the total legal evidence against him.

Richie Harker's informant had told him that the address of Graham's sister was current. It was the place Graham "was hanging out." He'd been seen there as recently as the previous day.

Quickly, they had all scrambled into police vehicles and headed there. The brick apartment building in the Crown Heights section of Brooklyn was six stories high and even in the flat, motionless dark of the hot July night it seemed to hang on its foundations like a tired old man whose years have bent his posture. It was one of several buildings on the street that in the moonless night looked like dominoes with window rectangles of light for the white spots.

Patti could hear the rumble of voices that belonged to the people who hung out the windows, "It's the cops. The cops are here."

You couldn't fool them, not ever. These people could spot an unmarked police car faster than she could say kiss my foot. They were street-wise, cop-wise. They knew the three cars carrying six plainclothes detectives and herself had come to get somebody. Somebody was in deep trouble. Somebody was going to be arrested. The cops didn't come in force unless they were after a real bad dude.

"Hey cops, why don't you fuck off," a loud metallic voice called out.

"Get lost," another joined in.

She ignored the insults, the whistles and cat calls as she stepped out of the car in which she, Sal Catalfumo, and Lieutenant Jim McGeown had ridden from the Seventy-Seventh Precinct. She took a deep breath and regretted it. The putrid smell reached into her, into her nose, mouth, and lungs. The smell was the community breath of Crown Heights. It was always amazing to Patti that when she met people in different surroundings who lived here that they smelled like anybody else. They didn't carry the Crown Heights odor with them. It was the breath of failure, disappointment and anger, and it smelled like a strong mixture of old rot, garbage, urine, feces, and moldering wood.

"Same old shit smell," Sal said as he came around the front of the car.

Jim McGeown looked down the shadowy street and saw Bruce Milau unfold his two hundred and eight pound bulk from the car in which he was riding with Lieutenant George Duke, of the anti-crime unit of the Seventy-Seventh.

The plan was for Bruce with Sal, Jim, Bob, and a

detective from the Seventy-Seventh to knock on the fourth floor door of Tyrone Graham's sister's apartment and demand that he come out. Patti and George Duke were going to head for the roof of the building via the elevator in case Graham got it into his head to try to escape by that route. Another detective from Duke's squad would post himself near the bottom of the fire escape and apprehend Graham there in the event the burglar was slippery enough to evade the detectives in the apartment and on the roof.

As Sal, Bruce, Bob, McGeown, and a quiet-spoken young detective from Duke's squad started up the stairs to the fourth floor, Patti, standing next to Duke, punched the elevator button in the foyer of the building. A ceiling light cast a weak glare around the detectives, throwing crouching shadows of them on the floor. As Patti entered the airless entrance hall she saw the evidence of forlorn defiance of the misery in the building in graffiti written on the scarred green elevator door.

Scrawled messages on the walls inside the elevator carried the same theme of desperation expressed in sprawling paint-sprayed messages announcing the superiority of one neighborhood gang over all others, and dubious telephone numbers for smack or snow, or sex. Trash was strewn on the elevator floor, red stains were flung across the base of one wall and the stench of urine punctuated it all.

Duke gasped for breath, and held up his arms in a surrender sign. It was a gesture that needed no explanation for Patti. She knew what the squad chief was thinking. The whole area was a sewer. The perp they were after had been raised in a poisonous environment of poverty, hate, envy, and the worst influence of all—hopelessness.

As the elevator came to a halt on the top floor, Patti

and Duke drew their weapons, snapped on their flashlights and climbed the one flight of stairs to the door leading to the roof. Before opening the door, Patti removed a walkie-talkie clipped to her belt and called for Sal. He was with Bruce and McGeown and the detective from Duke's squad.

"Yeah, who is it?"

"Sal? It's me, Patti. Are you in? Is he there?"

"Just about to, Patti. I'll call you back in a couple of minutes."

Sal Catalfumo replaced his walkie-talkie on his belt just as Bruce Milau knocked vigorously on the wooden door to Apartment 22. In a deep, authoritative voice, he said loudly, "Police! Open the door!" He stepped to the side of the door quickly. Jim McGeown was flattened against the wall on the opposite side of the door and Sal and Sergeant Frank Shields from the Seventy-Seventh were arranged behind the two men.

"What do you want?" a female voice asked harshly.

"Open the goddamn door!" Milau said in a threatening voice.

The door swung open on a chain about four inches wide, enough for Milau to see a copper-skinned woman's arm, part of her face and her maroon dress.

"Jesus, you're a big fucker for a cop. What do you want?"

"Tyrone Graham. Is he in there?"

"No, he's not here. What do you want him for anyway?"

"Just open the door, lady."

"I told you he's not here."

"We'll have to search. Open the door or I'll break it in."

There was a moment of silence followed by some muffled words Bruce or McGeown could not make out.

Then, the chain was removed and a sharp-featured, middle-aged woman stood partially blocking the open door with her arms folded. Bruce pushed by her, his gun drawn. He was followed cautiously by the other detectives.

"My brother's a good man," the woman said to Milau, following his broad back as he plunged into the apartment.

"I told you he's not here," the woman cried, raising her voice to a shrill protest when the four detectives returned to the living room after exploring the two bedrooms, the kitchen and the fire escape. She had worked herself into a fit of rage. Her outrage was shared by a red-lipped, afro-haired woman and gray-haired, ebony-skinned man who sat at the kitchen table staring at the detectives with sullen, tight-lipped fury.

Just before he stepped back into the apartment through a kitchen window from the fire escape, Sal called Patti on his walkie-talkie. "He's not here, Patti. We've come up empty."

Patti heard the message from Sal Catalfumo as she and Duke stepped onto the roof and quickly moved out of the rectangle of light cast by the circular lamp attached to the wall above the outside door frame. Patti switched on her flashlight, directing the beam at her feet until her eyes adjusted to the murky darkness. Duke's light came on a few feet away from her at the same moment and she could bet he was thinking the same thing she was.

Their flashlights made good targets of both of them. While Graham's MO did not indicate he carried a gun or had used one in any of the crimes he had committed, there was a first time for everything. They did know the knife was his favorite weapon. Patti shivered involuntarily. *God, she hated knives.* Through Patti's mind flashed Eileen Ross's description of how her attacker had never been without his knife during the entire time he was in her apartment.

"Damn!" she murmured to herself, it was so frigging dark it was like being in a tunnel. The only relief was the light she could see in the distance and the faint rosy glow of the city on the horizon. There was no moon; the stars were hiding; the roof was dark, evil smelling and hot.

In the few minutes it had taken for her and George Duke to get from the sidewalk to the roof, the thick heat had drawn perspiration from her pores like dew on a leaf. Her slacks seemed suddenly too tight. Her blouse clung to her skin and her waist-length police jacket with the slashed pockets imprisoned the heat against her body. The deep-down holster, snug inside the waist band of her slacks, felt stiff and awkward.

Shit! She thought quickly, glancing first to the left then to the right and back again. Hardly perfect conditions to find a rapist, who most certainly had his knife ready and had the terrific advantage of sighting her flashlight and using it as a beacon to her body.

She whispered to Duke, "Which side do you want, Lieutenant?"

"Shit! I can't see anything anyway. Let's do it side by side. I'll sweep about ten feet away from you. If he's here, we should be able to catch him within our lights in that distance."

Patti nodded in the dark; Duke didn't need to see her confirmation. They knew each other well enough to be able to count on the other's reaction. She elevated her flashlight so it formed an eight foot semi-circle of light from her body forward. She moved quietly, choosing her steps. Broken bottles winked in the path of her light. A gray tampon, a candy wrapper, the crumpled aluminum foil dish from a TV dinner formed a snarl of refuse which she nudged with her foot.

She was surprised when she saw the roll of blankets resting against the wall of the roof. For an instant she was confused. The rounded heap of dirty blankets was somebody's deserted bedroll. She stepped cautiously closer, puzzled, suddenly realizing there was a human form covered by the blankets. *A* street person probably, a vagrant, she thought.

Patti dropped the angle of her flashlight, leaving the top half of the sleeper submerged in darkness. She didn't want to startle whoever was lying there into wakefulness. Peering closer, Patti noted that the person swathed in the blankets on a hot night smelled like a ripe sausage.

Patti stepped back cautiously, then suddenly pointed her flashlight vertically at the sky. This was a signal to George Duke who came to her side quickly.

"In front of me," Patti whispered to him. "Somebody against the wall, covered with blankets and clothes. Could be Graham, could be a bum."

"It's your collar—I'll back you," Duke said. He shifted the pistol in his hand.

Patti tightened her grip on her .38 Chief and moved silently to the sleeping form lying against the wall of the roof. She played the light on the shoulders of the motionless figure and saw the back of the man's head. He was lying on his stomach with his head turned to the wall; she gasped. It looked like Graham. Patti knew his features. She had meticulously studied a picture of the man, as had the other detectives, in Duke's office at the Seventy-Seventh before they drove to his sister's apartment.

She scrutinized the man. It was Graham! Close now, she could smell the man; the odor was fierce, a commingling of sharp old sweat and new stained dirt, unwashed tennis shoes; he stank, she thought, of old fish and dead roses.

Three of the women who had described Spiderman had said he smelled high, stale and raunchy. A dirty man whose clothes held the odor of sweat and grime.

George Duke was at Graham's feet when Patti dropped to one knee, pressed the barrel of her .38 against Graham's forehead, and shook him with the hand in which she was holding her flashlight.

"Police. Don't you fucking move!" she warned, "or I'll blow your head off."

The man blinking in the glare from George Duke's flashlight, stiffened his body, then relaxed his muscles as the threat of Patti's gun convinced him to lie still.

"I hear you," he mumbled.

Patti's left hand was pressed hard against Graham's shoulder as a precaution against his decision to jump up suddenly and plunge over the wall into the dark. Now, holding the barrel of her gun steadily against the man's forehead, she shouted, "Get up, slowly."

As he obeyed her, raising his shoulders and chest, she saw it, the Rambo knife, sheathed in a slim leather case with an unfastened ankle strap. It lay in the impression his body had made in the blanket. Carefully, Patti, keeping her gun pushed into his forehead, reached out and kicked the knife out of the way with her foot.

For a moment Patti glanced at it. The knife was the kind deer hunters favored, with a grooved blade to drain blood. No wonder Eileen had been petrified.

Parted by no more than two feet, Patti stared at the man directly, her heart beating fiercely. "Are you Tyrone Graham?"

He mumbled an incoherent reply.

"Are you Tyrone Graham?" She pushed a little harder on her gun against his forehead.

"Yes, I am."

"Step away from the wall," she said, "toward me."

George Duke was now behind Graham as she backed toward the center of the roof. Deftly, Duke pulled the man's arms behind him and locked handcuffs on his wrists.

"Lay down on your stomach on the roof," Duke ordered Graham.

Patti walked to the edge of the roof and yelled to the detective waiting at the bottom of the fire escape. "We've got him. Up here!" On her walkie-talkie she contacted Sal Catalfumo.

"We've got him up here, Sal."

Patti realized her heart was still beating a little fast and she felt pumped up, the legacy from the adrenaline rush that always happened when she was involved in the arrest of a violent person. She walked back to search the belongings the man had been sleeping on. Partially rolled up, was a pair of pants, a wrinkled sweater, dirty blue sneakers, a broken comb. A few coins had slipped out of a pocket while he slept and lay in the blanket. If property was a measure of a man, the poor showing on the rumpled blanket indicated a bankrupt individual whose assets were so small that jail would be an improvement in his life.

Patti then walked slowly over to Graham, who stared at her intently. His voice cut like steel.

"If I'd heard you, you'd never have caught me. I would have dove to that tree and you never would have found me, or if you had, you'd have wished you didn't."

She stared back into Graham's hardened eyes and believed him. He was a man who had terrorized more than a dozen victims the police knew about, not counting sexual attacks and burglaries on people who didn't report them.

It was always a mystery to Patti why a man would turn rapist. Did the failure of his mastery of his own life drive Graham to desperately prove his mastery over another human? Was this the secret passion that motivated an act of violence so despicable and cruel that a raped woman seldom ever recovered from it?

The psychologists said rape was an act of violence that had little to do with sexual intercourse. It was a contest of power. A brutal bully and a defenseless victim. And many times, the attacker's need for proof of his masculinity escalated into murderous violence.

She pointed her flashlight at Graham, glanced at Duke, pulled a small card from her breast pocket, and said, "You have the right to remain silent . . ." As she recited the familiar words, she saw Sal, Jim, Bruce, Bob and the detective from the Seventy-Seventh come through the door to the roof. They formed a semi-circle around Graham, now pinpointed in the combined glare of several flashlights.

Here was the man who had mutilated a dog in a woman's kitchen, eviscerating the animal in an angry flaying of flesh and fur. He had raped at least four women, two of whom he had penetrated in the anguished presence of their husbands, bound and helpless to stop the hurt and humiliation of their wives. As Patti finished the Miranda warning, Bruce made the observation that was on everybody's mind: "He doesn't look like much now, does he?"

Several men and women had gathered on the front steps of the apartment when Patti and the others brought the handcuffed Graham down in the elevator. Bruce Milau led the way and the small crowd grudgingly opened a path for the big detective.

"Why you want to bust him, man? What's he done?" A tall bronze-skinned man asked.

"Yeah, you scuz, why don't you leave us alone," another chimed in.

"Go on home," Bruce said. "There's nothing here for you."

He pushed Graham into the back seat of an unmarked police car and followed him in. On the way to the Seventy-First Precinct, Patti kept glancing back at him just to be sure he made no sly moves. Sal was driving.

In the ten-mile ride to the precinct, Graham made only one statement: "I guess you know I'm the best. I'm the best burglar you've ever seen."

"Make that past tense, you were the best," Milau said. In the next few hours, Graham was fingerprinted, photographed, questioned, and jailed in a holding cell while the Sex Crimes Squad detectives contacted four of the Brooklyn rape victims and made arrangements for them to view a line-up the same night at the Seventy-First Precinct.

Patti Kehoe, who was the acknowledged expert in convincing street vagrants to pose as "fillers" in the Precinct line-ups, traveled with Sal Catalfumo to the Brooklyn Armory on Atlantic Avenue. The Armory served as a kind of half-way house for recovering alcoholics and drug-abusers.

When Patti drove up, she was greeted warmly by the derelict men, who liked her because of her sense of humor and her obvious lack of any pious attitude toward their addictions. Also, she always paid, in precinct funds, each man ten dollars for standing in a line-up for a few minutes. The men were transported to the precinct and returned to the Armory in a police wagon.

The line-ups began at 10:00 P.M. Procedure required a different set of volunteers for each separate complaint. The cops were taking no chances that Graham would ever have any legal recourse based on civil rights violations.

The four innocent men, with Graham sandwiched in, stood with similar cowed looks, as the first woman viewed them.

The small, trembling brunette had told Patti she didn't think she would be able to identify the man who raped her. "I was too frightened to think," she had commented.

But when she saw Graham among the men standing in a row, she screamed out, "That's him! It's him!"

Patti nodded her assent, comforting the woman who sobbed afterward on Patti's shoulder.

Adept at the voluminous paperwork required to process Graham through each legal step, Patti worked through the night. She and the other detectives broke for dinner, coffee, then later, breakfast.

The circus started at 7:00 A.M. when the news reporters and the police brass started flooding into the Seventy-First Precinct.

Several police executives were on hand to lend authority to the apprehension of a man who had become a figure of terror and fear in the minds of Crown Heights residents.

It was Captain Ralph Dumond, the commanding officer of the Seventy-Seventh Precinct, who gave assembled news reporters and television interviewers a description of the policework leading up to the arrest.

Richie Harker, the diligent police officer who had linked the Spiderman attacks with Tyrone Graham, was singled out for praise.

"Last night in Crown Heights, the man who has become known as 'Spiderman' was captured by a special anti-crime force from the Seventy-Seventh Precinct. His arrest was made on the roof of an apartment building located at 919 Park Avenue, Crown Heights, Brooklyn.

"The arrest brought to a conclusion months of investigative work which involved detectives from the Brooklyn Sex Crimes Unit, the Seventy-Seventh Precinct, and three Latent Prints police officers.

"On Tuesday, Police Officer Richard Harker received notification from Police Officer Frank Paganucci of the Latent Print Unit that prints lifted by Officers Harker and Baker at two burglary locations in Crown Heights were identified as belonging to Tyrone Graham. These burglaries were similar to a pattern of burglaries which were occurring in the Seventy-Seventh Precinct and surrounding areas.

"During several of the burglaries, sexual attacks took place or were threatened and in one case the occupant's dog was stabbed and killed by the intruder when it came to its owner's rescue. The most recent sexual attack occurred on Tuesday early in the morning at the location within the confines of the Seventy-Seventh Precinct.

"This attack matched a pattern of sexual attacks in the Crown Heights area and led to a press release Tuesday evening by Lieutenant James McGeown, commanding officer, Brooklyn Sex Crimes Unit, during which the attacker was described as the 'Spiderman Rapist'. Based on the information from Police Officer Paganucci, Police Officer Harker immediately notified Lieutenant George Duke, commanding officer, Seventy-Seventh Precinct Detective Unit, and Lieutenant James McGeown.

"An intensive investigation was commenced to compare all other fingerprint evidence in these cases with that of Graham's. This resulted in an immediate match to a print lifted by the crime scene unit at the July 15th attack. Information from Police Officer Harker was then developed by the Seventy-Seventh Precinct Detective Unit that indicated Graham might be residing at 919 Park Place, between New York and Brooklyn Avenues in the Seventy-Seventh Precinct. Last night, members of the Seventy-Seventh P.D.U. and Brooklyn Sex Crime Unit, responded to the location and apprehended Graham on the roof of the building."

While Captain Dumond described the arrest procedure Graham, handcuffed with his arms behind his back, his head lowered in a posture of defeat, was held between Sex Crimes Squad detectives Sal Catalfumo and Bob Merz. A few minutes later, Graham was taken down the stairs of the stationhouse to a waiting police car that would transport him to another Brooklyn Precinct with larger jail facilities. Patti Kehoe trailed behind Graham and the two detectives as they crossed through a bank of television lights and whirling cameras.

One of the cops who watched the small parade was Richie Harker. He had heard the plauditory words of Captain Dumond and he had been interviewed by two television stations. His version of the print work leading to the capture of Spiderman lacked the personal emphasis stressed by his precinct boss.

In front of the station house, a television camera was pointed at a news reporter who made comments while a crowd of angry Crown Heights residents—who had heard about the capture late the night before—surged around the reporter.

As Graham was slowly brought through the door into the street, the small bristling crowd pushed forward amid strident calls of "Castrate him," "Throw away the key," "Give him to us." The detectives shielded Graham from physical abuse, but they couldn't stop the threats. Both men knew that exposing a criminal who had attracted the anger of citizens, threatened by the idea that one of them might have become a victim, gave the people the emotional release of shouting at him, raising a fist, muttering threats.

While Graham was being taken to a car, Richie Harker was discovered again by a newsman. Standing to one side, in his day-off flowered sport shirt and light slacks, poised and satisfied, the veteran police officer efficiently answered the key question asked of him by a television reporter: "How did you guys break the case?"

"It was a matter of matching fingerprints," Harker said, explaining the process of recording fingerprints at a crime scene and comparing them manually against others until a hit was made.

News reporter Will Stens of the television Channel 7 news team learned the whereabouts of the building in which Graham had been captured the night before. He and a camera crew stationed themselves in front of the apartment house with the street number showing above the entrance door, and Stens spoke in a dramatic, sonorous voice.

"At nine o'clock last night in Crown Heights, Brooklyn, police scooped up the so-called Spiderman rapist. He has been identified as twenty-six-year-old Tyrone Graham. His attacks on women took place in upper floor apartments, sometimes with him jumping from building to building or from fire escapes to open windows. He is now facing twenty-four felony counts. He was picked up in this building. He had lived here since he got out of prison on parole."

The comment on the capture of Graham that most accurately reflected the exasperation of Brooklynites came from Deputy Police Chief Louis Raiford who said, "This man had no business being on the streets. His criminal activity could eventually lead to a killing. What he did was bad enough. Why he was free with the conviction record he has, is a question best left to the judicial system."

Two other women who had been raped also singled out Graham as their attacker.

It was 10:00 A.M. before Patti Kehoe was able to go home to her apartment. She had been up for thirty-one hours. Immediately, she called on the detectives at the Manhattan Sex Crimes Squad. It was an errand she anticipated strongly. She told the Chief of the Squad briefly that the Latent Prints Department at BCI had incontrovertible proof from fingerprints, that the Brooklyn rapist who had been charged with the sexual assault of four women in Crown Heights and several burglaries, was the same man who had raped Eileen Ross, the blind woman in Manhattan whose strategic thinking had resulted in Tyrone Graham leaving his prints clearly on a 7-Up glass in her kitchen.

"You'll be wanting to file against this guy, I'm sure," she said. Patti was aware that Captain Dumond of the Seventy-Seventh Precinct had already broken the news that an arrest was pending, so her announcement was not a big surprise. But it made her feel good. She had a sense of satisfaction she had seldom felt since becoming a cop sixteen years earlier. The last act she would perform to make her sense of accomplishment brim over was a telephone call to Eileen Ross.

Chapter 14

Eileen was sitting at the counter in her kitchen, spooning a heaping teaspoon of sugar into her cup of herbal tea, when the phone call came in.

"Eileen, it's Detective Kehoe. You know, from Brooklyn. I've got some news for you. We nailed Spiderman on a roof in Crown Heights. He's in jail. And we've matched him to five rapes for sure, four in Brooklyn and . . . yours in Manhattan. You trapped him just like you said you would. You'll read about it in the newspapers. You ought to be damned pleased with yourself, Eileen. Of course, they've got to charge him in Manhattan, but that will happen quickly. And there'll be another lineup. Well, I've got to go now. Good luck."

Before Eileen could properly thank Kehoe, the woman hung up. Eileen smiled to herself. She had a strong sense of empathy with Kehoe. The policewoman was very much like her, outspoken and frank. She was not the kind to linger over good or bad news. She had delivered her message. It was up to Eileen to sort out its ramifications.

Eileen sat there for a long while, trying to digest Patti Kehoe's information. It was strange, the idea of the man being in jail. Only days ago, he had sat where she was sitting now, with a knife in his hand. She remembered standing behind the stove waiting for the grease in the frying pan to heat on the burner. As if the moment had returned, she recalled with absolute clarity how she had weighed the idea of throwing the hot grease into his face. Burn his eyes and run for the front door.

The idea had seemed so real, so obtainable that she

had actually tested the weight of the pan, lifted it secretly, planning how she would have to throw it, holding her fingers just right on the handle. And she remembered giving up the notion, feeling scared and a little breathless that she had come so close to the instant of decision. In her mind she could see the pan flying, with the smoking grease spraying angrily out of it, hot enough to blister skin, scald and scar it. Then the thought had come to her. *What if she missed?* That's what had stopped her, the uncertainty of his exact location at the counter. He could dodge the pan if she didn't aim right. And then watch out!

It was amazing, she thought, that she could remember every detail of her calculations with the frying pan, but couldn't remember the details of his face. She couldn't reconstruct the features into a detailed mental picture. But she knew she would recognize Tyrone Graham if she were close enough to gather a total impression of the man—a combination of sight, hearing and smell. Her hearing was good, her sense of smell was sharp. But her image of a person was made up of blend of the visual, tactile and auditory messages she received from an individual. One woman she knew wore a favorite perfume, whose odor on her skin was distinctive. That was how Eileen remembered her. It unlocked in Eileen's mind all of the other stored image reminders of the woman.

Eileen's problem—the one she had thought about a lot in reference to her attacker—was the weakness of her vision capability, particularly under unfavorable circumstances. The news from Patti Kehoe certainly meant, as she had said, that the New York police also were going to have a line-up. Eileen would be called as the witness and she would be asked to identify a man among several posed ones as the person who had raped her.

"Unless I'm definitely one hundred per cent positive, *I'm not going to do it!*" She said out loud. Her secret thought process, which she had shared with no one, was a result of a lot of hard thinking. From the moment Patti Kehoe and Sal Catalfumo had left Eileen's apartment after interviewing her, Eileen had felt certain that Spiderman was the one who raped her. When Eileen had asked Patti if the man they were after in the Brooklyn rapes was the same one who has assaulted her, and the detective had said, "It looks that way . . ."

That had confirmed Eileen's feeling. When Patti called Eileen with the news that Spiderman was in jail, solidly linked to five rapes including hers by his fingerprints, Eileen knew decision time was at hand as to whether she could physically identify him. She waited impatiently for the morning newspaper; his picture would surely appear.

On Friday morning July 18th, 1986, four days after Eileen Ross was raped, the *New York Post* carried the story that reflected the culmination of the combined efforts of the Brooklyn Sex Crimes Squad, an indefatigable Latent Prints detective, a crime scene blue-suit who dusted prints and had a nose for details, and a victim who was absolutely determined that her rape would not disappear in the huge New York Police Department bureaucracy. The article, written by Anne E. Murray and Chris Oliver, read:

B-KLYN RAPE SUSPECT IS LINKED TO ATTACK ON BLIND WOMAN

The man charged in four sex attacks in Brooklyn's Crown Heights is a suspect in the beating, rape and robbery of a legally-blind

Manhattan businesswoman, The *Post* learned today.

Officials said fingerprints of Tyrone Graham—arrested for four sex attacks in Brooklyn—appear to match those of the man who terrorized 37-year-old Eileen Musumecci Ross.

She was raped and terrorized in her East Side apartment early Monday morning.

Cops said Miss Ross would be asked to try to identify her attacker, close-up, at a special police line-up as soon as the paperwork and legal proceedings are completed in the Brooklyn cases.

Graham, 26, of 919 Park Place, Crown Heights, was charged yesterday with 24 felony counts, including four Brooklyn sex attacks between May 15th and last Tuesday.

Miss Ross was attacked Monday after awakening at 2:30 A.M. to find a man standing near her bed in her ground floor apartment at 500 E. 77th Street.

He beat her with a hammer, threatened her with a knife, ordered her to make him breakfast and then raped her twice.

During the two hour ordeal, her attacker warned her: "I've robbed and raped before and I could kill calmly."

Before he left, he apologized for hitting her, "now that I know you're blind" and washed her head wound.

Then he tied her up and fled with a suitcase stuffed with a mink coat, a video cassette recorder, cash and some shrimp.

Miss Ross said she felt a moustache and goatee on her attacker's face.

The third Crown Heights woman attacked —on June 22nd—told police the rapist had a beard and a moustache.

The last Brooklyn victim—who was attacked early Tuesday—said her assailant sported a moustache, but no beard.

Police said Graham had a moustache when he was arrested, but had shaved off his goatee.

They credited one cop's perseverance with breaking the case.

Brooklyn's Police Officer Frank Paganucci pored over thousands of fingerprints to match those left behind after two of the four Crown Heights sex attacks to prints at an April burglary scene.

He then searched through fingerprints of known criminals and came up with a "hit"—Graham's prints, police said.

In addition to rape, Graham is charged with sexual abuse, burglary, robbery, grand larceny and a weapons possession in the Brooklyn case. If convicted he faces up to 25 years in jail.

When Eileen examined the picture of Tyrone Graham in the *Post,* holding the newspaper within four inches of her right eye, she could make out a black man whose face was almost concealed by the position of his head. Characteristic of many sex crimes suspects, he had dug his chin into his chest so the photograph had captured most of the top of his head and a foreshortened view of his forehead and his nose.

Disappointed, she realized she didn't recognize the man. As far as she could see in the picture he had no moustache or goatee. The manner in which he was holding his head down effectively hid any identifying features. The only fact about the man pictured of which she could be certain was that he was a black male whom she judged to be in his late twenties.

Then Eileen's growing resolve hardened. There was no way she was going to identify the man unless she was sure her testimony couldn't be shaken. And the chances of that were slim to none. She was not going to take any chances of making a mistake that would nullify the effect of the fingerprints they'd found in her apartment. The ones that matched Graham's. The set that was the strongest and clearest had been found on the glass she had handed to the man four days ago in her kitchen. Eileen remembered the moment: his reluctance to take the glass in his hand and how he gave in just as she had hoped he would.

She knew she was right about not taking a chance on letting him get off because, being blind, she couldn't make a positive identification. So far, her strategy with the newspapers had worked well. The Brooklyn Sex Crimes Squad had learned about her rape through the media, not from the already biased Manhattan police who had first questioned her.

It was Eileen's description of the rapist that had attracted Patti Kehoe and Sal Catalfumo to her. If her campaign to create publicity about her rape had accomplished nothing more than that, then it was still a smashing success. But now the legal hassles would start, and that worried her. Her concern about her ability to make an eyewitness identification of the suspect worried her greatly. She wanted to help the police create the strongest case possible against Tyrone Graham.

If she inspected the men in the line-up and said she wasn't sure about any of them because she couldn't see clearly enough to be certain, then the question would remain open. Graham might have an unjustified out. She shook her head.

She was not going to jeopardize her credibility and influence the case in a negative way. If she took a chance and identified the man who looked like Graham, and he wasn't the one, then everybody—cops, prosecutor, newspeople—would have good reason to doubt her judgement. They would say to themselves that she was grasping at straws, or worse was irresponsible.

The fact was the cops knew who Spiderman was. They had his fingerprints. It was probably not even legally necessary for her identification to make the case against Graham. Except that a positive identification would be another nail to hammer down the evidence. The stronger the case, the better the chance for a tougher jury verdict and a longer sentence.

There was another factor to be weighed: Even strong fingerprint evidence was open to interpretation by experts who were hired by defense lawyers to cast doubt on the ownership of fingerprints. She knew there was a whole area of conjecture about fingerprint comparisons. A sharp attorney, with a knowledgeable witness who expressed doubt about the valid points of similarity in two sets of prints—the suspect's and those found at the scene of a crime—could create enough confusion in jurors' minds to influence a verdict.

If the jury had previously learned that she had identified the wrong man in a line-up, she could be characterized as unreliable, and the twelve men and women might vote for acquittal of the suspect because the composite evidence was inconclusive. Her default might be enough to tip them over the edge if they were wavering. More than one guilty man had been freed by conscientious jurors who had been convinced by a persuasive attorney of the innocence of his client.

Well she wasn't going to let this happen in her case. She wasn't going to take any chance of providing Tyrone Graham's defense attorney with the ammunition to get him off.

She knew it could be argued that if she didn't identify her attacker she was actually benefiting her rapist. Identification by a witness of an assailant was strong evidence to a jury. But to Eileen the more important point was that her lack of vision made certain physical identification almost impossible. *And what if she were wrong?* This was the blunt question that had made her nights restless.

If they would only let her touch the man in order to identify him, run her fingers over his face. Her fingers were so sensitive, identification would then be certain, but she knew they probably would not allow that. They would insist on her being able to see him clearly. It would put her between a rock and a hard place. Damned if she did and damned if she didn't. She wasn't going to let that happen. She would allow nothing that would dilute the value of the fingerprints.

As Eileen finalized her decision on how she'd handle the line-up, she realized that some people might consider her behavior since the rape as unfitting for a rape victim, or for any victim when it came to that. She wasn't thinking about the Manhattan cops when she reached that conclusion. Their unspoken criticism of her was that she was creating a headache for them. They liked manageable victims. And in that respect, they were no different from policemen anywhere.

No, she was thinking about the general attitude of complacency to crime that seemed to have taken over in New York and everywhere else in the United States.

People had accepted crime in their midst and they were just glad it hadn't happened to them, often seeming to blame the victim for getting attacked.

People like herself who fought for justice, who demanded the apprehension of their assailants but kept people's attention riveted on the horrific consequences of crime and the price paid by its victims, were rare. They didn't allow the rest of the public to forget how dangerous life could be. It was a revelation many people didn't want. It made them fearful and uncomfortable. For they always knew in the back of their minds they could be next.

Eileen understood how they felt. Repression was an easy bandage to apply. Eileen knew it didn't heal the wound. It only let it fester. What bothered her was the lack of a sense of outrage. New Yorkers were particularly ambivalent. Some would walk past a dead man lying on the sidewalk as if they themselves were untouchable by death, and yet they would respond with praise to heroism or the pugnaciousness of a victim who fought back.

In her own case, thousands of letters expressing the approval of the writers for her decision to stand up for herself in full view of the public had reached her through the newspapers, which at first had not printed her Manhattan street address.

But Eileen would have been the first to say that her reasons for pursuing her rapist had little to do with the public benefit, or to improve the general attitude against crime. The object of her actions was to help other raped women who she felt would be treated more fairly if they emulated her example, spoke out and demanded quick action from the cops to catch their assailants.

She had pursued her unknown rapist for the same reason she had devised the strategy of the 7-Up glass:

She wanted punishment of the man for violating her personal self. She was her own private property. Nobody, *nobody,* had the right to hurt her, or shame her, or even threaten her. No one had the right to terrorize another human being and cause them such intense emotional and physical pain.

Nothing could sway her from that fundamental belief. It was as precious to her as the whole concept of individual freedom. She had expressed the core of that belief when she marched in demonstrations when she was younger. When she had defended the civil rights of blacks, she was defending her own personal right of individual sanctity.

She was stating that the safety of the individual surpassed any consideration of collective good or philosophical sanctions. Any faulty argument that gave an assailant indirect permission to injure on the grounds of his own deprivation was wrong. There was never any excuse, or justification for injuring another human being. It was wrong by definition. The person who committed such injuries should be punished.

Eileen was going to make certain that her rapist did not escape the fullest retribution the law allowed for his act of violence. She was going to be involved in the application of the legal process that led to his punishment. She was convinced that if other victims shared her unbending determination, there would be far fewer crimes.

Eileen continued her pursuit of justice. Three days after Eileen scanned Tyrone Graham's picture in the New York Post, she telephoned Nancy Patterson, the Assistant District Attorney who had been appointed to prosecute Tyrone Graham.

"Tell me how I can help," Eileen said after introducing herself. Patterson explained that the first step in the process was a preliminary interview in which Patterson would question Eileen about the rape. Following this meeting, a date would be set for the line-up, usually a day or so after the initial interview.

Number One Hogan Place in downtown Manhattan housed New York City's District Attorney. It was part of the complex of police, law and court buildings clustered together to form a convenient focal point for administration of justice in the system of police, prosecutors, judges and lawyers.

Eileen was shown into a large office with high ceilings, and large windows covered with venetian blinds that allowed the deflected sunlight of late July into the room. Nancy Patterson came out from behind her desk and extended her hand to Eileen. She was a woman in her mid-thirties with a calm face, little makeup, blonde hair and an unrevealing handshake. She smiled sparingly and pointed to a chair for Eileen to occupy.

"I'm Nancy Patterson. Thanks for being on time. The purpose of this meeting is for me to explain some things in the legal process now that we've arrested Tyrone Graham."

Nancy Patterson sat down behind her desk, clasped her hands together and leaned forward comfortably on her elbows. Patiently, she said, "You have to understand that while you're the complaining witness, the state is the prosecutor. In other words, the state is your attorney. We act for you. It's our job to get a conviction based on the evidence. Do you understand?"

"What you're saying is that what you say goes. I'm the victim, but you have the final word."

"Well . . . yes. I wouldn't put it exactly like that, but it's close enough."

"Are you going to be the one in court to present my case?"

"Yes."

"Okay, I just wanted to know."

Patterson smiled and said, "The next thing, Eileen, is for you to explain to me what your definition of rape is. I know that may sound foolish, but you're going to be asked the question in court: Did he put his penis in your vagina?"

"Yes."

"Well, you're going to have to say that in court. Exactly that way. He put his penis in my vagina. I'm not trying to be nasty or difficult, but the defendant has civil rights, also. So the court has to be clear that a rape happened, that penetration occurred."

"I understand," Eileen said. She liked the preciseness of the petite blonde whose soft-spoken voice had a steel undercurrent. She was obviously extending herself to make Eileen feel comfortable and at the same time carefully exploring Eileen's level of intelligence to determine her ability to comprehend legal subtleties.

"Of course," Patterson said, "if the case goes to trial, you'll be a witness, Eileen. And that means the defendant's attorney will ask you questions about your past, your sex life. Things like that. We try to keep that kind of exploration to a minimum. Actually, we're having more success in restricting inquiry of that sort than before. But there is still some of it and you have to know that it will happen. Now, why don't you tell me what happened the night Graham broke into your apartment."

In the next few minutes Eileen recounted briefly the events of the rape. Nancy Patterson listened studiously, occasionally making notes on a yellow legal pad.

When Eileen had concluded her narrative, Patterson said, "Well, I have no doubt about the strength of your case. It should hold up very well. That doesn't mean that we can sit back and relax. Graham has a good legal-aid attorney and he's not going to give this case away."

Eileen was gratified that the Assistant District Attorney had expressed a high opinion of her story and the evidence against Tyrone Graham. She was concerned, however, that Nancy Patterson may have made the common mistake of judging her blindness as a physical impairment that inhibited natural sexual encounters.

She thought it was important to correct this assumption if it was true. There had been several men in her life. Blindness did not convey celibacy on a person, or sexual deprivation. She realized many blind people looked vulnerable, inexperienced, almost devout with their closed eyes and contemplative expressions. The expression was misleading.

Blind people had the normal drives and appetites every other person had, and sex was certainly among them. Eileen leaned forward. She had no desire to speak about the intimate details of her own love life—not that there had been that many affairs—but she did not want Nancy Patterson surprised on the witness stand by Tyrone Graham's lawyer if intimate questions were asked and, in Eileen's usual forthright way, answered.

Except for her eyes, she was a normal, healthy woman who had nothing to hide and she was not going to allow anyone to make something dirty out of the private, intimate moments in her life, in which she had shared her body and her emotions with another person. She was fully aware that in New York's legal system, a woman's past sexual history was open to exposure to a jury, but a man's sexual history, including prior charges and convictions for rape, could not be introduced into evidence if he did not take the witness stand. It was unfair, but it represented the male attitude surviving in the law that placed the burden of proof on the rape victim to substantiate her moral character.

When Eileen expressed her feelings about possible sexual exploitation by the prosecution to Nancy Patterson, the woman listened intently and slowly said, "I think we can protect you from improper exposure, Eileen. We're going to concentrate on the strong points in your case. The fingerprints, the violent attack on you with the mallet, obviously the actual rape, and Graham's history of burglary. You will have to describe that he raped, that he made penetration."

"Yes, I understand that," Eileen quietly replied. "You told me I have to say he put his penis in my vagina."

Nancy Patterson nodded and studied the notes she had made on her yellow pad, then looked inquiringly at Eileen. "Let's talk about your vision, Eileen. It's going to have a bearing on how we conduct the line-up. How much can you see? I know you're legally blind, but how much sight do you have?"

"Out of my right eye, I can read the letters on a page if I hold the page close, and I can see television close up. It's tunnel vision, like looking through a keyhole. But it doesn't go very far. I know you're sitting behind your desk, but I can't make out any details. I really can't be more explicit than that. What would help is if I could touch him. Put my hands on his face."

Patterson leaned back in her chair, seemingly pondering Eileen's words. Then she shook her head. "I don't think they'll let us do that. I don't think it will be necessary and there may be precedents against the idea. We'll have to stay with procedure. We really can't do anything that may possibly violate Graham's civil rights. We don't want to jeopardize our case."

"Well, what about having him and the others say something out loud? A voice test so I can hear the way he speaks? That would help a lot."

"The same negative there," Patterson said her voice showed compassion. "You have to understand, Eileen, that there are precedents that have been established for identification of a suspect. If we try to introduce something new, we are inviting the defense to challenge us. We don't want that, or the delay that it could cause. I know that it all seems unfair."

Eileen broke in. "More than unfair! Being blind means substituting other senses for sight. My other senses are damned acute, but if you eliminate my using them and only allow me to use sight—the one sense I can least depend on for accuracy—how can I be certain?"

Nancy Patterson hesitated, then smiled, "Eileen, I wish we could do it your way, but we can't. The line-up will be the day after tomorrow. Someone from my office will call you with the time and place."

Eileen rose to her feet as she heard Nancy Patterson push back her chair. She shook hands with the Assistant District Attorney when the woman came around her desk. As Eileen walked to the elevator, she decided that when she got to her apartment she would call Peggy Pindar. The blind Iowa woman was a member of the National Federation of the Blind.

Eileen had been urged to contact her by Bill Gallagher, a member of the American Foundation for the Blind, who heard about Eileen's rape in the media. He had contacted her because, he told her, he had read between the lines and anticipated that she would probably encounter resistance from the District Attorney to any method of identification by Eileen that departed from the norm. He told her that Peggy Pindar, a former Iowa public prosecutor who was blind and had her own law practice, might be able to help Eileen with cases in the law which would establish the precedent for her touching a suspect and for vocal identification of him.

When Eileen contacted the woman in her Des Moines office, Pindar said she would be glad to respond to an inquiry from the Manhattan District Attorney, pointing out the case references that would substantiate the legality of tactile and vocal identification.

Excitedly, Eileen telephoned Nancy Patterson, conveying Peggy Pindar's information, and discussed it also with Patterson's boss, Linda Fairstein, the supervisor of the Sex and Crimes Prosecution Unit for the Manhattan District Attorney's Office. Fairstein dampened Eileen's enthusiasm. She thanked her politely but said it was too late to talk with Pindar since the line-up had already been set up and was slated to be conducted in a traditional form.

This was the moment when Eileen decided that she would probably have to refrain from pointing her finger at Tyrone Graham in the line-up, even if he definitely seemed to be the right man. The problem was she could *never* be absolutely sure, not by having to rely on her faulty sight alone.

The idea of deliberately withholding identification produced a strong conflict in Eileen. It went against everything she felt was right to do, her own credo of speaking out forthrightly and truthfully, not cowering in the corners. Moreover, the physical act of making the accusation in a traditional face-to-face confrontation was a righteous revenge scene in her mind that she had played over and over a hundred times.

Now she imagined how smug and self-satisfied Graham would feel when he heard her falter and say, "I don't know." *Laugh to himself like hell is what he'd do,* she thought, suddenly furious with Nancy Patterson, Linda Fairstein, the Manhattan cops, the whole bureaucratic system that was so cripplingly afflicted with archaic legal rheumatism that it impaired people like her more than blindness.

Chapter 15

Eileen was up early on Friday, July 25th. It was eleven days since the rape. She had called her attorney, Gary Trachten, to tell him about the line-up and he had insisted that he accompany her to the procedure.

"This is an important step. The newspapers will be there. I want to be sure you don't say anything that will compromise your civil case."

It was true that she had been giving interviews to newspeople about Graham's apprehension. By now Eileen felt comfortable with the press. She encouraged questions, answered them honestly, and knew her openness was appreciated. She also felt her continued openness was a signal to other silent victims who read the accounts and might be inspired by her example to come forward as she had done.

In the matter of publicity, Eileen was at odds with Gary Trachten and Norman Pearlman. "Don't rock the boat," was their advice. Don't do or say anything to attract attention and, as a result, furnish opposition lawyers with ammunition to shoot at her in front of a jury that would decide the fate of her lawsuit against the Navereign. To them, the most important factor was the large amount of money at stake.

Of course, the money was important to Eileen also. It was retribution for her intense pain and the building owner's gross neglect, the neglect which had resulted in her attack.

It was very important. It was just not the most important factor.

Punishing Tyrone Graham for his brutal attack was

Eileen's central focus. A close second was removing the stigma of shame and guilt from victims of rape.

Eileen was convinced that neither one of her lawyers understood the direct, and subtle, psychological benefits of publicity in achieving those ends.

Sympathetic publicity bringing out in the open the brutal aspects of the crime, as well as her determined efforts to apprehend and now have her attacker punished, would cause the public—some of whom had the power to change the callous, unsympathetic treatment of rape victims and the slap on the wrists punishment of most rapists—to pay attention.

Through a mixture of books on tape, readers and her own determined efforts Eileen read voraciously—she had planned at one point in her life to study law—and as a result had come to understand the conceptual link between sexual vulnerability and selected rape. On the same day she was raped in her apartment, the same crime happened to at least one hundred and seventy other women in New York City.

She knew one of the main reasons she had been selected for front page treatment was because she represented, what one astute observer of rape in the news, author Susan Brown-Miller, called "Glamour-in-destruction." Another, was that she had broken the caveat of silence that protected the identity of the victim, she was blind, which to others increased her vulnerability; and she was absolutely determined to see her rapist caught and punished. These factors made Eileen's attack front page news.

"You can't change a system unless you can bring attention to it," had always been Eileen's motto. She lived by it. As she saw it, her job was to put these words into action to the best of her ability. Now, by acting vigorously, publicly, for herself, she was representing the anger of thousands of women who wanted punishment for their rapists. By her publicized example, she was proving that the media—for whatever reason—could be the instrument of conveying the outrage of rape, thus making it less acceptable.

Eileen's conviction, that she should use her media appeal, received further confirmation in the story printed about her on July 22nd, three days before the line-up. The three-column picture, six and one half inches high, showed a touching photograph of Eileen holding her beagle, Bethie.

Even with a patch on her head covering the stitched wound where Tyrone Graham had struck her with the kitchen mallet, Eileen looked movie-star attractive. Her dark hair, dark eyes, the modeled Italian sculpture of her face, and the lovely shape of her lips projected the female image of desirability, of innocence attacked. It was an excellent photo that displayed all the mystery and vulnerability of adult womanhood. The story implied that the young, attractive blind woman had become inspirationally attainable to millions of newspaper readers.

Announcing the date of the police line-up, it repeated Eileen's forceful statement that she hoped she could touch her rapist and hear him speak to make her identification certain.

To Eileen, there was a certain irony in the *Post* story that ran prominently under a two-line bold banner that said: **Blind Rape Victim To Face Suspect in Line-Up.** The irony was that the by-line on the story was Anne Greason, the reporter who had called Eileen five days earlier with her announcement that the *Post* was killing its planned story on Eileen and her guardians.

For Eileen, the real value of the story in the *Post* was the pressure it created on the police and the prosecutors. Capping dozens of other stories, it made Eileen's attack a front page and media event. Eileen was absolutely convinced that if she had not originally contacted Rolanda Watts, the Channel 7 television reporter, through her friend Kay Ketchum, she would have become just another raped woman whose statement would have been recorded, filed, and forgotten by New York's police. The undeniable fact was that the interview had attracted the attention of the Brooklyn Police to the crime against her.

From the beginning of their investigation the Manhattan cops had demonstrated bias and indifference. This cavalier attitude demonstrated a universal fact about most cops that Eileen knew to be true: In a rape case, the woman was first presumed to be hysterical, a wife or girlfriend who was trying to cover up an affair, or a lonely woman who fantasized the intruder she reported to the cops.

She felt that most police accepted the predominately male viewpoint that viewed rape as "a little roughhouse that got out of hand;" that was the stereotype that women encountered when they reported a sexual assault.

Eileen remembered one of the letters she had received from a victim a few days after her story was first publicized. The woman, who described herself as a Plain Jane, said when she was interviewed in her apartment by two patrolmen, "One of them said, 'ah, who would want to rape you?' "

That was why Eileen had chosen publicity as her vehicle for getting justice. It focused public opinion on the victim and forced reluctant cops to give rape violators the same standard of professional investigative treatment that other major crimes received.

As far as Eileen was concerned, these benefits far

outweighed the concerns of her attorneys that she act submissive and shattered. She knew what she had suffered. She knew about her nervousness and the fear that stalked like a silent shadow behind her whenever she was alone in her apartment. She knew that if she gave in to her attorneys, she could easily give in completely and become a haunted wretch, afraid of every loud voice and unexpected noise.

As she stood in her bedroom on this Friday morning, Eileen thought again about Gary Trachten's insistence that she leave the talking to him when the two of them encountered reporters at the line-up. Eileen grimaced. He thought he understood her. Well, he didn't. He was a good man, a caring friend and he had her best interests at heart.

But neither he, nor Norman Pearlman understood the psychic burden of rape. That burden was inheritance of the myth made popular by men through legend, lore and history that all women secretly long for domination by a male and the ultimate act of that domination was rape. This fantasy received clever exposition in religion, marriage, the arts and inevitably in the law. The legal theory of collaborative evidence—slowly disappearing—in which the woman had to prove her innocence of complicity in rape was a cynical expression of male dominance.

Kind as the two lawyers were to Eileen, they did not understand the basic underlying motive in her campaign to find and prosecute her rapist. It was to strike a personal blow against the myth of female subjugation through rape fantasy—the "lust in pain" dogma that rape was something women desired. Perceived in its broadest and deepest applications, it was an overriding theme apparent in books, movies, popular songs and television serials in which women were most often portrayed as victims—seldom as survivors.

Well, it had to change. Women had to be freed from the burden of sexual exploitation. Rape was its most vicious manifestation. Eileen certainly had never had a perception of herself as a woman who would start a movement. But if one man was convicted for violence to a woman, it was a step in the right direction. The collaboration of media was essential to Eileen to publicize her cause and her determination for legal vengeance.

The lawyers had advised Eileen to choose something to wear which symbolized innocence and virtue. As if such outward signs proved anything. That was another stereotype people foisted on rape victims—"they asked for it." Eileen bit her lip remembering all she had suffered, and she thought for a moment of the agony of the other women who had called and written her. *Which bastard had the right to claim that wearing a certain kind of clothing or living a certain way entitled another human being to brutalize and terrorize a victim?*

Tears stung her eyes as she walked to the closet and opened the door. Still, just as she understood the value of publicity, she understood the value of presenting the right image on this day.

Her face flushed as she slowly pulled the white cotton dress with a scooped neck and wide cuffs from a hanger in the closet.

She dressed very carefully, brushing her long dark hair about her piquant face and clasping a strand of pearls around her neck. When she stepped into her living room to wait for Gary Trachten to come and for the police matron to be announced from the lobby, she looked sweet and vulnerable. But she stood ramrod straight and her will was steely. In her mind was a single thought. *I am going to see Tyrone punished.*

The first attempt at the precinct on West 82nd Street, to create a line-up that would enable Eileen to view Graham and five others, failed. She was unable to see through the one-way glass partition which separated observers in one room from suspects standing in another.

Nancy Patterson, patient and helpful, suggested finally that several metal chairs be stacked in a single row with their metal backs facing outward toward Eileen who could station herself behind each chair and look directly into the face of the man standing on the seat cushion side of the chair. If she leaned forward even slightly, her face would be less than six inches from the face of each suspect.

For Eileen's benefit, the Assistant District Attorney had devised an ingenious system of numerical identification for the six men who would be scrutinized. Large black numbers, two feet tall, were printed on yellow squares of paper and these placards hung from around each of the men's necks. The numbers were from one through six.

When the six suspects, all black men, played by volunteers—except for one, who was Tyrone Graham—stood languidly for Eileen's inspection, Nancy Patterson came up to Eileen and said, "Now, don't be nervous, and take your time. Nobody is going to rush you. If you look at a man and pass him by, but want to look again, that's all right. Just take your time. But don't touch anyone."

Eileen nodded and stepped in front of Number 1. Behind her stood Gary Trachten, Nancy Patterson, and several police officers from the Twentieth Precinct. They were on hand to prevent any violence should Graham, if identified, decide to lash out at Eileen.

Eileen could see immediately that Number 1 was

too big to be considered. She crossed him off mentally and moved to Number 2.

As she stood in front of Number 2, she asked herself honestly, "Is this the man who raped me? Is this the man who returned to kill me when he read my story in the newspapers?" She had a deepening sense of fear as she stared at Number 2, trying to see clearly or to locate in her memory a sign of recognition.

There was something vaguely familiar and menacing about the man, but there was certainly no rising conviction in her that he was Tyrone Graham. The man was breathing heavily; he seemed nervous, jittery. She was confused by his agitation. *He must be guilty of something,* she thought, *but she did not think it was her rape.*

She disqualified Numbers 3 and 4; one was too heavy, the other was at least six-foot-six; she had to look up to view his face.

Number 5 was the man Eileen pondered the longest. He remained perfectly still; his breathing was regular and unhurried. He did not seem apprehensive or distraught. She tried to absorb feelings, or emanations from the man. His face was smooth, no goatee or moustache. He could have shaved those off. He was a block of muscle and hair and flesh and he did not transfer any information. She raised her hand to touch him, then withdrew it quickly. That wasn't allowed.

She stepped away from him and moved to Number 6, the last man in the line. He had been staring at her boldly from the moment she had begun her examination. Was he daring her to pick him? To prove she was wrong? She had made a bet with herself that he was a cop who was overplaying his role as a volunteer. There was no question about disqualifying him. He was too short to be Graham.

Eileen revisited Number 5 and Number 2, and finally stood in front of Number 2, leaning forward, pondering him. If he was Graham, she wanted him to see she was not afraid of him, even if this was untrue. She straightened up at attention like an officer inspecting his men. Her straight posture was designed to dominate, to bring into focus the power of her accusations, backed up by the authority of the police and the prosecutors.

Eileen stepped away. It was just as she had feared. She couldn't positively identify her attacker on the basis of sight alone. *How could they expect me to? I am blind, damn it. They know that.* Her indignation was rising.

She tried to keep her voice calm, "If only I could touch them," she said, "hear them say something, I'm sure I could identify the man who raped me."

"I'm sorry, Eileen," Nancy Patterson said quietly, "You're not allowed to do that. I explained why. I can't give you permission to do anything but examine the men visually."

Eileen turned back to the standing men. She was angry and resentful. Didn't Nancy Patterson understand what today meant to her. She had finally triumphed over the man who had so brutally and cold-bloodedly bludgeoned and raped her. Moreover, she had spoken out, despite his threat to come back and kill her if she told. She knew he had counted on the strength of that threat. Yet he had been fooled by a woman who had trapped his fingerprints at a moment when he thought she was crushed.

Now, she ached for him to know that he had won nothing and was going to pay for it with a portion of his life. She had acted cowed, but never craven, and now she was here to make him pay for every minute of her terror. She wanted so much to identify him and because they wouldn't let her "see him" her way she couldn't.

She would have to keep her promise to herself not to identify her attacker unless she could be positively sure.

In the end she admitted defeat. She could not identify Tyrone Graham.

She was disappointed but glad that she had made that promise to herself. She kept her mind focused on her goal to have Graham punished no matter what.

Eileen turned to Nancy Patterson as the six men in the line-up marched out of the room in an orderly exit. She had to know. "Which one in the line-up is Graham?" she asked softly.

Nancy Patterson hesitated, then said, "I can't tell you that, Eileen. He hasn't been indicted. After that, if you still want to know, ask me."

Eileen started to protest and shrugged. She and Gary Trachten walked out of the room and down the hall to the front of the station house. They heard the voices of several people in mild banter.

"The media's here, Eileen," Trachten said. "I'll do the talking." He squeezed her arm for emphasis.

Dispiritedly Eileen nodded compliantly. "Who do you think was Graham, Gary?"

"Oh, Number 5. You thought he was 2, didn't you? You stood in front of him for a long time."

"It was a tossup," she said, "between 2 and 5."

The first reporter to reach Eileen was from the *New York Daily News*.

"Miss Ross, did you identify Graham? Is he Spiderman? Is he the man who raped you?"

Quickly, Gary Trachten intervened. "Miss Ross was unable to identify her assailant. She . . ."

Eileen stepped away from Trachten and said, "He's right, but they wouldn't let me touch the men or listen to their voices . . ."

It was fifteen minutes before the reporters let Eileen go. Angry, Gary Trachten who had tried unsuccessfully to act as a buffer between his client and the press, turned to her and said, "Why do I trust you to let me speak for you when you break your word every time? You've got to think about the civil case . . ."

"Gary," Eileen interrupted hastily, "you should know by now that I'm not going to let you run my life. I value your advice, but the newspeople are used to my being forthright. If it wasn't for them, Tyrone would probably not be in jail."

"What are we going to do with you, Eileen?" Trachten said half exasperatedly, half fondly as he grasped Eileen's arm and maneuvered her down the steps of the station house and opened the door to the police car that was waiting to take them to Eileen's apartment. The police matron was sitting behind the wheel.

As she sat in the back of the police car with Gary Trachten, Eileen realized that Graham's arrest, whether she could see him to make the identification or not, would always be inalterably attached to her determination to "get him." And her success. She began to feel better. After all, she was setting a precedent for women who were yet to be raped. The success of her efforts with the police and the prosecutor could be an example of determination for them. If they took courage by what she did, then the day would come sooner when violent men thought twice before raping a woman.

Eileen decided right then to press her advantage with the newspapers and radio and television, so that Graham's arrest would lead to his conviction and a new awareness by the public of the brutal reality of rape.

Eileen's convictions were soon rewarded despite

her inability to pick him out of the line-up. Later that same day, July 25th, Tyrone Graham was indicted by a Brooklyn Grand Jury on two counts of rape, two counts of robbery and two counts of burglary.

Chapter 16

Despite her rational, long-term strategy for other rape victims, Eileen was finding her everyday personal reality difficult and fear-ridden.

It was difficult to fall asleep at night. Often she woke up in a cold sweat. During the day she would begin trembling for no reason at all, jumping and starting at every noise.

It was even more fearful to be alone.

Had it not been for the tender ministrations of Rick who, noticing her nervousness, had assumed the role of her protector and was staying over at her apartment more and more, Eileen wasn't sure how she would have survived this period.

Finally, Gary Trachten, who was handling her civil case, recommended that she see a psychotherapist on the psychological damages of her rape. "We'll need her report later," he explained "to substantiate the extent and monetary value of the attack on you as a result of the negligence of the Navereign Apartments."

Hired opinions were apparently commonplace in civil law suits to determine personal injury. But Eileen found the woman to be sensitive and understanding. She was soon an active participant with Eileen in the process of helping Eileen adjust to the violence of rape, and to reach a point where she could diminish in her mind the threat of the man who stood over her bed with a club.

A tall, slim, blonde woman who had come to New York from Australia, Pamela Watson listened sympathetically and intelligently and answered Eileen's questions frankly. She made Eileen understand that there were identifiable symptoms of the shock of rape. They were shared by almost all women who survived the experience.

"You probably feel, Eileen," Watson said, "as if you had a close call with death. Isn't that true?"

"God, yes. That bastard held a knife to my throat. I thought he was going to slice open my throat."

"Well, you can't expect to survive an experience like that without some repercussions. Maybe if I explain how other women feel who have experienced the same thing, you'll understand more completely what you're going through and you'll be able to accept your reactions more readily."

Pamela Watson leaned forward, her voice gentle but firm, "You are terribly scared. You almost lost your life. There is a medical name for what you're going through. It's called post-traumatic rape syndrome. Other women who've been raped say they feel jumpy afterwards. A telephone call, somebody touching them, a loud noise, almost anything is enough to make them jump."

"I know," Eileen said, "I had to have Rick remove the new burglar alarm. It kept going off at the wrong time and I jumped out of my skin every time I heard it."

"Okay, don't be surprised if you experience mood swings, from anger to guilt, from revenge to shame. Feelings of humiliation are common and being more cautious about people you meet and where you go is also common. Nightmares and phobias can be expected. Changes in eating habits are another symptom. You may wake up several times at night and be anxious in the dark." Eileen interrupted, "I do." Pamela nodded, "Keep a night light on if that happens to you. I want to ask you about your nightmares, Eileen."

"I seem to have them all the time and I've been blanking things out."

"Don't let that upset you. It's part of the picture. Are you dreaming much?"

"Yes, one keeps coming back. I see Tyrone and I discover that he's really a white supremacist but he can turn himself black any time. He's a member of a group of people who can do that, turn from white to black. They go around fooling people that way. And then, suddenly, Tyrone says to me, after he's turned black, 'There's a man over there who can rescue you.' He's pointing and I turn and I see Hani and my heart sinks."

Eileen slumped back in her chair and signed. "It's a terrible dream."

"Hani is the name you called Tyrone isn't it?"

"Yes. It just slipped out."

"Who is Hani?"

"The man who betrayed me six years ago. Hani was a bastard. When we broke up I thought I'd die. I thought about suicide a lot. I lost weight, I couldn't sleep. A lot of the symptoms I'm having now, now that I think about it . . ."

"I met Hani Gabriel at a small gathering of handicapped men and women who were involved with the National Federation of the Blind. The occasion was to listen to the sound track of a new film the Federation was producing as a documentary. It was a congenial group of young people in their late twenties, early thirties, who were glad of an excuse to get together. While we were talking, I commented that I hate elevators with heat sensitive floor panel buttons. They created delays and confusions for a blind person whose exploring fingers could easily touch the wrong ones and light up the whole panel. It's a nuisance, I said, to have to stop on every floor when I accidentally activated the electronic eye.

"No sooner had I made that acerbic comment about environmental engineers, than I heard a rich voice with an English accent. He said, 'So you heat up all the buttons, do you?'

"I laughed, immediately interested in the speaker. He introduced himself to me. His name was Hannibal Gabriel.

"It was my friend, Pat Logan, who later that night took me aside and warned me about the man, blind from a swimming pool accident in his native Israel when he was ten and educated in England.

" 'He's got a bad reputation, Eileen. He's got lots of money and he's a romantic. On the surface he comes on great, but watch out. He's hard on women, they say, condescending and deceitful. I know you're interested. I can hear it in your voice. Just be careful is all I'm saying.' "

Eileen thanked Pat, but knew in her heart that it was too late. She was already irresistibly drawn to Hani. It was as simple and straightforward as that and as mysterious. She had been with men, had enjoyed the excitement of flirtations and petting, even sex, but she had never been so completely in love before. She felt buoyant, lighter than air, full of hope and awed at the depth of her feelings for a man she hardly knew.

They took long walks, went to movies, investigated restaurants he recommended, kissed self-consciously and discovered the attraction was magnetic, strong and absorbing. When, finally, they made love, Eileen was delighted to discover that Hani was a masterful lover who spent enormous effort arousing her own passion, giving her pleasure before and after intercourse and holding her in his arms as if he were afraid she would break.

The period of blissful delight lasted five weeks before the first signs of disharmony. That was when Eileen began to notice that Hani had a roving eye. He continually admired other women and would comment extensively on their attractiveness. Eileen tried to accept his words and not take them personally—some men were that way. It didn't mean they wanted to fornicate with every woman they saw. When, however, he began to speak of how they would be in bed, she suggested, as an attempt to bolster her slipping ego, that perhaps, "we should both date other partners."

Hani's reaction was swift. He told that their relationship must remain as it was. He would rather break off with her than share her with other men. Soon he became more possessive. Whenever she received a telephone call from another man and he answered the phone, he would turn to her and say sarcastically, "One of your lovers is on the line."

In the next few weeks, Eileen learned with deeper misgivings the true character of the man to whom she had given her heart. She discovered he hated his boss, a woman, at the company where he was an executive. Then he began criticizing her. She disliked blind people, he claimed. That was the reason for her criticism of him.

Finally Eileen realized as the weeks passed that the man who pretended to advocate for blind persons, was an active charismatic officer and speaker for the National Federation of the Blind, was in fact a neurotic who deeply hated his mother and resented bitterly the act of God that had taken his sight. His mother, she learned, had been unable to adjust to her son's handicap when he struck the cement in a swimming pool. The accident deprived him of his ability to see, and her of her image of having a perfect child. She had packed him off to boarding school when he was ten, unable to cope with his blindness.

Eileen reasoned to herself that perhaps his attitude toward women derived from his mother's failure to support him when he needed her most. He had been punishing his mother in every woman he met. If what she heard about him from other women was true, he was a misogynist who took delight in leading a woman on until she was infatuated and vulnerable. Then he planned her destruction, subtly at first by undermining her confidence in herself, alienating her from her friends by encouraging her dependence on him, and finally, deserting her when she had trusted him with her heart and feelings.

The strong urge for him to control people, women especially, was demonstrated to Eileen one day when he returned to his apartment where Eileen was visiting with a hand full of wide rubber bands. When he was nervous he bit his fingers and wrists, or he would use his teeth to punch a row of holes in a rubber band, then he would tear the weakened band apart with his fingers.

Holding up a macerated rubber band, he said to Eileen, "That's what I do to people when they don't obey me. I make them fold up."

As Hani became more critical of Eileen, he became more demanding. He ordered her to do things for him she would not have done for another living soul and she obeyed. On one occasion, he instructed her, imperiously, to lead him out of a restaurant where they had been dining. When she did not move quickly enough to suit him, he grabbed a belt on the back of her coat and gave it a brisk wrench, and shoved her rudely. She stumbled and lost her footing. When she turned to confront him, he admonished her not to raise her voice. It wasn't ladylike.

On the following day, they were both marching in a demonstration when Harold, a friend of Hani's, whispered a few words in her ear. Hani had immediately come over to say he didn't like her joking with a friend of his, and had struck her on her leg.

Eileen was astonished, angry and disappointed by Hani's cruel treatment of her. He behaved as if he was purposely trying to drive her away from him. He made up things to do that would hurt her feelings and lower her estimation of him. When she asked him for an explanation he treated her requests as if she were stupid and had no rights in their changing relationship. Eileen became more desperate as she saw his affections deteriorate, his condescension grow more constant and his contempt for her more apparent.

One day as they walked side by side on the street, a hulking man in a hugh mushroom-like coat, walked up with hurried intent. A premonition of trouble flashed in Eileen's mind. Suddenly, a lifted hand flashed into her range of tunnel vision. The hand held a bottle of clear liquid. Eileen grabbed the person's wrist. The struggle was over in a moment, the bottle fell to the pavement and the person ran. Even before she picked it up, Eileen knew it was acid. It had been meant for Hani. If she'd been slower, it would have been thrown in his face. As it was, a few drops had burned holes in his shirt; there was a rank, bitter smell in the air.

Eileen was shaken by the experience. She urged Hani to go to the police. He refused. It was then Eileen realized Hanibal Gabriel was not the man she had thought he was. Obviously he had a hidden past and had vicious enemies. In the weeks to come, she discovered a reversion of his personality so complete that his hate for her was displayed in cunning treachery, lies about her to people who had been their friends and in a treacherous campaign to destroy her confidence in herself as a desirable woman.

She understood the true meaning of the statement she had heard from women before her affair. Hani turned lives upside down. He was a vicious misogynist. What made him deadly were his attractive qualities. He used his smile, cultivated voice, charm and intelligence to flatter a woman. When she exposed her secret feelings, he wounded her.

But none of his conquests were so brutal as his actions towards Eileen. He had let down his guard far enough for Eileen to see the frightened, insecure man hiding beneath the lustrous exterior. He could never forgive her for discovering his shallowness. He had to punish her for that.

"Yes" Eileen said to Pamela Watson, "I did call Tyrone, Hani. It may sound melodramatic, but Hani raped my mind and my heart. Just as viciously as Tyrone did my body. Tyrone selected me at random. Hani set out to harm me on purpose."

She said huskily to Pamela Watson, "I have not had relations with a man for six years until Tyrone forced himself on me."

Pamela Watson encouraged Eileen to participate in the Mt. Sinai Rape Crisis Center Program as a beneficial way to rid herself of her fears. The experience would also be helpful, Pamela suggested, because it would expose Eileen to the cases of other women who were going through various stages of rape adjustment.

At the Crisis Center Eileen met Iona Segal, an energetic blonde woman in her mid-forties who was director of the Rape Crisis Intervention Program. She immediately told Eileen how much she admired Eileen's decision to publicize her rape. She had read the progress of Eileen's case through the newspapers. She was fascinated to learn from Eileen how she had contrived to get Tyrone to leave his fingerprints on the 7-Up glass.

Eileen felt relief and a sense of freedom with Segal. She could speak plainly, spontaneously, about what had happened to her. She did not have to qualify her remarks as she did for the attorneys, for the police, for Nancy Patterson. It was a good feeling to say what was on her mind.

The decision to become a volunteer at the Rape Crisis Center was almost instant for Eileen. She felt at home, protected, understood. She attended classes, listened to other women tell their frightful stories, and most fascinating of all, she learned a lot about Tyrone Graham. This discovery happened as a result of material she read and discussed with Segal and others that clearly identified three basic patterns of rape: Anger rape, power rape, and sadistic rape. Graham fell mostly in the second category.

It was anger and power expressed as sexual behavior that Tyrone Graham had demonstrated. Typically, she learned, a rapist motivated by a need to dominate attacked his victim by physically knocking her to the ground, tearing her clothes, then raping her. In another approach, the rapist was calm, assured the victim by his quiet mastery that she had nothing to fear from him, then suddenly he changed and became aggressive and mean. The rape followed.

This last behavior is closer to Graham, Eileen thought. In one book she found in the library of the Mt. Sinai Rape Crisis Center, she located the description of rape behavior that seemed to fit Tyrone Graham almost as if the authors had him in mind. The book, published by Plenum Press in 1979, was: *Men Who Rape: Physiology of the Offender,* by A. Nicholas Groth and H. Jean Birnbaum. For such offenders sexuality itself is typically regarded as "something basically small, 'dirty' and offensive at some level of subjective experience, and, therefore, it becomes a weapon, a means by which he can defile, degrade and humiliate his victim."

Eileen remembered the detached manner of Graham. He had actually shrunk violently from contact with her before the rape. He did not want her to touch him. And during the act, he had performed almost mechanically. When she deliberately fell against him in the kitchen, with her hand touching his neck and face, he had jumped out of his chair as if he had been stung.

Eileen thought, their analysis was an accurate the description was of Graham's personality. Indeed, he had seemed to disassociate himself from the assault.

Not long afterward, Eileen fell into a conversation with a recovered rape victim named Roberta who listened patiently when Eileen explained her discovery.

"It's amazing," she said. "They have identified Graham exactly. I wonder if other women you've talked to have had the same experience?"

Roberta smiled. "Yes, quite a few of them. Since it happened to me I've talked to a lot of women and have learned about the kind of man Graham is. He may have fantasies about sexual conquest and rape. He's a burglar, you say, and has learned that entering homes gives him the opportunity to live out his fantasy. I'll bet he spied on you while you were asleep, sizing you up before he woke you."

Eileen stared at the woman, realizing she was probably right. The idea of Graham exploring her apartment before he woke her with the mallet had occurred to her. Coming from another victim, it made sense and it gave her a funny feeling. Graham seemed more menacing.

"The main characteristic with a man like Graham," Roberta said, "is that he probably sees himself with his victim in her kitchen or bedroom. When he makes his rape intention clear, the woman naturally resists his advances and he overpowers her and achieves penetration. As part of his power fulfillment fantasy, the victim is overwhelmed by his ardor and comes on to him, actually encourages him in the act of coitus. She opens herself to him.

"To someone like Graham, the attraction of his fantasy is strong," Roberta said. "The power rapist has convinced himself that his victim is really enjoying herself and he finds clues in the woman's behavior to support his idea that she really wanted sex. She was clearly enjoying it, or was wet, or aroused, or made sounds which he interpreted as moans of pleasure."

Eileen thought about how Tyrone Graham had acted in her kitchen, playing the role of the "man of the house." He had talked with pride about stealing for a living, explaining that he was an experienced break-in artist. He pointed out that there were a lot of "mugs on the street" that a single woman had to look out for.

He had looked at her and said seriously, with no trace of irony in his voice, "You really should get a big dog to guard you when you go on a walk. A woman by herself can't be too careful . . . Why, somebody could mug you."

As Eileen prepared for bed that night, she felt she understood the man who had raped her far better than she had supposed would have been possible. In her mind she reviewed what her new friend, Roberta, had said about the compulsiveness of men like Graham.

"Of course, Eileen, no matter how much he tries to convince himself that the rape experience was great, there's a doubt in his mind. Since it represents a test of his maleness, his competency, he's got to convince himself that the act of sex with a stranger was terrific.

"The man who raped me," Roberta said, "bragged about several of the women he had attacked. 'They never said anything to the police because they liked the way I did it,' he told me. Actually, the power rapist feels something is lacking in his own performance or in his response. Failing to ejaculate, as most power rapists do, is a big worry. He's got to go out and find another victim, the 'right one', and that starts a series of rapes which may not end until he gets caught."

If what Roberta said about men like Graham was true, then why did he come back to kill me?, Eileen wondered. She knew in her heart that the man had returned. Her dogs had smelled his presence in her apartment and had gone absolutely wild. Then she realized she had already found the answer to her question in the *Men Who Rape* book.

She remembered the passage: "Frequently, the power rapist denies that the sexual encounter was forcible. He needs to believe the victim wanted and enjoyed it. Following the assault, he may insist on buying the victim a drink or dinner, or express the wish to see her again. In some cases, this may be understood as a way of 'fooling the mark', that is, a gesture of friendliness and 'no hard feelings', or a way of discrediting any subsequent report of rape by her . . ."

Graham's gesture of friendliness, Eileen realized, had been to clean the wound he had made in her head. That was supposed to make everything all right. Now she knew, indelibly, why he had returned to kill her. Having assured himself that she liked him, forgave him for striking her—an accidental blunder—approved of his sexual prowess in retrospect, he felt enraged and betrayed by her vow in the papers to catch her rapist. He had to come back to punish her for turning on him.

With a sudden shiver of deep fear, Eileen realized

that Graham had risked almost certain discovery to come back to get her. He'd come back again if he was free. Her upcoming Grand Jury appearance suddenly took on even greater importance. She had to convince the people on the Grand Jury—without any doubt—how dangerous Graham was and how he deserved to be indicted, tried and convicted. It was up to her to obtain his long-term imprisonment—and assure her and other women's safety.

Chapter 17

"The Grand Jury will meet on July 30th," Nancy Patterson advised Eileen. "It will be up to them to decide if a major crime has been committed. If they believe in you as a witness and are convinced the evidence collected by the police was conclusive, then they will render a 'true bill'." In Eileen's case, it would mean an indictment of Tyrone Graham.

The Grand Jury. To Eileen the name conjured up fearful images. If even members of the press who had seemed so supportive could so easily turn against her as had Anne Greason, how would twenty strangers whom she could not see or touch react to her and to her story? She dreaded the idea of testifying before them. One part of her felt as if she were to be put on trial, her own guilt or innocence to be decided.

Of course, deeper down she knew that this was not the case. That such feelings were the result of her own subconscious fears, those that were so akin to the fears of the other rape victims from whom she had heard and met when they were asked to convey the agony they felt to those who decided, after judging victims' veracity, their attackers' fate.

For Eileen it was the worst of times, and during it she was also grappling with self doubts magnified by her feeling that she was losing control of her business. Though Rick Rivera was doing a remarkable and valiant job of keeping the small medical transcription service going, it suffered from the lack of Eileen's personal attention.

Moreover, despite her therapy sessions, remaining

alone in her apartment had become all but impossible. Whenever she tried to transcribe medical dictation tapes at her familiar desk with her back exposed she would begin shaking, the hair raised on the back of her neck, chills ran down her spine and she would hurl herself out of her chair, staring wildly at the room closing in on her.

Sometimes she locked herself in the bathroom and talked for hours on the extension phone to friends until Rick came back.

She had looked cool and poised at the police lineup, but now that it was behind her, her arms and legs often felt like they were made of lead. She had performed for the cops, the prosecutor, even for the men in the lineup—the brave woman who had restored her sense of self by an act of will power.

What a laugh that was. At any moment during the day the threat of tears moistened her eyes and she found herself trembling all over.

Tired and jumpy as she was, she greeted eagerly every opportunity to absent herself from the apartment, and spent most of her evenings upstairs gaining solace from talking with her friend David, whose own physical condition continued to weaken.

Then, two days before Eileen was to present herself before the Grand Jury, David Wilson, the man who had dragged himself painfully out of his sickbed to untie and comfort her the night of the rape, died. It was a wrenching blow to Eileen. Few people in her life had ever meant as much to her as David. She especially valued the cheer and comfort of their intimate, unpretentious talks together. They talked about everything and nothing in particular, and never found it necessary to define the gladness each felt in the presence of the other. His death—even though she knew it was coming—left an empty void in her life.

It was like pulling the rug from beneath her feet when she had few emotional reserves left with which to deal with more loss or new disappointments. When she heard the news she ran into the bathroom, locked the door and sat on the closed toilet lid, then wrapped her arms around herself. Her body shook as tears fell and grief rolled over her in waves.

Foolish as it may have been to think of a dying man as an anchor, the fact was David had been hers. His steadfastness had been her source of resilience, humor and renewal. What would she do without him?

There was a wake for David Wilson in Newark, New Jersey. Eileen attended with Pat Sulsona, Bill Clemmons, and Chantal Gruber. They were not surprised that a crowd of more than two hundred people had come to pay their last respects. David lay in an open coffin and she remembered with a teary smile his joke the week before about the arrangements. "Yeah, I think I'll have an open coffin so I can see if anybody shows up."

Now feeling more alone than she ever had in her life, Eileen steeled herself for the ordeal of testifying before the Grand Jury.

The day she appeared for the Grand Jury hearing, accompanied by her Aunt Ann, a petite woman with graying hair and a trim figure and the optimistic decisiveness of her brother, Eileen's father, Eileen discovered that Linda Fairstein, the Assistant District Attorney who supervised sex crime prosecutions for the Manhattan District Attorney, was being interviewed for television. Eileen had not expected to be part of a television film for the Hugh Downs/Barbara Walters 20/20 Show, but as a rape victim who was willing to be identified, she was asked to answer some questions as background for the 20/20 story on the powerful personality of the prosecutor.

Eileen was not surprised that the producers had chosen to create a television segment around Fairstein. The woman was a tall, attractive blonde who spoke with distinction and candor, a perfect example of the successful female lawyer who had created a reputation for herself as a fair, vigorous public servant dedicated to prosecuting sex offenders who took cruel advantage of women and children.

Eileen was amused when the segment director abruptly cancelled the interview portion of her part in the film and asked instead that they be allowed to film her in a "fade-out" walk. Eileen was filmed walking slowly down the hall toward the Grand Jury room which she would actually enter a little later that day. The camera came for a close-up of her face, then she began her stroll, growing smaller in the lens until she stepped through the door and disappeared.

There was a symbolic irony to the fade-out procedure that appealed to Eileen. A rape victim's life was never the same after the event. The scene showing her getting smaller as she drew farther away captured the idea of the diminished woman, reduced in emotional stability and in her possession of herself by the act of rape.

During the rest of the morning Linda Fairstein interrogated Eileen on the substance of the attack that took place in 1979.

"I need to know this, Eileen," Fairstein said, leaning forward. Tyrone Graham's attorney has the right to know about any relevant information. It's up to me to determine that.

Obediently, Eileen described the attack on her at a remodeling site near East End Avenue. She had left the apartment of a boyfriend after he had gotten so drunk that he had passed out, unable to walk Eileen home to her apartment a few blocks away.

She explained that a wild-acting man had jumped out at her with a knife in his hand.

"I haven't got any money," she had screamed.

"Well, I don't leave bitches alive. Now that you've seen me."

"But I'm blind. I can't identify you."

"I'm going to beat you up to make sure you don't remember."

He had started punching Eileen in her face. The blows were partially deflected by the heavy woolen hood Eileen was wearing. Painful was the metal on a scaffolding that had cut into her face every time her head rocked with a blow from her assailant. With his knife he had slashed her corduroy pants, then pulled out his penis and in a frenzy had suddenly ejaculated on one leg of Eileen's pants. Furious, disappointed, he had run away, and Eileen had heard a car's motor start a few seconds later.

"Well," Linda Fairstein said after hearing Eileen's story, "I certainly don't think there are any grounds for provocation in that encounter. And you reported it to the police, didn't you?"

"Yes, I did."

"But please don't think," Nancy Patterson whispered to Eileen, "that just because Graham was indicted in Brooklyn that this is going to be a shoo-in. There is no such thing as a rubber-stamped Grand Jury. At least I've never seen one. We've got to prove to twenty-two people that Tyrone Graham abused you sexually, raped you by force, entered your apartment illegally, and stole from you. There can't be any questions in the jurors' minds that he did these things.

"I'm not asking you to be dramatic, but I am asking you to be convincing. Tell your story with complete frankness and honesty. The jurors will see the truth in your face, hear it in your voice if you tell your story in a straightforward way, answering the questions I'll be putting to you. Do you have any questions for me?"

"No, I've got it straight. I think we've covered everything in our rehearsal," Eileen said, "just describe the room."

Quickly, Patterson filled Eileen in.

Afterwards Linda Fairstein thanked Eileen and her aunt, who then walked with Nancy Patterson to some benches outside Room 40 of the courthouse building. The two women sat close together while Patterson went inside and Ann patted Eileen's hand.

"It won't be long now, dear." Ann, who had no vision impairment, scanned the corridor.

"I'll nudge you so you'll be ready."

A few minutes later, Nancy Patterson opened the big yellow oak door and beckoned to Ann who immediately conveyed the news to Eileen. Trembling, Eileen stood up and smoothed the lap wrinkles in her dress, mentally squared her shoulders and placed her hand on Nancy Patterson's forearm. The Assistant District Attorney guided her to a solitary table and chair in the large room.

Though she couldn't see her surroundings beyond the table, Eileen had fresh in her mind the benefit of Nancy Patterson's description of the room. A semi-circular platform contained several ascending rows of wooden seats. As many as fifty to sixty person could be seated, with the highest row perhaps twelve feet from the bottom. The jurors would be looking straight at Eileen.

Nancy Patterson positioned herself, as she had told Eileen she would do, at a lectern in the back of the room. She was separated from Eileen by a distance of thirty or so feet. Her questions to Eileen would be made in a loud clear voice.

Through Eileen could not see the large windows in the room, she could see the light that came in through them from the hot July day outside. She was aware of their sunshine brightness, and the faint traffic sounds that floated up from the street level four stories below. She also heard the rustle of clothes, the soft sibilance of fabrics rubbing against fabrics, a cough, a murmur, the sounds of paper sliding, as the jurors settled into their seats.

Nancy Patterson began by asking Eileen to identify herself.

"Will you please tell the jurors your name and where you live."

"My name is Eileen Ross." Eileen gave her address.

"In the early hours of July 14th, 1986, were you awakened from sleep by an intruder?"

"Yes, I was."

"Will you tell the jurors what happened?"

In a steady, determined voice, Eileen described the intrusion of Tyrone Graham, how he struck her head with a wooden mallet he had discovered in her kitchen and how he brutally wounded her pet beagle, Bethie.

Then she said, "I could hear the popping sound when the mallet struck Bethie. She screamed, but I couldn't comfort her because I was dazed from the blows he had given me. Bethie was knocked unconscious.

"I put my hands on Bethie," she said in a low voice, "and I could feel the blood. She was bleeding and I thought she was dead. That was one of the worst moments in my whole life," her voice rose plaintively, tears rushed to her eyes and fell down her cheeks as she remembered the terrified squeal of Bethie before she fell unconscious on the bed and the sinking feeling that came over her when she thought Bethie was dead.

Eileen looked up apologetically in the direction of the jurors, her voice caught in her throat. She was momentarily overwhelmed. She heard soft snuffling sounds among the jurors and realized some of them had been moved by her breakdown.

Eileen recovered her poise and Nancy Patterson deftly brought her step by step through her ordeal with Graham from his erratic behavior in the kitchen—how he had insisted Eileen cook eggs for him, then left them to burn as he instructed her to remove her clothes,—to the moment when he touched her breasts. Nancy lingered carefully on the details so they were impressed on the minds of the jurors.

"Are you saying he touched your breasts with his fingers?"

"Yes."

When Eileen described Graham's strange ritual with the screwdrivers she heard sharp intakes of breath among the jurors. They did not miss the significance of the screwdrivers as weapons.

"Did Tyrone Graham try to hurt you with the screwdrivers? Did he touch you with them in any way?"

"No," Eileen said. "I couldn't help thinking about the Boston Strangler who forced sticks into the vaginas of his victims, and I was afraid. But he didn't do anything with the screwdrivers."

Nancy Patterson patiently and adroitly led Eileen to the moment when Tyrone Graham raped her.

"Will you please describe, Eileen, how the man raped you."

"He put his penis in my vagina." This was the phrase Eileen and Nancy Patterson had been over so carefully. The wording was important from a legal standpoint to establish the act of rape as described by the law. It was also important to the victim because it required her to make a public statement to twenty-two strangers.

Patterson had explained to Eileen that many women were emotionally incapable of saying the words. They were horrified and ashamed at the idea of having to tell them to complete strangers. Not only did they cringe when describing the physical act of forced entry, but for many all of the highly charged personal, private feelings, and the awful rage that was associated with the act of rape, broke loose.

At that point some women, Patterson had told Eileen, were so distraught, so wounded and nervous that they were physically unable to form the words on their tongues. They shuddered and squirmed, tear-stained and cowed in the witness chair, feeling as pinned to that awful seat of inquisition as they had been by their rapist.

For women who were unable to speak the words, Nancy Patterson had devised a different strategy. The law required that the complaining witness accuse her assailant in plain words of the act of sexual penetration. There could be no exceptions. But the law was willing to accept a full description that required only an affirmative answer.

Had Eileen decided she was unable to say the emotion-charged words, then Nancy Patterson would have asked her: "Are you telling this jury that Tyrone Graham put his penis into your vagina?"

That form of the question would only require a one word, "yes" answer.

Another question at which many rape victims cringed was a similar one, in which the witness was asked, "Will you explain to this jury what you mean by the act of rape?" This usually preceded the previous question, but not always. It was the responsibility of the Assistant District Attorney to make absolutely certain that no doubt existed in the minds of any of the jurors that the rape had occurred and that the victim had been an unwilling participant.

Eileen, her determination to speak out strengthening her resolve, had held together through the most trying part of her testimony about Tyrone Graham's brutal attack on her. Now that it was over, she waited impatiently to reveal her own plan to trap her attacker.

Finally, Nancy Patterson asked her if she had deliberately contrived to convince Tyrone Graham to take a water glass in his hand.

"Is it true you planned to trap Tyrone Graham's fingerprints on a water glass, by handing it to him as you would to any other visitor to your kitchen who was having a drink with his breakfast?"

Eileen smiled triumphantly, "Yes, that's true."

"Weren't you afraid that he would realize you were trying to collect evidence of his visit and punish you?"

"Yes. I was terrified."

"How did you retrieve the water glass from him after he had taken it from you?"

"Carefully!" Eileen said with depthless irony.

Laughter filled the room and the faces of the Grand Jurors.

Nancy Patterson deftly let the moment linger and then went on. "Is it true that you placed the glass unwashed in the kitchen sink with some other dishes and told the police later when they came where it was to be found?"

"Yes. That's true," Eileen said slowly, deliberately.

Nancy Patterson turned directly to the Grand Jury and said, "I have here certified copies of fingerprints taken from the water glass and the telephone in the bathroom. They are a match to prints of Tyrone Graham on file at the Bureau of Criminal Identification."

A few minutes later, Eileen was excused from the Grand Jury room. Exhausted but satisfied she sat down next to her aunt on the bench outside the room where the cloistered jurors remained and heaved a deep sigh. Her Aunt Ann beamed at her and squeezed her hand, "It's all over now. You can breathe easier."

Nancy Patterson had informed Eileen that the Grand Jury would probably vote very quickly on the indictment and that if she would wait, she could take the news home with her.

When the Assistant District Attorney appeared in front of her twenty minutes later, she smilingly announced, "They indicted him, Eileen, on seven counts: rape in the first degree, two counts; robbery in the first degree; burglary in the first degree; assault in the second degree; and sexual abuse in the first degree."

Eileen listened intently, took a deep breath, then asked, "How long can he get?"

"Theoretically, added together, Eileen, he could get as much as ninety years. As a matter of practice, sentences usually run concurrently. With good behavior?" she shrugged.

Eileen thought about Nancy Patterson's last statement as she and her aunt rode the elevator down from the fourth floor. Eileen felt furious over the idea that Graham, who had brutally raped her and so many others, might serve only a few years and then get out.

As the doors opened she turned slowly to her aunt. "I want Tyrone Graham locked up for the rest of his life," she said emotionally. "I won't give up until I have done everything in my power to ensure that."

Chapter 18

Eileen went home convinced that while the Grand Jury had indicted Tyrone Graham, his trial still lay ahead. That would not happen for months while his public defender attorney took his jailed client through the baffling and, for those awaiting his prosecution, frustrating steps in the law designed to provide defense alternatives for an accused.

Meanwhile, Tyrone Graham occupied a jail cell in a city prison system which was located, as the crow flies, not more than four or five miles from Eileen's apartment. The man had a prison record of attempted jail breaks. Eileen could not stop imagining what would happen to her if he broke free.

As the days went on she relived many times the feelings of absolute terror that had seized her the afternoon her dogs started barking wildly, sensing that he had been there when she brought them back home after a walk in the park.

At odd moments when she was alone in the apartment and heard an unfamiliar sound, fear jumped at her. Her legs turned to jelly, she was gripped with panic and her throat seemed to close. She couldn't scream or breathe until the fright attack passed.

Then she would sit down in the kitchen with the radio playing for companionship, while her fears about Tyrone Graham threatened to undo her. Dr. Pamela Watson had carefully explained that rape victims suffered post-assault anxiety attacks—all part of the rape trauma syndrome. Imagining the rapist returning was commonplace among victims whose nerves had been shattered.

That might be so Eileen acknowledged, but she was certain the stark fear she still suffered was far more acute. It was the kind of terror that physically took her breath away.

Eileen was also sure she would never be able to convey to another human the absolute certainty in her heart that Tyrone Graham planned to get even with her. That's why she was uneasy about him sitting close by in a jail cell, while the wheels of justice slowly turned.

How could she explain a dread sense of expectancy? An event that seemed so real, so familiar to her because she saw it in her mind, that it was like reviewing a memory of something that had already occurred?

She knew how Graham felt about getting even. He had told her that repeatedly during the two hours he had spent in her apartment. Now, he knew Eileen had not only reported the rape to the police but by attracting so much media interest had brought about his arrest. That was what made her believe he would try to get her if he ever got the chance.

Now as he languished in prison he had plenty of time to reflect on all that had occurred and the woman who was responsible for sending him away.

Eileen shivered. Graham, if he got out, would be sure to come back to punish her for his imprisonment. And Nancy Patterson's words echoed in Eileen's mind. *The sentences could run concurrently. With good behavior?* Who knew what the outcome of the trial would be. He could claim that if she hadn't screamed, he would never have struck her. That his blow and attack on her were things that just accidently happened, like dropping a hot iron on your toe, or scalding your hand on a hot plate.

It wasn't planned.

They might argue that as a result, the punishment should fit the crime. He wouldn't mind taking a rap for burglary. That was part of the risk of his profession. If he had to serve some time for rape it should be a light sentence. Nothing heavy.

Yes, Eileen knew what Graham and his lawyer might say in order to get him off. She also had learned that some judges in New York were inclined to give local jail time for jury-convicted rapists rather than sending them to prison. It didn't happen all of the time, but once could be enough if the rapist was Tyrone Graham.

Eileen pondered the problem of Tyrone Graham's prison sentence many hours. She wanted to do something to increase the chances that he get more than a few years behind bars, but she didn't know what. She believed if she kept applying herself to the idea that eventually a workable solution would pop into her mind.

She didn't know if it was unusual or strange for a rape victim to be instrumental in the promotion of a stiffer prison sentence for her assailant. She only knew what she had to do and that her action would be condoned by every rape victim. Hundreds of letters from sexually assaulted women had told her so.

It was not vindictiveness that drove her. It was her personal safety. She was scared to death of the man. Every instinct in her being told her the man nursed a terrible anger for her. In his mind, she had not only broken the promise of silence he had tried to force on her, but she had made the *little rape,* as he saw it, something far worse than it was. She had made things hot for him by going to the cops. It was bad enough for her to report the rape, but she had added insult to injury by appealing to the newspapers for his capture and arrest.

More than any other person she was responsible for where he was now.

To Eileen's knowledge none of the other women had made the kind of big deal of his raping them that she had. Some of them had probably not even reported what he did to them. She was to blame for his troubles . . . and she would pay. These thoughts weighed heavily on Eileen's mind.

Moreover, not only was there the pressure of knowing Tyrone Graham was imprisoned not far from her; there was also the pressure of his impending trial and there was increased pressure from the Navereign Apartment owners and their insurance agents to get her out of their building.

A few weeks after she appeared before the Grand Jury an incident at the Navereign involving Rick convinced Eileen that the daily personnel of the apartments had been coached by the management to go out of their way to be rude to her, unkind, and contemptuous of her and anybody who visited her.

If ever she had been in doubt about the biased attitudes of the guards, doormen, gardeners and utility workers at the apartment, the day Rick's car stopped dead in the curving driveway in front of the glass entry doors of the apartment building proved their cruelty.

Rick had purchased a used car whose battery was failing. It wasn't an attractive vehicle, its shine and newness long ago having disappeared under the grime of New York. Compared to the sleek limousines, Rolls, Mercedes, and Cadillacs that swept grandly up to the entrance, it was a droopy out-of-place nag among haughty thoroughbreds.

When it refused to start one day after Rick had deposited Eileen in the passenger's front seat, both she and he got out and pushed. As they strained to budge the lumpish car, other vehicles lined up to take on or disgorge passengers. Soon a group of doormen, guards and utility workers were gathered and they threw insults at Rick and Eileen. They refused to lift a hand to help push the heavy machine clear of the driveway.

"Get a horse!"

"Move that wreck!"

"Where'd you find that? At the city dump?"

With a burst of effort Rick and Eileen got the car rolling and pushed it out of the driveway into a space next to a curb on the street. When Eileen recovered her breath, she was furious and resentful. Those people had no right to act the way they did. She realized the futility of complaining to the management. Ever since the rape, even requests by her for routine maintenance calls on her apartment had been ignored.

It was obvious the management had adopted a policy of trying to make her life in their apartment building so uncomfortable that she would leave. She vowed to herself that it was going to take more than a few unpleasant remarks to drive her out. Still, her cheeks burned from the taunting insults. As for Rick, his anger was explosive.

A few weeks later, an incident with a strange man convinced Eileen that the apartments' insurance carrier was trying to prove that her morals were questionable. If they could show that she took "just anybody" into her apartment, then her character might be successfully attacked and her value as a witness for herself in the impending civil suit trial for damages resulting from their neglect might be considerably reduced.

On this particular morning, Eileen was about to enter the Navereign through a rear service door. She had Bethie and Bonnie with her. Suddenly a black man dressed in a wild, yellow paisley shirt, short pants and white boat shoes, looking like a pimp, appeared. Around his neck were gold chains and on his fingers were several rings.

"Hey babe," he said in a sing-song chant, "How ya doing? Lookin' real nice today. I want to help you, be your man, go shoppin' for ya, hold your hand, be nice to ya."

Eileen was astonished and repulsed by the man. He had a creepy, swaggering, exaggerated smoothness and his vernacular seemed put on as well.

He tried to put his arm around Eileen's waist. She pushed it away. He tried to sidle past her through the door, but she blocked his way with her body. "Get away from me," she said, more angry with a security guard who was standing nearby doing nothing than with the man himself.

When she finally got away and returned to her apartment with the dogs, she realized what it was about the man that was false. He was an educated person trying to sound like a hip, sweet guy. It didn't work. As she thought about the flawed performance, she realized he was a fake. Gary Trachten and Norman Pearlman had warned her to be alert for tricks and strategies by the apartment management or their insurance company that might besmirch her character in some fashion.

She felt this little act was a ruthless attempt to sabotage her that the apartments' management was her enemy. They were afraid of what she was going to cost them as a result of their negligence. In her opinion they were trying to escape the financial punishment that a large jury verdict in her favor would cost them.

While Eileen coped with the hassling incidents at her apartment building Nancy Patterson, the Assistant DA, called once or twice a week to fill Eileen in on their progress or lack of it in bringing Tyrone Graham to trial.

Graham was a trickster. Because he was a parole violator, he was being held without bail, but he had showed up for one of his hearings ranting and raving, obviously being cued by one of his fellow prisoners to act crazy, claiming through his public defendant he wasn't competent to stand trial.

The court had had to schedule a psychiatric evaluation. Then, a short while after this didn't work, Graham had suddenly announced that he was going to defend himself.

Disgusted by the continual delays and her continued harassment, Eileen had begun to seriously consider moving from New York, and this decision was seconded by Rick Rivera.

Chapter 19

Just when Rick's and Eileen's relationship had moved from simple friendship to something more serious, neither was certain.

At first, Eileen had thought she was imagining his attraction to her. He was so young. She was skeptical. At his age she had thought herself in love everyday. Moreover, she had not been physically involved with anyone since her disastrous affair with Hani.

When Eileen's young guards finished their protective tour of duty, Rick took on that role himself. By this time his tender treatment of her had began to warm her heart. One day he brought her a tiny porcelain beagle and, hugging her, said, "I'll buy you a real beagle puppy one day." She wondered if she should approach the subject of their attraction with him, but was afraid he might say *Don't flatter yourself, you old bag.*

Then one night, he confessed to Eileen that one of her friends had asked him if Eileen liked him, and he had replied, "I don't know, but I like her."

All of a sudden they were both caught up in a relationship which was becoming more intimate. Then Rick caught a terrible flu and she made him move from the living room couch to the bedroom where she could nurse him.

Going back and forth from her den to the bedroom was exhausting. One night as she lay down beside him to talk and relax he reached over to her, his voice filled with tenderness, "You're beautiful, you know."

"I really don't think we should be doing this," she had replied. "You're much too young for me and—"

"I'm not asking you to marry me," he interrupted her.

She was good to Rick and Rick was kind, non-threatening—a gentle patient lover. He treated her better than any man she had ever known and because he had had a difficult life, had been working since he was twelve, he was mature beyond his years.

By Christmas they were a couple and had decided to move to Oregon. Away from the brutality, fear and hassles New York had come to symbolize.

Right before Eileen left to find them a house, Nancy Patterson told her, "The prosecution has decided to try to cut a deal with Tyrone Graham."

Because Eileen couldn't definitively identify him, perhaps they'd have him plead guilty to robbery and burglary, for which the sentence would be the same as rape.

"Please don't do that," she pleaded with Patterson. Eileen was furious. "That will leave a question in everyone's mind as to whether a rape really took place."

"If you let him cop a plea," Eileen threatened, "I'll go back to every television channel and newspaper and tell them about the injustice," her voice broke.

Patterson, who was both compassionate and weary, promised to do everything she could to make the rape charges stick.

Meanwhile, Eileen moved to Oregon. The beautiful clear air, the green lush scenery brought both her and Rick renewed enthusiasm for life, and a new peace.

Shortly thereafter, Nancy Patterson called, "Tyrone Graham has agreed to plead guilty in your case to two counts of robbery and rape."

He had pleaded guilty to Eileen's rape, the assault and burglary charges against him on March 30, 1988.

When he stood before the bench with his eyes fixed stonily on the toes of his shoes, he was accompanied by his attorney, Doug Lyons. He had exhausted all the legal strategems to avoid going to trial or to answer in the affirmative the legal allegations against him.

His plea was entered a year and a half after he raped Eileen Ross and represented the defeat of the delaying actions he had employed through two attorneys to lengthen the period between his grand jury indictment and his confrontation with Eileen, or with a judge, if he chose to admit his guilt and take his chances that his sentence might be moderate.

In New York law on criminal procedure there is a rule known as the 30/30 rule. It requires the prosecutor in a criminal case to be ready for trial within six months from the time a suspect is charged with a crime. Defendants' attorneys are well aware of the rule and devise every legal strategy to delay the prosecutor "in chargeable time".

The prosecutor is always aware that he is fighting a deadline. He must prepare his case and have it ready for trial within the prescribed six-months period or risk that a judge will dismiss the charges against the defendant because the prosecutor has violated the 30/30 rule.

There is another reason the defendant's attorney prefers delaying going to trial on a case as long as possible. The prosecutor's witnesses may get tired of waiting to testify. At the very least, a drawn-out waiting period will dim the memory of witnesses and they won't be as effective when the trial date actually arrives.

Adjournments requested by the defendant's attorney are not chargeable as time against the prosecution under the 30/30 rule.

Tyrone Graham requested five adjournments. One,

a routine delay, was in May of 1987. The second in July of the same year was for the purpose of determining whether he was psychologically fit to go to trial. He was found not legally insane.

On October 14, 1987, a delay was ordered on a motion of his lawyer to determine if he were competent to assist with his own case. Such a request is usually a routine delaying ploy to allow the defendant's attorney or the prosecutor "thinking time" to decide what to do, finally, about a case.

Another delay was granted because Graham's court-appointed attorney, Tom Kline, had to leave the case for personal reasons.

Finally, with no cards left to play, Tyrone Graham stood before Judge Edwin Torres on March 30, 1988 and heard his attorney, Doug Lyons, say: "My client has authorized me to enter a plea of guilty on all counts of the charges and specifications listed against him."

Judge Torres accepted the plea and set May 4th, 1988 as the date for sentencing.

It was like a benediction for Eileen's and Rick's new life.

Eileen had been living in Oregon City, Oregon for several months by the time the deposition hearing with the attorney representing the Navereign Apartments was held on June 3rd, 1988.

Eileen had been warned by her attorney Robert Kappel, whose law firm, Schneider, Klinik, and Weitz, had replaced Norman Pearlman, that the adversary attorney was going to try to establish that Eileen had been suffering from severe emotional trauma stemming from her relationship with Hanibal Gabriel when she was raped by Tyrone Graham. His questions were going to arrow in on the issue. If he could prove to a jury that significant psychological injury existed prior to the rape, then the amount of the cash award might be reduced.

The lawyer, whose name was Richard Eniclerico, had taken Eileen step by step through every detail of the rape and had been relentless with questions concerning her psychiatric treatment following the shock of separation from Hani.

Several hours of questions had exhausted her, but in the end Kappel squeezed her hand and told her she had done fine.

Apparently, her testimony had convinced Eniclerico that a court trial was simply going to add unneeded additional expense to his client's legal fees.

The Navereign Apartments offered a cash settlement to Eileen's attorney on September 5, 1988. The original amount of the civil suit was for eleven million dollars. The settlement was for an undisclosed amount, but Eileen would never have a financial worry for the rest of her life, if she invested the award wisely.

Eileen agreed as part of the settlement terms never to reveal the amount.

Eileen's final solution to her quandary, about how to ensure a long prison sentence for Tyrone Graham, occurred one morning while she was alone in the library of the medical transcription department at Willamette Falls Hospital where she had begun to work.

A date had finally been set for a judge to sentence Tyrone Graham.

On this particular day, Eileen had signed out. Afterward, she sat quietly for a few minutes, then began talking slowly into a cassette recording machine that physicians used to transcribe medical notes. Forty-five minutes later she sat down and started typing a letter to Judge Edwin Torres, letting her own words reveal the anguish in her heart.

Dear Judge Torres:

Currently, I am not in a position to return to New York City for the sentencing of Tyrone Graham. Therefore, in my absence, I send this letter, which I trust will serve as an adequate substitution. I request that you read it carefully and in its entirety, and if you feel it is appropriate, please read it aloud, as Graham stands before you today, May 4, 1988. I think perhaps this written document will be easier for us all, as words may have failed me, had I been present in your courtroom today.

JULY 14, 1986,

Approximately 2:00 A.M.

A savage breaks into my home, beats me, nearly kills my dog Bethie, then ties Bonnie (fourteen) to the terrace rail; rapes me, terrorizes me, robs me; eats a meal, turns on the stereo; talks to me about his life and his various criminal activities and the revenge he'll have upon me if I ever tell anyone. He leads me to the bathroom, where he carefully cleans the bloody wound he has inflicted upon my head, leads me to my bleeding dog and then tells me "everything will be okay." He then ties me up with an electrical cord and escapes into the night, leaving me bound, bloody and terrified.

What else can I tell you about the facts that you don't already know? Probably, nothing, for I realize you've worked long and hard hours on this case, and I thank you very much for it.

Two Hours:

In the course of one's life, a very short span of time. Yet, those two hours have changed my life forever, and have caused me irreparable damage. Herein, I can only give you a brief outline as to what I, only one individual in a string of many, continue to go through, long after the dust has supposedly settled.

After the incident, I was immediately faced with the cold, hard reality that I had to somehow go on with my life such as it would be from that moment on: "What am I going to do now, what am I going to do now," I thought over and over again in my mind. Yet, it was necessary that I function, go on; somehow be the survivor that I always thought I was.

My network of support systems included some very faithful friends (especially my two beagles), those people who worked with me in my business, my father, the media, and most importantly myself (who I always considered to be my best resource). Later I became active in the Rape Crisis Intervention Program at Mt. Sinai Hospital. There I shared the pains and the triumphs of those who had been in similar situations. It was there that I found the most comfort.

Those two hours have changed my life forever. My life, no matter what the future may hold, will never again be the same.

I gave up my small word-processing business of ten years, ultimately had to leave my apartment and even felt it necessary to move out of New York State, where I had lived my entire life.

My new life has not been too easy for me, either. I'm trying to rebuild and start again as if from scratch. Sometimes I am so scared and tormented I don't know what to do.

Other times I feel like running. The problem is, where do I run to? As a woman, although handicapped, I always enjoyed my independence, freedom and even solitude. Would you believe I have not spent one night alone since July 14, 1986?

Subjectively, I feel no sympathy for this creature of the night who, with a free will, chose to be a personal messenger of torture and devastation to the lives of so many.

I do, however, feel thankful that my life and the lives of my dogs were spared, particularly since I learned that he brutally stabbed to death another person's dog.

Judge Torres, I am asking you when you look upon this individual who has confessed not only to this, but other rapes also, to sentence him to the longest period in prison the law allows. For my safety and the safety of other women, he should never be paroled.

Thank you for reading this.

Eileen Ross

Eileen had obtained Judge Torres' address from Gary Trachten. She arranged to have the letter delivered to Judge Torres before 10:30 A.M. on Wednesday, May 4, 1988, the day Tyrone Graham was to be sentenced.

In court that day, Judge Torres's reaction to her words was swift and strong. "It seems to evoke in me certain sentiments that I had thought, in my thirty-one years in this criminal justice system, I had put behind me," Torres said. "It is truly heart-rending. Truly."

Supreme Court Justice Edwin Torres' angry remarks boomed across the courtroom: "The parole authorities should never set this individual free to rape, plunder, pillage or rob—ever again. That is my conviction," Torres said.

His remarks made no apparent impact on the sweatshirted rapist, Tyrone Graham, twenty-seven, whose eyes remained glued to his shoes.

The next morning, on May 5, 1988, Mike Pearl wrote an article in the *New York Post* " 'Spiderman Rapist' gets 15-to-life" which described what had happened in New York Supreme Court because of Eileen's letter.

> A Manhattan judge yesterday sentenced the "Spiderman Rapist" to fifteen years to life in prison for raping a blind woman—and recommended he be kept permanently behind bars. . . .
>
> Graham—who already is doing 18 years to life for raping four Brooklyn women—broke into Ross' Upper East Side apartment in July 1986.
>
> He beat the legally blind woman and one of her dogs, raped and robbed her, and forced her to cook him breakfast before tying her up with an electrical cord and leaving.
>
> At the time of the savage attack, Ross, thirty-nine, identified herself as a rape victim because she felt that the stigma belonged on her attacker.
>
> She became an articulate spokesperson for victims' rights and gave a detailed description of her rapist, which greatly enhanced the police case against him.
>
> It wasn't until later that Ross fell apart, suffering the consequences she described in her letter.
>
> Yesterday's sentence will run concurrent

with the time Graham received for the Brooklyn rapes.

"But it is unlikely that he will be set free after eighteen years," said Assistant District Attorney Nancy Patterson.

"The proper authorities are fully informed of Mr. Graham's history and will recommend that Mr. Graham will serve well in excess of the minimum term," she said. . . .

When Eileen read the story which had been forwarded to her by Gary Trachten, she thought back to the night the man had clubbed her when she screamed. She cringed inwardly at the memory and she realized that while he might never be free to live outside bars, she would live the threat he represented in nightmares for the rest of her life.

But now, they were nightmares that could be banished at first light.

Epilogue

When Eileen Ross arrived at Bill Budd's Restaurant to meet all of the former members of the Brooklyn Sex Crimes Squad, there was a special significance to the get-together. It was a reunion with the five detectives. But it was also a ceremony of thankfulness for the rape survivor to express her gratitude to five people who not only understood how important the arrest of an assailant was to a victim, but went against their own bosses in order to bring an end to Spiderman's brutal career.

Officer Richie Harker and his partner were the recipients of the New York Finest Foundation Award for their outstanding work which led to the arrest of the Spiderman Rapist. He is married, the father of two children, and resides in Staten Island.

Much had happened in the preceding three years. On September 3, 1986, three months after Sal Catalfumo and Patti Kehoe had interviewed Eileen Ross in her living room, investigators raided the sex crimes squadroom, scooping up the team's memo pads, the unit's log books, and cartons of other materials. Shortly afterward, Jim McGeown was transferred to another Brooklyn detective unit. Within weeks he suffered a serious fall. After a couple of months of recuperation, he retired from the N.Y.P.D. on half pay.

Back at the Sex Crimes Squad, the Patterns Crime and Special Investigations team was disbanded, its files stored away, and its members reassigned to regular catch-team duty. Bob Merz, who like McGeown already had twenty years of police work under his belt, also chose retirement.

Patti Kehoe, Sal Catalfumo, and Bruce Milau accepted reassignments and they each retired within the next three years. They joined up again in pairs and singly, Sal Catalfumo and Patti Kehoe as private detectives in partnership; Bruce Milau working alone as an investigator; and Jim McGeown and Bob Merz, partners in a Floral Park, New York detective agency (Jupiter Investigator Group).

In civilian life, as private investigators, the members of "Fancy Dans" were quickly successful attracting clients who valued the original thinking and bravery of these cops "who knew the ropes".

Walking into the restaurant dining room, Eileen was feeling glad the team was reassembled. As she sat down at the table, McGeown was raising his glass to salute the four detectives with whom he had worked on the Spiderman rape case. They were all there: Patti Kehoe, small, sharp, feisty, a fine detective with a great gut instinct; Bob Merz, the durable cop who believed in the averages and was proud of his badge; Bruce Milau, the two-hundred-and-eighty-pound giant who looked like an offensive line backer; and Sal Catalfumo, the Italian cop with the operatic mustache and the ability to see the character in a person's eyes.

Tears came to her eyes as Eileen focused on each one. These were the detectives who had bolstered her own conviction that her decision to publicly pursue her rapist had been correct. In the three years since her rape, Eileen had talked to many women who had been raped and had discovered the ones who had been active in pursuing their attackers legally after the rape were usually the women who adjusted better to life following the violent event.

Eileen felt she had come to the end of a long road when she was seated with the "Fancy Dans". They had done far more than their jobs required to remove the threat of three notorious rapists, one of whom was the man who had changed her life.

When she said "thank you" to them, the article that appeared in the *New York Daily News Magazine* was on her mind. The article on the detectives had disclosed the sacrifices they had made to pursue Spiderman at a time when their careers were in jeopardy because the police brasshats were convinced they were "show boating". She knew they would be embarrassed if she mentioned it.

As she greeted the detectives Eileen realized more deeply than ever how fortunate she had been to have had the "Fancy Dans" in her corner—tough-minded cops who got angry about rapists and did something about them with the fervor of a personal crusade. They pushed when caution told them to pull back. They were cops. *Real cops.*

Eileen began to talk about the arrest of Tyrone Graham. During this time she had increasingly been involved with the Mt. Sinai Rape Crisis Center in New York, and in rape counseling activities while she was in Oregon. She completed training to become a rape advocate, then a facilitator, and worked in outreach programs to help survivors of sexual assault adjust. She also worked with hospital emergency personnel to increase their sensitivity to rape examination trauma.

She discovered that too many people held the attitude that women got raped only because they "asked for it".

In rape information programs for cops in precincts in New York, she was generally pleased that her audiences, largely men, were open to suggestions that would enable them to handle rape victims better. When she told them about the cops who had entered her apartment mistaking David Wilson for the assailant, most of them agreed that the cops on the scene had had to judge by appearance. Being forewarned by erroneous information volunteered by the security guard of the apartment complex, they were convinced when they came in that they were dealing with a domestic squabble.

Eileen was able to comprehend the cops' point of view, but it didn't remove her own conviction that the crime scene investigation had been handled improperly at the beginning and that influenced official attitudes about the probity of her story. She advised the cops to not always judge the situation by first appearances and try to pay closer attention to what the victims are saying.

As Eileen reviewed her own feelings about how she had handled the rapist in her life, she gradually developed recommendations for those who might be confronted by a sexual attack.

Eileen felt that her decision to attempt to control her rapist by treating him like a human being was largely responsible for keeping her alive.

She often told women that they were their own best resource, to try to "keep cool", to retain their emotional stability; and that there was no "right or wrong behavior" in the face of rape.

Every rape, she had told women, consisted of three factors: the rapist, a place where the rape was happening, and the victim.

Try to read the rapist or take effective or rational actions against him. Try not to miss those clues that could help you gain information or even slip out of danger," Eileen said to women.

One can capitalize on the rapist's lack of stability by trying not to panic. Eileen felt it important to try to regain control as she did. The fact was, Eileen stressed, when a woman retained her emotional stability in a sexual confrontation, she had more control. If a person can retain her composure and draw the rapist out, she may gain an important edge.

When Tyrone Graham was in her apartment Eileen deliberately got him to talk about himself, posing herself as a interested listener. A woman could minimize the damage to herself if she follows this rule, she observed. Even when emotionally disturbed, people tend to live up to what other people expect of them. If you treat a person like a mad dog, he will probably do his best not to disappoint you, Eileen said. If you call him a disgusting brute, very likely he'll be disgusting and act brutally. If a woman confronted by a rapist reacts to him as if he is inhuman, then he won't feel the need to stay within normal human limits.

Another important strategy, Eileen told women, was for them to gain the potential rapist's confidence.

Few women realized it, but in general, the rapist was just as frightened during the assault as his victim. He may be worried that the woman will scream and draw attention. He may be afraid that if she struggles she might end up with a weapon, in which case he can be the one who gets hurt. He may fear that the woman will report the assault to the police, identify him and send him to prison.

He may be worried that the woman is not going to

give him what he wants, or what he thinks he needs. And he may be frightened by his own impulses.

Eileen stressed that for their safety, women have to try to ease the fears of an assailant. If they find a way to reassure the man that the victim represents neither a mental nor a physical threat to him they may escape or minimize their danger. Unless a woman can gain the confidence of her potential rapist, she will be in danger throughout the assault.

The rapist, like all of us, deals with threats in just two ways: fight or flight. If he sees his victim as a threat he may run. On the other hand, he may strike out readily and kill her.

No one ever recovers completely from a rape. Eileen hasn't. Her recovery has been aided by the women to whom she has talked and from whom she has come to understand the nature of the violence that happened. Tyrone Graham is in jail. But what about others? Rape is on the increase. Violence against women reaches new heights every year. What can be done?

Eileen believes that all of us have to take a new look at how to deal with a convicted rapist. Our real aim should be to prevent rape, rather than to have to fight to see justice done once a rape is committed, as she had to in the case of Tyrone Graham.

Eileen feels the best way to stop the rapist, the intruder with a knife or gun and a savage compulsion in his breast, is to treat him psychiatrically. Discover his problems and attempt to help him solve them. It is either that or condemn him to prison for life. Eileen feels if enough pressure is exerted on legislators, they will devise a rational, mandatory treatment program for rapists. A long-term program, combined with confinement in a hospital for several years, seems to Eileen to be the most rational approach, the one most likely to work, the one most likely to be accepted by our society.

According to her, "Once you survive a sexual attack you should think of yourself as a survivor, because that's what you are. You have taken the most important step to recovery by surviving the ordeal. I don't think I did anything others can't do. If you can manage to keep your 'cool', you will find your courage."

Eileen Ross continues as a rape activist and public speaker, responding to many invitations to talk about "crimes against women". She lives with Rick Rivera, the companion of her crisis years.